The Market for College-Trained Manpower

Richard B. Freeman

The Market for College-Trained Manpower

A Study in the Economics of Career Choice

Harvard University Press
Cambridge, Massachusetts
1971

Distributed in Great Britain by Oxford University Press, London
Library of Congress Catalog Card Number 70–139726
SBN 674–54976–7
Printed in the United States of America

Acknowledgments

As with other works of research, this study has benefited from the direct and indirect inputs of numerous persons in addition to the principal author. I would like to acknowledge a debt of gratitude to the people and institutions who generously aided me.

First, Professor John T. Dunlop was exceedingly helpful in advising me throughout the work. He helped set the path which the research followed and, with suggestions and criticism, improved the content of the final essay.

Several other faculty members and students in the Department of Economics at Harvard, including Yoram Ben-Porath, Chris Sims, James Scoville, Lladd Phillips, Suresh Tendulkar and Peter Doeringer, also assisted me by discussing and criticizing certain aspects of the study. The initial impetus for the study came from Professor W. W. Leontief's Seminar at Harvard.

Part of the study was presented at seminars at the University of Chicago and Carnegie Institute of Technology. At both of these schools the comments of participants, including Professor H. G. Lewis, Theodore Schultz, Mary Jean Bowman, Robert Lucas, Leonard Rapping, and Myron Josephs, led to improvements in the work.

The study would have been impossible without the aid of several research assistants: Linda Wilcox, Judy Topping, Dorothy Furber and, most particularly, Franziska Amacher. James Zeanah skillfully handled much of the computer programming.

Lindsey Harmon of the National Academy of Sciences, Robert Cain of the National Science Foundation, and Betty Vetter of the Scientific Manpower Commission helped me obtain statistical data.

Finally, the first year of the study was supported by the National Science Foundation. The second year I was supported by the Department of Labor, Office of Manpower Policy, Evaluation and Research.

Richard B. Freeman

Cambridge, Massachusetts

Contents

List of tables xi

List of figures xvii

Introduction xix

1 The Economic Theory of Occupational Choice 1

1.1 Distinctive aspects of occupational choice 1
1.2 The individual choice of a career 2
1.3 Expectations 8
1.4 Aggregate supply 11

2 Models of the Labor and Education Markets 16

2.1 The time structure of supply response 16
2.2 Lagged adjustment models of the labor market 18
2.3 Availability of training facilities 28

3 Developments in the Market for Highly Specialized Workers after Word War II 33

3.1 Specialized occupations 33
3.2 Educational qualifications 39
3.3 The relation between education and occupation 46

4 The Cobweb Pattern: the Bachelor of Science in Engineering 55

4.1 Employment and training of engineers 55
4.2 The cobweb model in B.S. engineering 58
4.3 Supply of B.S. engineers 65
4.4 Demand for B.S. engineers 70
4.5 The cobweb mechanism 72

5 The Income of Doctorate Specialists 76

5.1 Doctorate labor market 76
5.2 Change in income, 1935–1965 77
5.3 Discounted lifetime income 86

6 Stipend Income and Educational Subsidies 100

6.1 Subsidization of graduate students 100
6.2 Stipends and labor supply 107
6.3 Financing higher education 111

7 The Incomplete Adjustment Pattern: Doctorate Manpower 116

7.1 Supply of graduate students under incomplete adjustment 117
7.2 Additional dimensions of doctorate supply 123
7.3 Capacity of graduate schools 134
7.4 Summary of the findings: doctorate manpower 137

8 Cobweb and Incomplete Adjustment in Other College Markets 139

8.1 Cobweb of adjustment in accounting 139
8.2 Cobweb adjustment in the MBA market 144
8.3 Incomplete adjustments in chemical professions 148
8.4 Incomplete adjustment in mathematics 156

9 Demand for Education and Market for Faculty 160

9.1 The interfield composition of faculties 160
9.2 The faculty labor market model 168
9.3 Doctorate faculty 175

10 Career Plans and Occupational Choice **180**

10.1 The survey questionnaire 180
10.2 The career decision 181
10.3 Interrelation of specialties 188
10.4 Information in the college market 194

11 Expectations of Marginal Decision-making **202**

11.1 Expectations of college students 202
11.2 Expectations of income by specialty 209
11.3 Perceptions of other characteristics 218
11.4 Marginal decision-making 223

12 Policy and Research Implications **227**

12.1 High-level manpower policy 227
12.2 Labor market research 229

Appendix A: Computation of Incremental Taxes **233**

Appendix B: Questionnaire and Representative Response **235**

Appendix C: Analysis of the Response Bias **241**

Notes **243**

Index **261**

Tables

3.1	Proportion of male workers in professional and science-oriented occupations, 1947–1967	34
3.2	Employment and education of male engineers, scientists, and professionals in 1960 and the changes in employment and education, 1950–1960	35
3.3	Distribution of college-trained scientists and engineers, by degree, 1964–1966	37
3.4	Percentage of male PTK workers employed in business, government, and professional services in 1960	38
3.5	Percentage of college-age persons with college training in U.S. and in OECD countries, 1959	40
3.6	Doctorate degrees awarded to males, by major, 1950–1965	41
3.7	Master's degrees awarded to males, by major, 1950–1965	43
3.8	Bachelor's degrees awarded to males, by major, 1950–1965	45
3.9	1960 occupations of June 1958 male college graduates, by field of study	48
3.10	1960 occupations of June 1958 male graduates: social sciences, psychology, humanities majors	50
3.11	Percentage of doctorate recipients remaining in the same field from baccalaureate to doctorate and doctorate to job	52
4.1	Distribution of employment of engineers, by major industry, 1950–1966	56
4.2	Correlation evidence of the lagged effect on starting salaries of the number of engineering graduates, 1949–1967	66
4.3	Supply of first-year students to engineering, 1948–1967	67
4.4	Supply of engineering graduates, 1951–1967	69

4.5	Determination of changes in engineering starting salaries, 1948–1967	70
4.6	"Cobweb Equation" for supply of first-year students to engineering, 1948–1967	74
5.1	Percentage change in starting salaries of doctorate graduates and in general economic conditions, by quinquennium, 1935–1960	78
5.2	Changes in doctorate salaries by field compared to changes in manufacturing wages, 1935–1960	80
5.3	Compound annual changes in salaries and wages, 1948–1957 and 1957–1967	80
5.4	Monthly earnings of nonsupervisory scientists, average hourly earnings of production workers and changes in earnings, by industry, 1949–1965	81
5.5	Percentage change in doctorate starting salaries, 1935–1960, 1956–1960	82
5.6	Salary and annual changes in salary of doctorate scientists, by field of specialization, 1948–1966	83
5.7	Salary and changes in salary of doctorate workers in industry, government, and education, and the salary advantage of industry, 1948–1964	85
5.8	Lifetime income of doctorate workers, discounted to the time of graduation at varying rates of interest, by specialty, 1960	88
5.9	Estimates of compensating income differentials in the doctorate market, 1960	89
5.10	Comparison of ability of the B.A., the Ph.D., and the high school student and effect of ability on rates of return to education	92
5.11	Lifetime income of scientists and engineers in 1962, discounted to present value at age 26 with a 6% rate of interest	94
5.12A	Lifetime income of scientists in the National Register, discounted to present value with a 6% rate of interest, 1964	95
5.12B	Discounted lifetime income adjusted for the nonpecuniary value of working in educational institutions, 1964	96
6.1	Direct subsidization of students, 1963–1965	101
6.2	Educational loans and fellowships at Harvard University	102
6.3	Value of stipend income in 1960, compounded at 6% upon graduation	103
6.4	Contribution of stipend income to the median total income of graduate students in 1963	104

6.5	Proportion of graduate students supported by federal agencies in 1963	106
6.6	Effect of stipend support in 1959 on growth of Ph.D. degrees, 1959–1964	108
7.1	Incomplete adjustment supply equations	120
7.2A	Changes in median annual salaries, 1948–1957, and in doctorate degrees, 1953–1963	124
7.2B	Changes in doctorate salaries, 1935–1960, and in doctorate degrees, 1940–41 to 1965–66	125
7.3	Change in specialization from doctorate major to field of work	126
7.4	Mobility of Ph.D.'s among fields and income of fields of In- and Out-Migration	128
7.5	Effect of the capital value of degrees on the educational composition of science and engineering fields	131
7.6A	Proportion of Ph.D. scientists employed in education, industry, and government in 1948 and 1964	132
7.6B	Rank correlation of the relative change in salaries and in sectoral employment, by field	133
7.7	Capacity of graduate schools to increase doctorate enrollment in 1959–60	135
8.1A	Supply of bachelor's degree accountants, 1951–1965	143
8.1B	Demand for bachelor's degree accountants, 1951–1965	143
8.2A	Supply of Master of Business Administration graduates, 1949–1966	147
8.2B	Demand for Master of Business Administration graduates, 1949–1966	148
8.3	Degrees in chemical professions, 1950–1965	149
8.4	Incomes in the chemical industry	150
8.5	Acceleration of change in number of doctorate degrees in chemistry compared to changes in ratio of Ph.D. chemist to Ph.D. engineer-scientist salaries, lagged five years, 1952–1966	152
8.6	Supply of doctorate and master's chemists, 1955–1966	153
8.7	Demand for chemical specialists: salary determination regressions, 1951–1966	155
9.1	Percentage changes in enrollment and in new faculty, by major field, 1960–1964 and 1954–1964	161
9.2	Incremental vacancy rates in academic institutions compared to the ratio of industrial to academic salaries, 1964	166
9.3	Reduced form employment and salary equations of the faculty labor market model, 1920–1964	169

9.4A Structural supply equations of the faculty labor market model, 1920–1964 171
9.4B Demand equation with dependent variable $\Delta\ln$ FAC, 1934–1942 and 1952–1964 171
9.4C Demand equations with dependent variable $\Delta\ln$ SAL, 1934–1942 and 1952–1964 172
9.5 Determinants of faculty employment for 42 institutions and departments 174
9.6 Distribution of doctorate workers between academic and nonacademic employment and percentage changing place of employment, 1935–1963 178
10.1 Career plans of college students, by major field of study 184
10.2 Education-occupation matrix 1967: percentage of students intending to work in specified occupations 190
10.3 Percentage of students considering various careers as the closest alternative to their intended career 192
10.4A Student perceptions of the earnings in five well-known careers 196
10.4B Student perceptions of changes in earnings over the life cycle in five well-known careers 197
10.4C Student perceptions of changes in job opportunities and need for workers in five well-known careers 197
10.5 Student information on the doctorate labor market compared to actual conditions 198
11.1 Student expectations of income, 1967 204
11.2 Variations in expected and actual income 206
11.3 Estimated foregone income, 1966–67 207
11.4 Perceived importance of job characteristics in choosing career 209
11.5 Income expected by students, according to field of study in 1967, and analysis of variance of expectations 210
11.6 Incomes expected by students, according to intended career in 1967, and analysis of variance of expectations 212
11.7A Rank order comparison of expected and actual starting salaries, by undergraduate major 214
11.7B Rank order comparison of expected and actual starting salaries, by intended occupation 215
11.8 Perceived and actual life-cycle earnings curves 216
11.9 Student perceptions of relative income position of intended occupations 217
11.10 Measures of expected and actual variation in income and

	opportunities for wealth compared to variation and skew of income distributions, by occupation	220
11.11	Expectations of personal economic success	222
11.12	Income in the career choice of marginal and other suppliers	224
11.13	Expected levels of income of marginal and other suppliers	224

Figures

1.1 The individual supply of labor to an occupation: a step function depending on the reservation wage 3
1.2 A programming model of the role of preferences and job characteristics in career choice 5
1.3 Ability endowments and the determination of potential earnings 7
1.4 The connections among market conditions, expectations, and labor supply in economic analysis 10
1.5 Aggregate supply curves to an occupation under alternative assumptions of the distribution of "reservation wages" in the labor force 13
2.1 Equilibrium in the basic model 23
2.2 Adjustment of new entrants 24
2.3 A comparison of paths to equilibrium in the market for new entrants with paths to equilibrium in the market for the stock of workers 25
2.4 Linkages between the education and labor markets 28
3.1 Percentage change in male degree recipients, 1950–1965 40
4.1 Proportion of freshmen in engineering and changes in engineering salaries, 1947–1967 61
4.2 Proportion of engineering freshmen graduating four years later, 1947–1963 62
4.3 Lagged adjustment of salaries to shifts in supply when firms expect supply to equal last period's 64
4.4 The percentage of freshmen in engineering compared to the proportion predicted by the cobweb supply equation, 1948–1967 68

5.1 Disequilibrium in the doctorate labor market in 1960, as indicated by the deviations of expected from actual discounted lifetime income 90
5.2 Present value of earnings, discounted at 6%, accruing to scientists and engineers, and year in which capital value of the Ph.D. exceeds value of the M.S. and B.S. 97
5.3 Variation in the cross-sectional earning of scientists, by degree, field, and age in 1964, as measured by the interquartile range of earnings divided by the median 98
8.1 Bachelor graduates in accounting, relative to all graduates, all business and commerce graduates, and all graduates in nonengineering programs, 1951–1965 142
8.2 Percentage of male master's degrees awarded in business administration, 1948–1966 145
8.3 Post-bachelor's degree work and study patterns of chemistry majors in the class of 1958 compared to the class of 1951 154
8.4 Post-bachelor's degree work and study patterns of mathematics majors in the class of 1958 compared to the class of 1951 157
8.5 Proportion of Ph.D. degrees awarded to males in mathematics compared to the ratio of starting salaries in mathematics to the average doctorate starting salary five years earlier, by quinquennium, 1940–1965 158
9.1 The proportion of new faculty and of enrollment in four major fields of study, 1953–1965 162
9.2 Percent of new college teachers with doctor's degree 164
9.3 Faculty-student ratios, 1920–1964 170
10.1 Selected aspects of the career decision process, undergraduate and graduate males, 1967 182
10.2 The relation of college studies to career choice 187
10.3 The importance of channels of job information to undergraduate and graduate students in 1967 195
11.1 The incomes students expect in their career compared to explorations of 1966 incomes, by level of education and life-cycle status 203

Introduction

The high-level work force of the United States has been expanding rapidly in recent years. In 1947, 6.6 percent of total employment was in professional, technical, and kindred jobs; in 1967, 14.4 percent. During the same period the number of young persons enrolled in institutions of higher education jumped from one fourth to over one half of the population aged 18–21, and the number in graduate education quadrupled. These developments denote a fundamental change in the nature of the labor market and of the modern economic system; the transformation of the proletariat of traditional capitalism into a college-trained professional work force.

This book is a study of the changing labor market for high-level, primarily college-trained, manpower in the United States.* It focuses on the career decisions of college students, with particular emphasis on scientific and related specialties. The study is addressed to the basic question: "Can an economic theory of labor supply explain postwar developments in the market for high-level manpower?" Since salaries are an important factor in supply decisions some attention is also given to the process of salary determination.

Methods and Data

The approach taken is that of "traditional" price theory, which explains the allocation of resources by price or wage differentials. Since noncompetitive institutions like unions or monopsonies are generally absent

* The terms "high level" and "professional" are used interchangeably in this study.

from the market for college graduates,* price theory is more applicable here than in the unionized markets usually studied by economists.

Two research tools are used in the study: econometric model-building and a survey questionnaire. The econometric analysis relates the number of students choosing different curriculums to economic incentives and shows how supply and demand interact to set the starting salaries of college graduates. The data used in these calculations include estimates of enrollment and graduation compiled by the Office of Education and salary figures gathered by placement offices, professional societies, and federal agencies. For the most part these data have not been previously exploited by economists investigating the labor market and career choice.†

The questionnaire was mailed to several thousand male students in the Boston area. It gathers *new* information about several aspects of career decisions: the timing of decisions, their amenability to change, the alternative careers considered by students, the role of foregone income, occupational information, evaluations of occupational characteristics, and estimates of future income. By focusing on persons in the process of selecting a career, the survey provides especially useful insights into the decision process and a good test of the "micro-foundations" of the economic theory of occupational choice.

Structure of the Study

The book consists of twelve chapters, the first three of which set out the theoretical and empirical base required for the study. Chapter 1 presents the economic theory of occupational choice in a linear activity framework. It attempts to clarify the role of abilities, preferences, income incentive, marginal decisions, and expectations in supply theory. Chapter 2 develops a triad of market models to guide the econometric analysis; a *cobweb adjustment* model in which variables oscillate toward equilibrium; an *incomplete adjustment* model, in which they approach but fail to attain equilibrium in the period under consideration; and a *simultaneous equations* model, where the allocation and salaries of workers among sectors of the economy are jointly determined. The cobweb and incomplete adjustment patterns focus on supply lags due to the time required to train

* While some college graduates, pilots, teachers, and government officials are union members, most of them work in nonunionized markets. Increased unionization of teachers may change this in the future.

† Two earlier studies are: D. Blank and G. Stigler *The Demand and Supply of Scientific Personnel* (National Bureau of Economic Research, 1957) and M. Friedman and S. Kuznets, *Income from Independent Professional Practice* (National Bureau of Economic Research, 1945).

new specialists. The simultaneous equation model deals with allocation of a fixed stock of workers between academic and nonacademic jobs. Chapter 3 — the antithesis of these theoretical discussions — describes the postwar developments that a theory of supply should explain: the growth of high-level occupations, the changing number of students in educational curriculums, and the relation of college major to occupation.

The remainder of the study applies the economic theory of career choice and the labor market models to developments in the postwar market for college graduates. In Chapter 4, the cobweb model is used to explain fluctuations in the enrollment and salaries of engineering specialists. Chapters 5, 6, and 7 examine the operation of the market for Ph.D. graduates. The financial status of graduate students and Ph.D.'s is examined, and changes in the supply of Ph.D.'s to diverse specialties and sectors explained in the context of the incomplete adjustment model. By relating supply to discounted lifetime income (corrected for the nonpecuniary value of university employment), the model provides a test of the "human capital" theory of behavior. Chapter 8 extends the analysis to four other college specialties: the cobweb model is estimated for accountancy and MBA management; the incomplete adjustment model for chemistry and mathematics.

A critical postulate in the econometric analysis is that individual career decisions, not the availability of places in universities, determines the supply of students to diverse specialties. This assumption is tested in Chapter 9, where the simultaneous equations model is used to study the effect of changes in the demand for specialized education on the employment of faculty.

Chapters 10 and 11 present the principal results of the survey. The former contains evidence regarding the timing and certainty of decisions, the adequacy of occupational information, and student perception of the market for five "well-known" careers and ten doctorate specialties. Chapter 10 deals with student expectations of future income, their perceptions of the variability, risk, and chance for great wealth in various fields, and with the marginal aspects of decision-making. The final chapter evaluates the results of the study for policy and future research.

Principal Findings

The main empirical findings of the study may be summarized as follows:

1) Expansion of the college-trained work force has been accompanied by great shifts in the composition of specialties and of levels of education.

The proportion of men in various curricula changed dramatically over time, often in different ways at different levels of training. The number of bachelor's degree engineers, for example, declined greatly relative to the total college population from 1950 to 1965, while the number of Ph.D. and M.S. engineering students increased (Chapter 3).

2) The role of the college major in preparing students varies by field and degree. Baccalaureate study in engineering and accounting is confined almost entirely to persons planning careers in those fields. By contrast, most social science majors obtain jobs in occupations only remotely related to social science disciplines. At higher degree levels, areas of study are closely linked to specific occupations, with a near one-to-one correspondence between the doctorate or professional school major and area of work (Chapters 3, 10). The intention of graduates to seek employment in a field is influenced by the state of the labor market, especially at the bachelor's level (Chapter 8).

3) The doctorate market has flourished in recent years. From the mid-1950's to the current period (1968–69) doctorate incomes increased more rapidly than those of other workers. Mathematics, engineering, and economics recorded especially large gains. Throughout the period the rate of return to the doctorate was substantial, particularly after adjustment for the nonpecuniary value of university employment. It has been in the area of 10–14 percent (Chapter 5).

4) The lifetime income of doctorate specialists, discounted at rates ranging from 0 to 10 percent, differs noticeably among fields of study. Part of the variation is due to nonpecuniary income associated with the distribution of jobs between industry and education. The rest may be attributed to disequilibrium in the market (Chapter 5).

5) Stipends account for a sizable fraction (5–6 percent) of doctorate lifetime income. The availability of stipends varies across fields, with the biological sciences offering the most awards per student. After *Sputnik I*, the value and number of awards increased greatly. Both the inter-field and time series variation in awards is primarily attributable to the fellowship policies of the federal government (Chapter 6).

6) Stipends significantly affect career decisions. Fields with a relatively large number of awards attract more students than would otherwise be the case. Moreover, by making full-time study feasible, stipends reduce the time spent obtaining a degree. In the long run the effectiveness of stipends drops, as the induced growth in the number of graduates in supported fields lower salaries and the incentive to enter (Chapter 6).

7) Foregone income is an important factor in the decision to enroll in higher education. Student estimates of foregone income are closely aligned with the earnings reported by comparable workers. Comparisons of estimated foregone income and potential future earnings reveal a high subjective rate of return, which is consistent with the decision to attend school. Many students volunteer foregone income as the principal cost of schooling (Chapter 6).

8) While students receive substantial subsidies in the form of stipends and below-cost tuition charges, they are not "freeloaders" on the non-student taxpaying public. Most of the cost of schooling is attributable to foregone income, which is paid by students. The taxes received on the additional earnings of persons induced into college by subsidies repays nearly all of the remaining cost. Since much of the repayment is through higher federal income taxes, funds are transferred from the states with public education programs to the federal government (Chapter 6).

9) The supply of young men to high-level occupations is governed by economic incentives. All else being the same, increased wages attract students to a field and add to the supply of specialists several years later. Lags in supply are due primarily to the length of educational programs. Both econometric and survey data indicate rapid response to changes in market conditions (Chapters 4, 7, 8, 10).

10) Students in the "pipeline of production" also alter career plans in response to changes in economic incentive. When salaries increase rapidly in a field, more students are likely to complete their studies than would otherwise be the case. In engineering, for example, the dropout rate is a function of the state of the market for graduates in the junior year relative to that during the freshman year (Chapters 2, 4).

11) In specialties with narrow vocational curriculum, lengthy cumulative training, and moderate long-term increases in demand — engineering, accounting, and MBA management in postwar years — the market operates under cobweb adjustment. The fraction of students choosing these fields fluctuates cyclically: a large graduating class depresses salaries and causes a relative decline in the number of entrants; when a small class graduates, salaries are increased, causing a jump in enrollment, and so on. Cobweb fluctuations follow a stable dampened pattern. "Random shocks" produced especially large fluctuations in engineering in the 1948–67 period (Chapters 4, 8).

12) In specialties with more dramatic shifts in demand and/or longer training periods — mathematics, and chemistry and most doctorate fields

— the market operated under incomplete adjustment in postwar years. Short-run changes in supply can be explained by the level of disequilibrium in a market (as measured by discounted lifetime income relative to incomes in comparable fields). Long-term changes in supply appear to result from changes in salaries caused by shifts in demand (Chapters 7, 8).

13) Experienced workers also respond to the economic incentive of market disequilibrium and/or changes in equilibrium incomes. When salaries are high or rapidly increasing in an occupation, older doctorate graduates enter from related specialties. Similarly, high or rising salaries cause shifts in the allocation of Ph.D.'s among employers (Chapter 7).

14) Changes in the salaries of college graduates are explicable by shifts in supply and demand schedules. When a large number of students graduate in a specialty, the rate of increase in salaries is reduced; when industries that normally employ graduates expand, salaries are increased. In any given recruitment period, however, salaries do not clear the market. Salaries adjust relatively slowly to shifts in supply that are not foreseen by firms (Chapters 4, 8).

15) The availability of places in universities, as reflected in teacher:student ratios and the size and inter-field composition of faculties, adjusts to the demand for education within the limits set by the internal and external labor markets and university budget constraints. The internal market operates through the desire of administrators to have an "equitable" salary scale, with narrow inter-field variation in salaries. Rates of promotion and nonmonetary perquisites are used to circumvent the internal constraint. They are not perfect substitutes for differential salaries: specialties with especially strong nonacademic demand report relatively many vacancies in the university system (Chapter 9).

16) Faculty salary and employment levels are determined simultaneously in the faculty labor market. The supply of new and experienced specialists to universities is relatively elastic. Salaries are flexible within certain limits, adjusting with a lag to supply or demand shifts. Increases in the demand for education induce large enough increases in the number of places that capacity limitations in higher education do not seriously limit the supply of specialists (Chapters 7, 9).

17) Corroborating the econometric evidence, survey data show the career decisions of students to have the flexibility and responsiveness to economic incentive required for an elastic supply curve. Most students choose a career while they are in college and give serious consideration

to alternatives. Many are willing to alter their plans when information or conditions change. A wide variety of possibilities is considered by men with different career intentions.

18) Students appear to be well informed about economic opportunities in the market for college graduates. Subjectively, most consider the information available at the time of their career decision to be adequate for a sensible selection. Objectively, their evaluation of the economic characteristics of such well-known professions as medicine or law and of specialized doctorate fields is in accord with economic reality. The perceived positions of careers with respect to starting salaries, growth of income over the life cycle, and changes in job opportunities are nearly perfectly correlated with statistical measures of these characteristics (Chapter 10).

19) Student income expectations are realistic when compared with actual market incomes. The levels expected for the future are in accord with reasonable projections of current salaries. Differences in income expectations among students with different career plans mirror the actual structure of salaries. Students in fields with high current remuneration expect above-average earnings and rank their career high in the income distribution of college specialties. Awareness of economic opportunities extends to the entire life cycle of earnings (Chapter 11).

20) Perceptions of other occupational characteristics, including the chance to earn great wealth and the risk or variability of income opportunities, are also in accord with market phenomena. Students planning legal careers, for example, are aware of the income variability and risk involved in law, while those intending to teach recognize the relative security of that profession. Past changes in income are expected to continue into the future, which suggests that students extrapolate rates of change as well as levels of income in forming anticipations of lifetime income (Chapter 11).

21) Persons who are identified as "marginal suppliers" by their willingness to change careers upon receipt of additional information appear to be especially sensitive to economic stimuli. These students express dissatisfaction with economic opportunities in their chosen career and seem to be searching for a superior alternative. Students with especially high evaluation of monetary incentives also make career decisions in an a priori sensible way, flocking to occupations where salaries are high and expected to increase greatly. Fields which students view as offering especially good income opportunities relative to comparable alternatives tend to increase most rapidly (Chapter 11).

In broad perspective, these results present an arresting picture of the market for high-level manpower. Here, the market operates in accord with economic theory, with an informed group of suppliers responding rapidly to economic incentives and salaries determined, albeit with a lag, by supply and demand. The imperfections, immobilities, and institutional rigidities often regarded as characteristic of labor markets do not prevent the price system from allocating students to professions. The contrast between these findings and those from studies of "blue-collar" markets suggests that the trend toward an increasingly professional, college-trained work force will produce a more "classical" labor market.

The Market for College-Trained Manpower

1 The Economic Theory of Occupational Choice

"If the advantages of any one occupation . . . are above the average, there is a quick influx of youth from other occupations."
Alfred Marshall, *Principles of Economics,* p. 216.

How does the labor market transmit needs for highly trained workers to the individuals choosing an occupation? What is the role of economic incentive in career choice? What determines the supply of college graduates to the professions?

The economic tools relevant to these questions are set out in Chapters 1 and 2. The former applies the economic analysis of choice to the problem of selecting a career and shows how the aggregation of individual decisions yields a supply curve. Chapter 2 considers the lags inherent in supply behavior and develops testable models that embody these lags.

1.1 Distinctive Aspects of Occupational Choice

Because workers are human beings, with finite life spans, freedom in decision-making, and nonmonetary as well as monetary preferences, occupational choice differs from other supply decisions. Characteristically, it is an "all-or-nothing" decision in which one career is selected from a set of mutually exclusive alternatives. There are three reasons why the worker investing in human capital normally limits himself to a single occupation. First, the time required to learn the skills used in most careers is lengthy enough to preclude simultaneous or seriatim study of several specialties. If the individual divides his time among careers, he is in danger of being a "jack of all trades and master of none" who will be unable to compete with fully specialized workers.[1] Second, the finite work span of human beings limits the period over which returns to investment in work skills are earned and thus discourages such investments later in life. Occupational mobility is generally restricted to alternatives with considerable transfer of skill.[2] Third, in the absence of a lien on human capital, few persons will diversify their human capital portfolio by investing in others. Exclusive of professional athletics, there is no human asset market equivalent to those for financial or physical assets. The only way in which a coal miner can invest in the human capital of a doctor or engineer is through purchases of claims on firms that employ those specialists and not by direct investment in the individual.

As a result, "learning a trade or profession [which] requires training and experience . . . renders the choice of an occupation a momentous decision which few can afford to make more than once in a lifetime." [3]

Indivisibility in career choice makes an individual's supply decision a simple step function with respect to each occupation. In Figure 1.1 the individual is shown to supply labor only when the wage (w) exceeds his reservation wage ($\overline{w}$).* The aggregate supply schedule to an occupation depends on how reservation wages are distributed in the population and thus on the underlying distribution of preferences and abilities.

The investor in human capital earns income in his career by devoting time to the work process. Since he has nonpecuniary preferences regarding the characteristics of work, nonpecuniary factors will be especially important in the career decision. As Alfred Marshall observed, "The seller of labor must deliver himself . . . so it matters a great deal . . . whether or not the place (of work) is wholesome or pleasant . . . while it matters little to the seller of bricks whether they are used in building a palace or a sewer." [4] Problems in evaluating nonpecuniary factors make the economic analysis of career choice especially difficult. Since persons "purchase" pleasant work with foregone income, monetary differentials may be inversely related or unrelated to the real attractiveness of alternatives.[5]

1.2 The Individual Choice of a Career

The factors that influence the career decision can be classified into two groups: those inherent in the individual, such as preferences and abilities;

* Throughout this book the terms "wages," "income," "salaries," and "earnings" are used interchangeably except in specific applications.

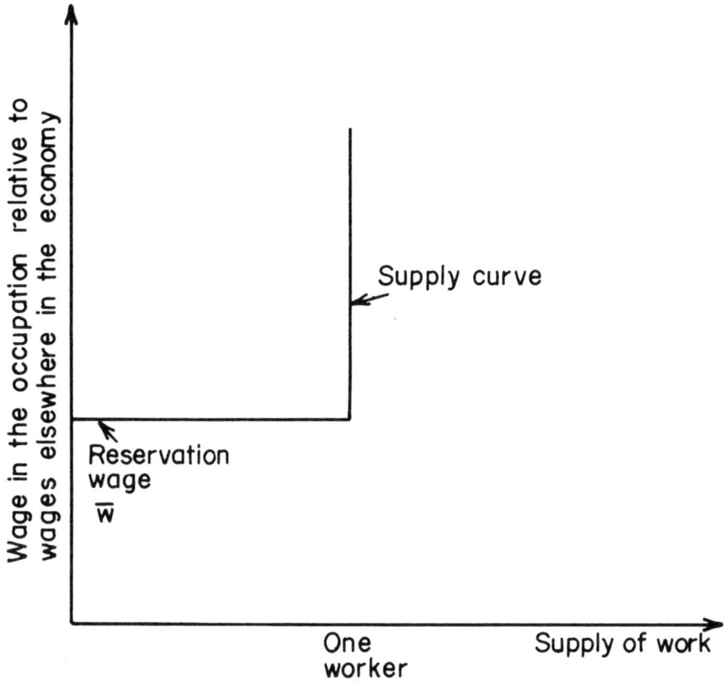

1.1 The individual supply of labor to an occupation: a step function depending on the reservation wage

and the wages and job characteristics that are determined by the market. The economic theory of choice assumes that within the constraints set by the market and by personal abilities, the individual selects the occupation that maximizes his utility function. Schematically, the career decision is made as follows: (1) on the basis of market wages and ability endowments, the individual calculates *expected lifetime income* for all relevant occupations; (2) he compares the utility of the commodities which can be purchased with this income and with potential nonwage income to the nonmonetary value of working in each of the careers; (3) he selects the career which offers the greatest total utility. The process can be summarized as the maximization of a functional form:

$$\operatorname*{Max}_{i} U(x_i, w_i + W),$$

where U is the indirect utility function; x_i is the vector of job characteristics in occupation i; w_i is the lifetime income expected in occupation i; and W nonwage income. The index i runs from 1 to N for N occupations. For simplicity w_i will be termed wages and W nonwage income.

Even in this very general formulation, the theory has one interesting implication for career choice. It suggests that wealthy persons, those with substantial nonwage income *W*, will select different careers from those chosen by persons with less wealth. Since their initial money income is high, the wealthy are likely to elect occupations with greater nonmonetary rewards. Casual observation shows this to be a reasonable description of behavior: very wealthy families are often devoted to public service and allocate more time to charities and volunteer work than other families; students from upper-class homes are over-represented in aesthetic professions and under-represented in fields like engineering.

Preferences and Abilities

The role of preferences and abilities in career choice can be examined furthur in a model that distinguishes different job characteristics and types of abilities. To capture directly the indivisibility of the decision, linear activity analysis, in which alternatives are rejected entirely, is employed. Every occupation is assumed to offer fixed amounts of job characteristics (for example, pleasant working conditions) and to reward abilities such as intelligence or physical strength at fixed prices per unit of ability. The individual chooses his occupation by weighing the relative value of nonmonetary characteristics against the earnings potential of each alternative.

Panel A of Figure 1.2 depicts the operation of this model in the case of two occupations and a single nonmonetary job characteristic.[6] The rewards in occupation I consist primarily of monetary characteristics such as opportunities for good earnings, while those in occupation II are nonpecuniary-intensive. The third possibility is leisure, which offers nonmonetary pleasures only. If the monetary characteristic is measured in dollars, the slope of the activity rays representing the occupations relates money income to nonpecuniary income.

Utility is limited in the model by the finite time available and the restriction of choice to a single career. Allocation of all time to leisure brings an individual to point Z, the maximum possible production of the nonpecuniary good. Allocation of all time to occupation I brings him to point X, where money income is maximized. The difference between actual income and the maximum is the foregone income, or cost, of pleasant working conditions. As occupation I offers the maximum income, its wage rate exceeds that of occupation II.

Lines XZ and YZ show the possible ways of combining work and leisure by dividing time among the activities. Since indivisibility rules out combina-

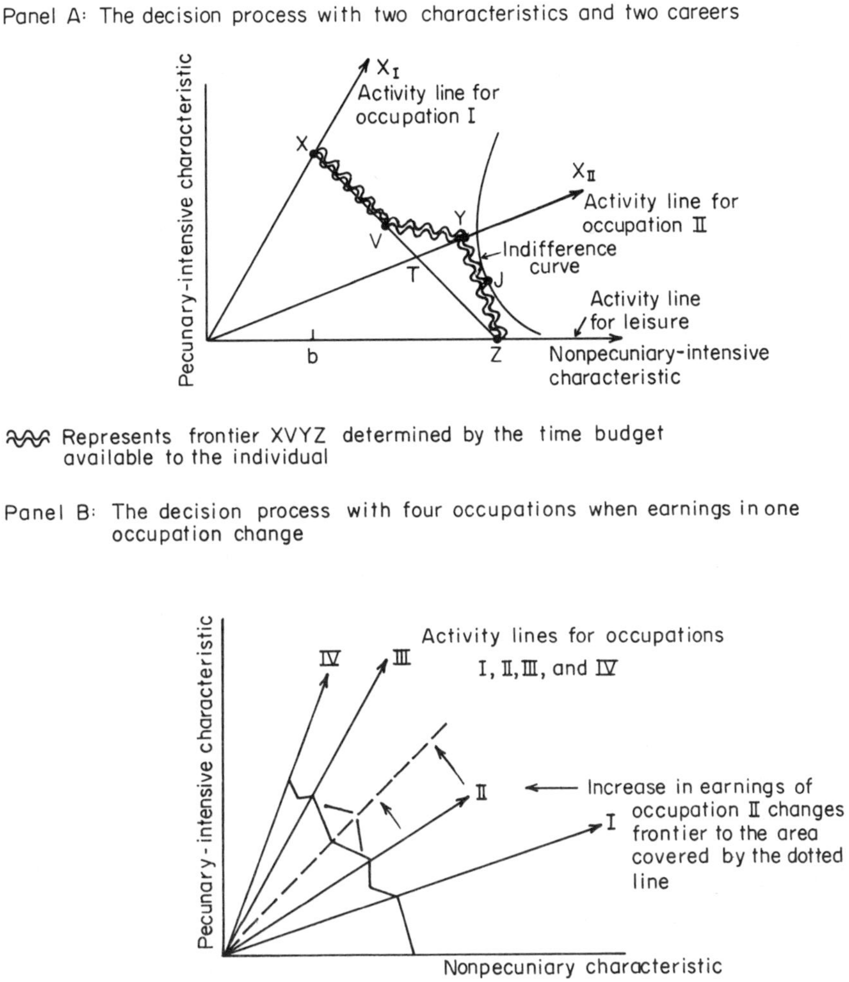

1.2 A programming model of the role of preferences and job characteristics in career choice

tions of occupations I and II, XY is infeasible, and the frontier of attainable combinations consists of points on the XZ and YZ boundary. Efficient combinations of career decisions, work, and leisure lie along the broken line XVYZ. The decision maker chooses the combination placing him on the highest indifference curve.* In the figure he selects point J, dividing his

* Analytically, the decision process may be described as the maximization of a utility function as follows:

$$\max U(\lambda w_i x_i,\ (1-\lambda)L + \lambda x_i n_i),$$

subject to the single occupation constraint $x_i = 1, 0$, and the maximum time constraint

time between work in occupation II and leisure. The closer J is to the X_{II} ray, the greater is the fraction of time spent at work.

Although relatively simple, this model offers several insights into supply behavior. First, it points out the close relation between career selection and the allocation of time to work.[7] Since the point Y dominates the TV segment of possible work–leisure combinations, persons who might work few hours in occupation I will elect instead to work full time in occupation II. As a result, the occupation offering great nonmonetary benefits will contain many "full-time" workers and a positively skewed distribution of hours. This is sensible because work is pleasant and wages low in that occupation. Second, in the case of several occupations, the activity analysis shows that the short-run effect of changes in the wages of one field will be limited to "neighboring" occupations with similar characteristics and wages. In panel B of Figure 1.2 an increase in the wage offered by occupation II draws persons from occupation III and perhaps from occupation I also. In the short run, occupations like II and III, with middling characteristics and several neighbors, will have greater elasticity of supply than those with extreme characteristics and few neighbors. Long-run elasticities depend on the way in which the entire wage structure adjusts to the change and cannot be calculated in this model.

Linear activity analysis can also be used to investigate the determination of potential earnings in diverse careers. In this case we assume that individuals have an initial fixed ability endowment and that careers reward abilities in accordance with a linear ability requirements vector and the shadow price of abilities in the market.[8] In each occupation the income potential of an individual is a linear function of the rate at which abilities are remunerated and his ability endowment:

$$W_i = \Sigma_f R_{if} P_f A_f,$$

where W_i refers to income; R_{if} refers to the ability requirements of the occupation; P_f is the shadow price of abilities; and A_f the units of ability with which the individual is endowed. The $_i$ index relates to occupations, the $_f$ index to abilities.

The distinctive aspect of this formulation is the coupling of a requirements vector, which differs by occupation, with a market-determined

$0 \leq \lambda \leq 1$. In this formulation U is the utility function; λ the fraction of time devoted to work; x_i the occupational choice variable; n_i and w_i the rate respectively of pecuniary and nonpecuniary pay in occupation i; and L, the nonpecuniary compensation of leisure. Nonwage income could be added to this model without affecting its essential structure.

shadow price of abilities identical in all occupations, to show how abilities contribute in different ways to incomes in different careers. The R vector is measured in fractions which vary from zero to unity. When $R_{if} = 1$, ability is fully required or used in the occupation; when $R_{if} = 0$, it is of no value. Intelligence, for example, probably has a near unit coefficient in research and a near zero coefficient in farm labor. In a more realistic non-linear model, the elements of R might vary with scale, with rapidly diminishing returns to such qualities as intelligence in farm labor and possible increasing returns in such occupations as the biological sciences or management.

Figure 1.3 depicts the setting of earnings potential in the linear model

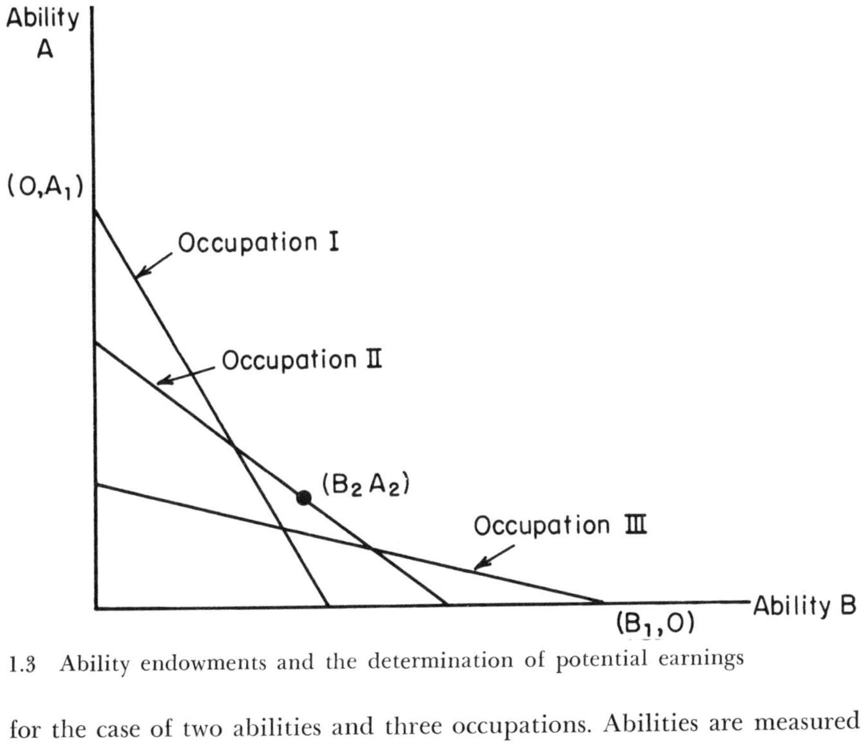

1.3 Ability endowments and the determination of potential earnings

for the case of two abilities and three occupations. Abilities are measured along the axes; the dependence of earnings on ability endowments is shown in the "iso-earnings" lines. Each of these lines tells the amounts of abilities required to earn a given level of income. For example, the lines for occupations I, II, and III show that A_1 units of ability A and 0 units of ability B permit a person to attain the x dollar level in occupation I but not in II or III. For a person with this endowment, potential earnings are higher in the first occupation than in the second, and higher in the second than in the third. At point (B_1, 0) the opposite holds, with occupation III offering the highest potential earnings; at (B_2, A_2) II is the most remunerative.

Iso-earnings lines for specialized occupations such as professional athletics or opera singing have peculiar shapes. Since these fields make use of a very limited set of abilities, the ability requirements vector has unit coefficients for the relevant abilities and zero coefficients otherwise. The slope of the earnings line relating required to unnecessary abilities will be very steep, possibly infinite. Only persons with similarly skewed ability endowments are likely to choose these fields. If persons with the relevant abilities are scarce, income will be especially high, and "most of the highly paid people will utterly specialized in some occupation that is socially advantageous at the moment." [9]

The quality of the work force in specialized fields varies inversely with the level of demand in this model. Increased demand draws persons with fewer units of the required abilities into the occupation, and since incomes reflect the remuneration of abilities, increases the dispersion and skewness of the occupational income distribution. Much of the increased demand ends up as economic rent for the more able. In less specialized occupations, on the other hand, increased demand induces person of varying abilities into the field. The average quality of the work force and the skew and relative dispersion of income need not change.

1.3 Expectations

Since individuals respond to *expected* future rather than current incomes, expectations must be introduced into the analysis. It is necessary to consider how expectations, market conditions, and decisions are interrelated, and how the risk and uncertainty associated with the future affect supply.

The Market, Expectations, and Behavior

It is usually assumed in economic analysis that expectations depend explicitly or implicitly on past market conditions. In the context of the career decision, we postulate that the principal variable, expected lifetime income, is the function of three market variables:

1) The income of workers at the time expectations are formed. In this

study, cross-sectional age–earnings curves are used to index future income over the life cycle under the postulate that the position of workers is extrapolated into the future.[10]

2) The rates of change of income. We assume that persons extrapolate past rates of change into the future in such a way that they adjust completely to long-term and relatively continuous market developments. In the short run, however, the possibility of transitory shifts in income is likely to make the "expectations elasticity" less than unity.

3) Nonwage information, such as changes in employment, vacancy or unemployment rates, recruitment efforts, and the like. Since in the usual situation of market disequilibrium prices or wages do not convey all the information needed for rational decision-making, individuals are expected to pay attention to other indicators as well. In general, the term "wage" should be interpreted broadly as a *vector* of pecuniary and nonpecuniary variables describing the overall state of the market.

There are two ways to build an analysis of supply on the assumption that market phenomena determine expectations. The first and prevalent methodology treats expectations as a "black box" that rationalizes the market variables whose effect on decisions is actually estimated (arrow A in Figure 1.4). The second, more complex method of analysis requires, *separate* study of the formation of expectations (Arrow B) and the way in which they influence decisions (Arrow C). This methodology permits finer tests of theories of choice and pinpoints weaknesses in the underlying behavioral postulates. In periods of structural change, when the past is not a safe guide to the future, it may be the only sensible means of analyzing behavior. It suffers, however, from the difficulty of obtaining reliable measures of expectations. The expectations that people report in questionnaires may not reflect their true feelings about the future. In the present study both methods are used to uncover the effect of income expectations on career decisions.

Expectations are likely to affect future labor market behavior as well as the initial selection of an occupation. When, for one reason or other, expectations are unfulfilled, workers will modify their initial plans, possibly shifting to new occupations.[11] If there are no costs to mobility, changes will occur until the expectations of marginal suppliers are fulfilled. Like the smile of the Cheshire cat, expectations are self-verifying in this situation. When costs to mobility are high, on the other hand, faulty expectations create long and costly disequilibria, which make it worthwhile for persons to invest substantially in career information before

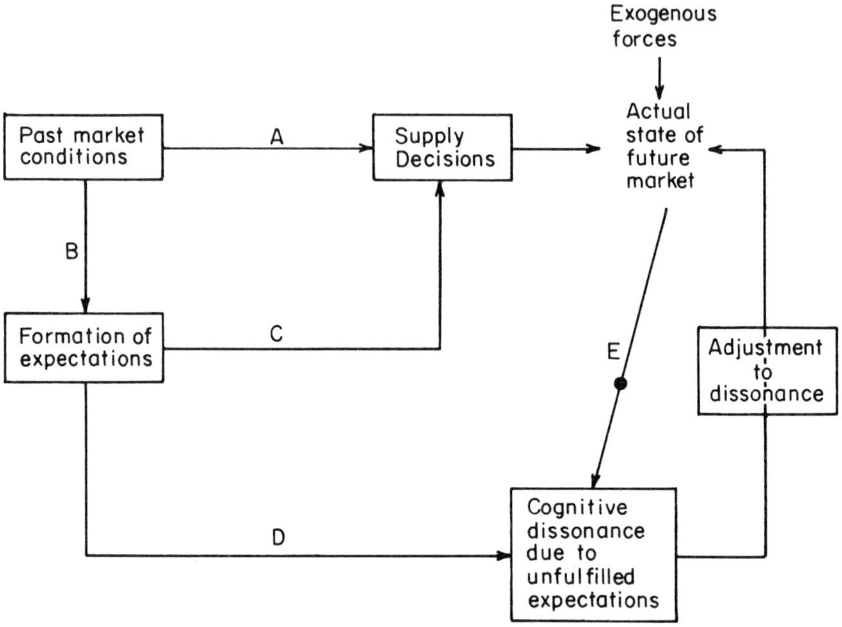

1.4 The connections among market conditions, expectations, and labor supply in economic analysis

choosing a field. Their investment should produce especially realistic expectations and thus limit the likelihood of disequilibria.

Risk, the Chance for Wealth, and Uncertainty

Except for the clairvoyant or telekinetic, expectations of the future necessarily involve risk and uncertainty. Future earnings are risky because persons are unsure of their eventual position in occupational income distributions and because occupations fare differently in the uncertain future. Operationally, risk due to personal economic status can be measured by the variation of income in a cross section of workers, or by the variation of individual incomes over time.[12] Risk due to the status of an occupation is reflected in the variation of mean earnings or changes in earnings over time.

It is usually held that risk deters people from particular occupations: "As a rule," Marshall writes, "the certainty of moderate success attracts more than an expectation of an uncertain success that has an equal actuarial value." [13] If *all* persons are risk-aversive in this way and if they correctly perceive risk, risky occupations will be high-paying, and average income positively correlated with variability in the labor market. If *some* persons are risk-loving or indifferent, or if they have, as Adam Smith and others claim, "an overweening conceit of their own abilities . . . (and) . . . good fortune," [14] the relation between income and risk breaks down. The ultimate effect of risk on income depends on the demand for risky occupations relative to perceptions of risk and the supply of risk-lovers.

Anticipated opportunities to garner great wealth are also likely to influence career decisions. All else being the same, "if an occupation offers a few extremely high prices its attractiveness is increased out of all proportion to their aggregate value." [15] Statistically, skewness of income distributions ought to be negatively correlated with average incomes.[16]

Finally, the main result of the empirical analysis of uncertainty — that individuals have an "irrational" preference for certainty[17] — suggests a bias in career choice toward established professions. As a result, increased information may reallocate persons from certain to uncertain alternatives and reduce the wages in new occupations and industries. The tendency of high wages to prevail in new sectors of the labor market may be due in part to the effect of uncertainty on supply.

1.4 Aggregate Supply

For the analysis of market phenomena the results of individual career decisions must be added together to form supply functions. This is most easily accomplished by assuming a given distribution of reservation wages determined by abilities and preferences and by examining the effect of wages on aggregate supply.

A Single Occupation

Consider first the supply of workers to a single occupation associated with alternative distributions of reservation wages. At one extreme, all prospective entrants may have the same reservation wage. If they do, the aggregate supply schedule is a step function with everyone or no one in the occupation. The existence of many occupations refutes the general validity of this distribution. At the other extreme, reservation wages may be zero to one occupation (possibly differing by person) and infinite to all others. In these circumstances "supply curves would be completely inelastic and . . . all wages would be price-determined instead of price determining and so be rents." [18] Since, conceivably, preference and abilities could severely limit the significance of wage incentives, this distribution cannot be ruled out a priori; it is invalidated by the empirical work of this study.

Central limit theorems and the shape of income distributions suggest the normal, log-normal, and Pareto-type distributions as more plausible representations of reservation wages. Each of these is the limit of (weighted) sums of independent, identically distributed random variables. Each adequately describes part of the distribution of income among individuals. If many independent factors influence preferences and abilities and if incomes reflect reservation wages, distributions are likely to be well described by these curves.

Aggregate supply functions for the three "tailed" distributions are depicted in Figure 1.5. Since aggregate supply is the cumulative distribution function, the supply curves are S-shaped, which suggests a decline in elasticity as an occupation grows beyond a critical size.

Occupations Taken Together

When events in the market for a given occupation significantly affect others, a simultaneous or general equilibrium analysis of supply to all fields is required. The main links between occupations are conveniently exhibited in the behavior of an individual "on the margin" between two alternatives. *A fortiori,* the careers offer the individual the same real income. Assume, however, that money wages differ between them:

$$U(W^{\mathrm{I}}{}_{np}, W^{\mathrm{I}}{}_{m}) = U(W^{\mathrm{II}}{}_{np}, W^{\mathrm{II}}{}_{m}) \quad \text{and} \quad W^{\mathrm{I}}{}_{m} > W^{\mathrm{II}}{}_{m},$$

where U is the individuals utility function; W_{np} refers to nonpecuniary characteristics; and W_m measures money wages. The superscripts denote occupation I and II.

As long as the marginal evaluation of nonmonetary or monetary goods declines for the individual, and is either independent of the consumption of other characteristics (as with additive utilities) or is altered in a positive or slightly negative way by such consumption, identical changes in money income will affect the career choice. Since the marginal value of money is relatively higher in the lower-paying occupation, equal *absolute* increases in wages make it more attractive, while equal absolute decreases do the reverse. Similar behavior is possible when incentives change by *equal percentage* amounts, though in this case the greater absolute change incurred in the higher-paying field may balance out the smaller value of money.

Extending the argument to differential changes in wages suggests pos-

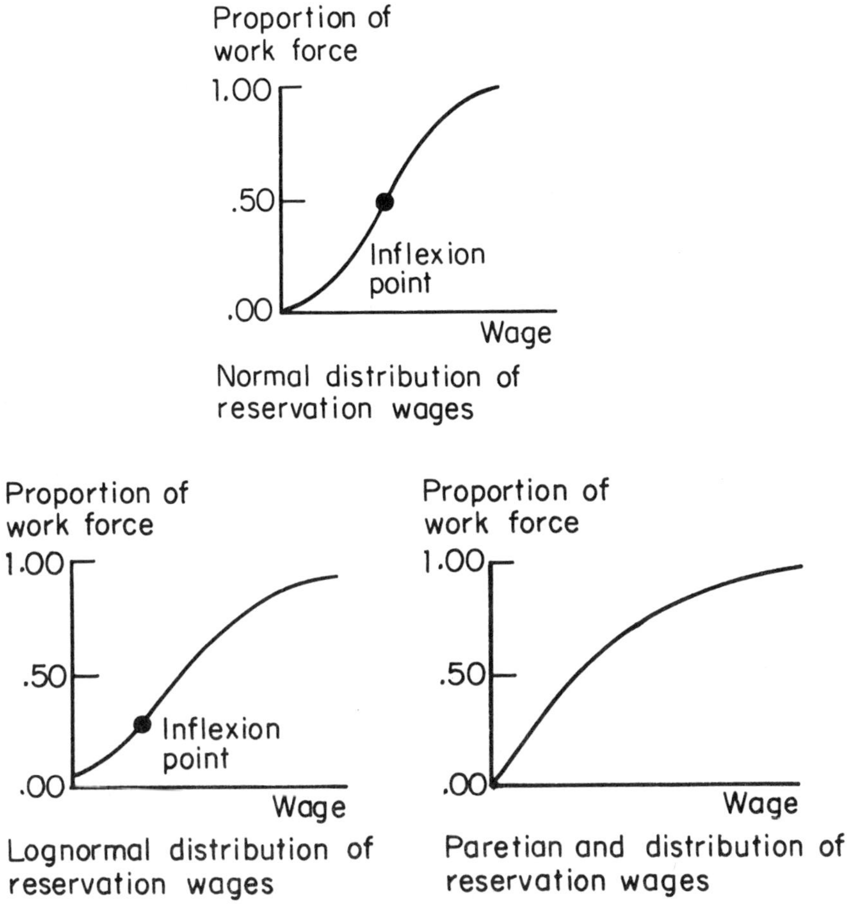

1.5 Aggregate supply curves to an occupation under alternative assumptions of the distribution of "reservation wages" in the labor force

sible "anomolous" responses to relative wages. An increase favoring higher-paying fields could, for example, induce marginal suppliers into lower-paying alternatives if the value placed on pecuniary characteristics diminishes rapidly. Intuitively, continual increases in real income may favor nonpecuniary opportunities by reducing the marginal utility of additional money. Pleasant working conditions and other desirable aspects of jobs may be superior or luxury goods.[19]

When more than two occupations are considered, the likelihood of anomolies increases significantly. With several options, the number of persons "on the margin" will differ across occupations. The effect of changes in money income on the allocation of workers depends on the extent of the margin and the rate of decline of the value of pecuniary goods. Either one of these factors can create "peculiar" correlations between supplies and wages: even with economic behavior and upward-sloping supply curves, changes in supply might be inversely or only modestly related to changes in wages.

These arguments have three implications for empirical work. First, they suggest that percentage changes in income are better indicators of supply incentive than absolute changes. With percentage measures, the likelihood of inverse relations between changes in money income and in real income is reduced. Second, they raise the possibility that relative wage terms are inappropriate measures of incentive. By forcing coefficients on separate wage figures to be identical, relative wages may mask the differential income elasticity of the characteristics of relevant alternatives. Third, since it is difficult to take account of the size of margins or the income-elasticity of job characteristics in comparisons of income and employment in many careers at two points in time, moving cross-sectional and time series estimates of supply parameters are likely to differ. The cross-sectional analysis can be expected to yield smaller estimates of responsiveness.

Social Science Analyses of Career Choice

As set out above, the economic theory of career choice is based on the interaction of abilities, preferences, and monetary incentives and on the response of marginal suppliers to changes in monetary incentives. The theory does not postulate, as sometimes claimed, a peculiar *homo oeconomicus* whose sole concern in life is money; who always chooses the more remunerative alternative. It asserts only that there exist some persons on the borderline between careers who, all else being the same, respond to economic stimuli. The vast majority of persons may be unaffected by alterations in wages, with their career choice primarily determined by preferences or abilities. Even the marginal supplier may not weigh money heavily in evaluating alternatives; money need be important only *at the margin.*

Viewed in this way, the economic theory of career choice is consistent with the approaches of the other social sciences. It does not deny the importance of abilities or preferences in the career decision nor does it underestimate the role of sociological or psychological phenomena. What it does do is to take these factors as given in order to focus on the effect of wages on aggregate supply. As long as the distribution of preferences and abilities in the total population is relatively stable, economic forces will have an independent and, likely as not, significant role in determining the allocation of workers among jobs. The methodology of this study thus complements rather than competes with sociological or psychological studies.

2 Models of the Labor and Education Markets

In this chapter I am concerned with time lags in the adjustment of the labor market to changed conditions and with the manner in which educational facilities affect supply. The models of the labor and education markets developed here guide the empirical calculations of Chapters 4–9.

2.1 The Time Structure of Supply Response

"The supply of labor in a trade in any generation," observed Marshall, "tends to conform to its earnings not in that but in the preceding generation." [1] There are two reasons for this: the years of training and education required for specialized work and the time needed to learn about and adjust to new conditions. Delays of the former kind, *training lags,* operate on the supply side only and give the market for high-level manpower a *recursive* structure, with supply ordinarily lagging behind demand.[2] Delays of the second type, to be called *information-decision lags,* affect both suppliers and employers.

Training Lags

The training lag for most high-level jobs is set by the period of production in the university system and, for institutional and technical reasons, is well specified by the educational process. Bachelor's training, for example, typically takes four years, with the sciences and engineering requiring the entire period in the major, and social sciences or humanities, just two years. Professional training in law, medicine, or business also has definite periods of production, ranging from two to four years. Only in the doctorate program, where many students spend more than four years, is there noticeable variation in the length of training.

Under some circumstances the lead time needed to train specialists will exceed the college delay. College students must, after all, have appropriate high school preparation before undertaking a college major.[3] Because the educational system is shaped like a pyramid, however, with the bulk of students at lower levels of training, most adjustments in supply do *not* require changes in pre-college training. Even in the sciences the number of students with strong high school training far exceeds the number in college programs. A shift of just one per cent of high school students taking mathematics in their senior years into the college major would, for example, increase the output of B.S. candidates by *one third*.[4] Thus, the college delay is an appropriate measure of the lag between the decision to supply specialized labor and actual supply.

The pipeline of production in the university system also facilitates adjustment with a minimum lead time. In fields with cumulative, rigorous training — engineering, pre-medicine, science — many freshmen and sophomores with indefinite career plans enroll to preserve the *option* of choosing the specialties. If the decisions of these students to continue in a program are influenced by market incentive, the number of graduates can be altered without changing the number of enrollees. Similar adjustments in the behavior of graduate students "with all but the dissertation" permit flexibility in doctorate production. For limited periods of time the "effective training lag" can thus be shorter than the period of formal study. The smaller the fraction of qualified persons that normally go on to advanced study, and the more flexible decisions to change majors, the shorter is the adjustment delay.

Information-decision Lags

Information-decision lags are complex phenomena whose extent is difficult to determine a priori. It seems reasonable, however, that they will be greater the greater the *random variation* of wages or employment in a market, the greater the *economic resources* committed by a decision, and the greater the *nonprofit* motive of enterprises. In the first case, variability confuses permanent with transitory developments, making it wise to wait for additional facts before reacting to change. In the second case, the dollar value of resources affects the time devoted to search by increasing the payoff to obtaining correct information.[5] Finally, the absence of clear economic signals and goals probably makes nonprofit enterprises slower to respond to market developments than profit-maximizing firms.

Short-run Adjustments

In addition to changes in the supply of new entrants there are several other mechanisms by which the labor market adjusts to new conditions. These relatively short-run mechanisms allow for greater flexibility and smaller lags in the market than are depicted in models of career choice. Some of the principal short-run mechanisms are:

1) *Allocation of time among activities.* By shifting the amount of time devoted to different work activities such as research, teaching, or administration, the manhours in activities can be increased or decreased. This mechanism is especially important in fields where many persons teach, since university faculty have summers free and spend relatively few hours in the classroom.

2) *Alterations in labor participation.* Retirement decisions and the work decisions of marginally committed women offer a way of expanding or contracting the work force in the short run.

3) *Occupational mobility.* In specialized jobs, mobility may occur among related specialties (physiology and zoology, for example) or between managerial and professional work.

4) *Alteration of job content.* By adding or subtracting tasks, employers can change the skills required for a job to make best use of the available work force.

5) *Training older workers.* Since older workers often pick up additional skills needed for more advanced work, on-the-job training or retraining may upgrade the work force more quickly than training the young.

6) *Substitution among different work skills or between labor and capital.* The degree to which this adjustment mechanism can be used depends on technical production possibilities.

2.2 Lagged Adjustment Models of the Labor Market

The effect of lagged supply response on the operation of the labor market is examined next with a recursive model of the supply and demand for workers in a single occupation. The disequilibrium adjustment paths generated by the model provide the framework for empirical investigations reported in later chapters. Throughout the analysis the possible impact of training facilities on supply is ignored.*

The Basic Labor Market Model

The essential features of the labor market are represented by a six equation "basic" model:

1) Career-decision equation, relating occupational choice to expected discounted lifetime income:

$$T_t = \alpha_0 W_t^* - \alpha_1 A_t^*$$

2) Income expectation equation, linking expectations to market phenomena:

(a) $W_t^* = W_t$ and $A_t^* = A_t$

(b) $W_t^* = W_{t-1}^* + B_0(W_t - W_{t-1}^*)$, and analogously for A_t^*

(c) $W_t^* - W_{t-1}^* = B_0(W_t - W_{t-1}^*) + B_1(W_t - W_{t-1})$, analogously for A_t^*

3) Training-supply relation, linking initial career decisions to entrance in the labor market:

$$Q_t = rT_{t-1}$$

4) Stock of labor, relating the stock to the previous period's stock and new entrants:

$$N_t - N_{t-1} = -\delta N_{t-1} + Q_t$$

5) Demand for labor, dependent on wages and output:

$$N_t^d = -a_0 W_t + a_1 A_t + a_2 Y_t$$

6) Market clearing

$$N_t^d = N_t$$

The symbols are defined as follows:

Variables

T_t = number of students selecting training in year t. Training lasts for one time period;

* The assumption that individual supply decisions, rather than the availability of training facilities, determines the output of universities is supported by the evidence in Chapters 7 and 9.

W_t^*, A_t^* = expected lifetime income in the occupation and in alternatives, respectively, discounted to present value. The subscript t is the period in which expectations are formed;

W_t, A_t = vectors of wages and other economic conditions determining the state of the labor market for the occupation and its competitors, respectively;

Q_t = number of entrants in year t;

N_t = stock of workers in the occupation in year t;

Y_t = output in industries hiring the specialists.

Parameters

$\alpha_0, \alpha_1, a_1, a_1, a_2 > 0$

$0 \leq B_0 \leq 1$ B_0 is an adjustment coefficient relating expectations to previous expectations and conditions;

$0 \leq B_1 \leq 1$ B_1 is a trend extrapolation coefficient showing how changes in wages influence expectations;

$0 \leq r \leq 1$ r is the fraction of students completing a course of training;

$\delta < 1$ δ is the depreciation of stock resulting from deaths, retirement, mobility, and changing marginal productivity over the life-cycle. δ can be negative.

Endogenous variables: $T_t, W_t^*, W_t, N_t, Q_t, A_t^*$

Exogenous variables: A_t, Y_t.

The recursive structure of the model is easily exhibited. By equations (1)–(3), supply is predetermined by previous supply and wages. Through market clearing, demand becomes a wage determination equation relating wages to lagged endogenous and exogenous variables:

$$W_t = -(1/a_0)N_t + (a_1/a_0)A_t + (a_2/a_0)Y_t. \tag{7a}$$

Substituting for N_t with equations (2a) and (3),

$$\begin{aligned} W_t = {} & -(1/a_0)[N_{t-1} - \delta N_{t-1} \\ & + r\alpha_0 W_{t-1} - r\alpha_1 A_{t-1}] + (a_1/a_0)A_t + (a_2/a_0)Y_t \end{aligned} \tag{7b}$$

Thus, $W_t \rightarrow N_{t+1} \rightarrow W_{t+1} \rightarrow N_{t+2}$, and so on.

Expectations rules (2a–c) relate expected income to market phenomena in increasingly complex ways. The first rule sets expected income equal to past income, which, in view of increasing real wages, is best interpreted as assuming that economic growth has no effect, *ceterus paribus,* on expected relative incomes. The second rule allows for the adjustment of expectations to past differences between expected and actual income. Presumably each cohort modifies prevailing expectations in the direction of the latest information.* The final rule (2c) adds extrapolation of past changes (ΔW_t) to the adjustment process, under the assumption that past trends are expected to continue.

Demand is represented in the model as demand for a *stock* of workers, preferably measured in "effective work units," depending on productivity. The usual difficulties in measuring the stock of an input can be handled by weighting numbers of workers by a predetermined index of productivity such as wages,[6] eliminating stock terms through judicious substitution,[7] or by modifying the model to focus on new entrants.

Modified Model: New Entrants

There are several conceptual and empirical advantages to focusing on recent graduates as a separate group of workers. First, their economic status is probably especially significant in the career choice of young students, who are likely to anticipate similar experiences. Second, the salaries of new entrants are less dispersed about the average rate than those of older workers, and so should be a more meaningful indicator of returns to specialized training. Third, the salaries of recent graduates are given an especially heavy weight in discounted lifetime earnings. Fourth, the mobility of young workers may produce an exceptionally active, responsive market, offering particularly good clues to future developments.[8] Finally, data on the number of new entrants (e.g., graduates) and on starting salaries are readily available while those on stocks of workers and lifetime income are harder to come by.

To modify the model to concentrate on new entrants, equations (2), (5), and (6) are replaced by:

(2′) Expectations equation: $W_t = f(W_t^N)$ and $A_t = f(A_t)$, where f is any of the three rules presented earlier;

(5′) Demand for new entrants: $Q_t^N = -a_0W_t^N + a_1A_t^N + a_2Y_t$.

(6′) Market clearing: $Q_t^N = Q_t$,

where Q_t^N = demand for new entrants;
W_t^N = wage of new entrants;
A_t^N = wage in substitute occupations.

* Note that the usual justification of adaptive expectations in terms of *individual* response to experience with past expectations is invalid in the present context, for different persons make career decisions over time.

As before, the demand equation is rewritten as a relation between wages as the dependent variable and the number of entrants and exogenous factors:

$$(7') \qquad W_t^N = (-1/a_0)Q_t^N + (a_1/a_0)A_t^N + (a_2/a_0)Y_t.$$

If starting salaries index lifetime earnings, and the substitutability between young and old workers is small, or the stock of older workers relatively constant in the short run, this model will provide a tolerable picture of market developments.

Equilibrium Conditions and Disequilibrium Adjustment

An occupation is in labor market equilibrium when its stock of workers remains fixed over time[9] — that is when the flow of new entrants equals the outflow from depreciation:

$$N_t = N_{t-1} \quad \text{or} \quad Q_t = N_{t-1}.$$

When this condition is satisfied, expected and actual wages are equal in all time periods so that no cohort has the incentive to change supply.

Figure 2.1 depicts the equilibrium situation. Quadrant I shows the demand curve, a short-run, inelastic supply curve, and long-run supply. Quadrant II shows the relation between actual and expected wages and between expected wages and the number of new entrants. Quadrants III and IV show the determination of stock. All variables are constant in equilibrium.

The model generates two adjustment paths to equilibrium: a *cobweb* path, in which variables oscillate toward equilibrium, and an *incomplete adjustment* path, in which they approach but fail to attain equilibrium for several periods of time. Figure 2.2 depicts the paths in the market for new entrants: Panel A is the usual cobweb diagram, in which an initial shift in demand raises wages, leading to additional entrants and an ensuing reduction in wages; over time, wages and the number of entrants move toward the $(\overline{E},\overline{W})$ point; Panel B shows incomplete adjustment, with the increased wage having a modest impact on expectations and supply and with disequilibrium continuing for several periods.

Since new entrants represent the change in stock, the path of adjustment for new entrants may differ from that for the market as a whole. For instance, the number of new entrants may fluctuate from period to period, while the total stock approaches equilibrium along an incomplete adjustment path. The principal relations between the flow and stock adjustments

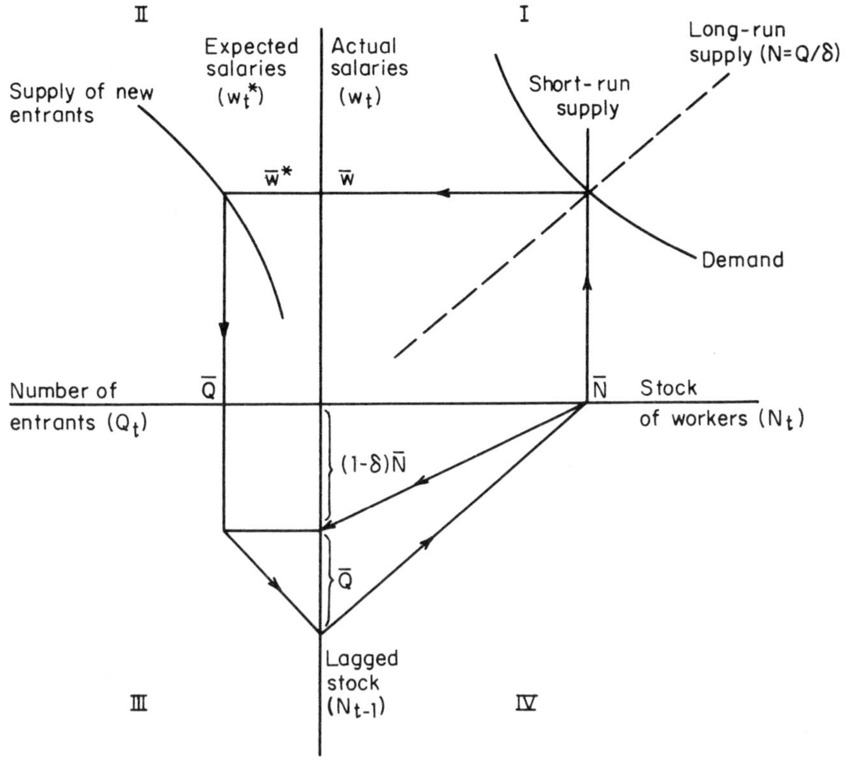

2.1 Equilibrium in the basic model

are set out in Figure 2.3. Panels A and B show incomplete adjustment in the market for stocks of labor and in the market for new entrants. In Panel A the number of entrants is increasing toward $\delta\bar{N}$ so that the growth of stock accelerates. In Panel B the number of entrants is large and declining; as a result, the rate of growth of the stock decelerates. In Panel C are shown fluctuations of the cobweb type in both parts of the market. The final two panels depict fluctuations in the rate at which the stock approaches equilibrium accompanied by cobweb (panel D) or cobweb-type fluctuations around a trend line (panel E) in the new entrants market.

Determinants of Disequilibrium Adjustment

The conditions governing the path to equilibrium are found by solving the difference equation system and analyzing the effect of parameters on the solution. Judicious substitution yields a single first-order equation

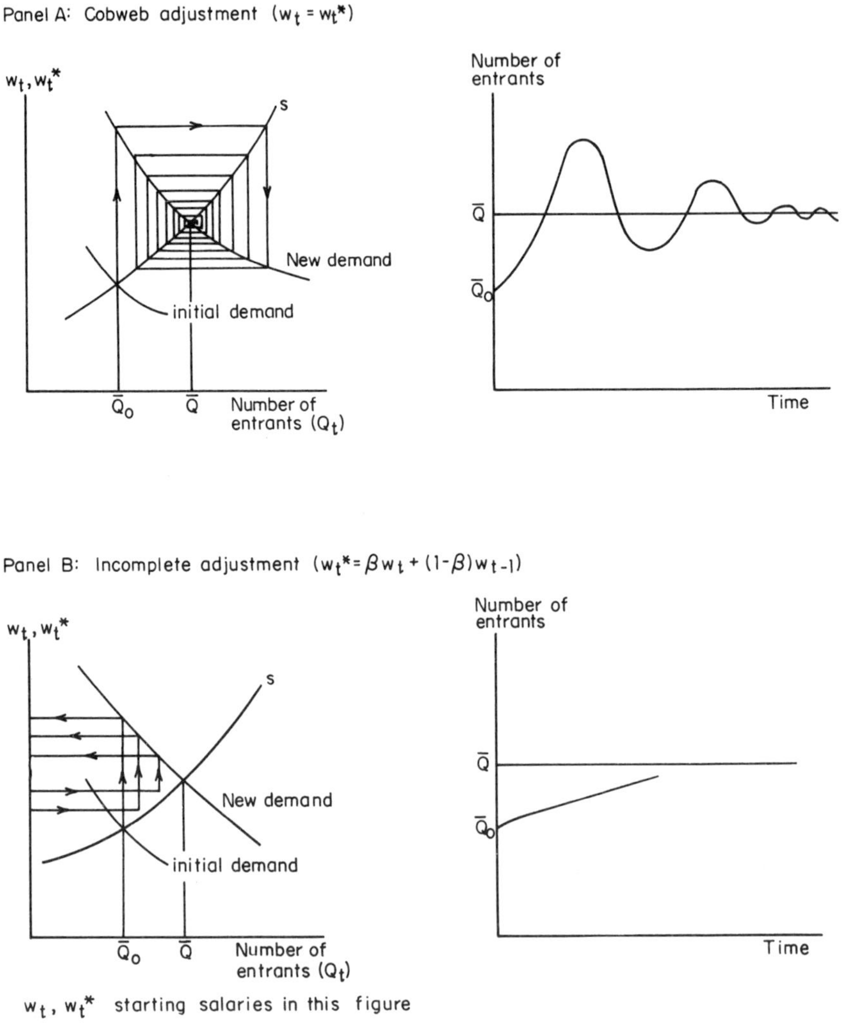

2.2 Adjustment of new entrants

under expectations rule (2a) and a second-order equation with rules (2b) and (2c).[10] The principal parameters have the following effects on the nature of the path:

1) The smaller the demand parameter (a_0), the more likely is cobweb adjustment. This is because inelastic demand places the burden of adjustment on wages, which can then motivate excessive supply response.

2) The greater the supply parameters (r, α_0), the more likely is cobweb adjustment. Elastic supply is needed to overshoot equilibrium.

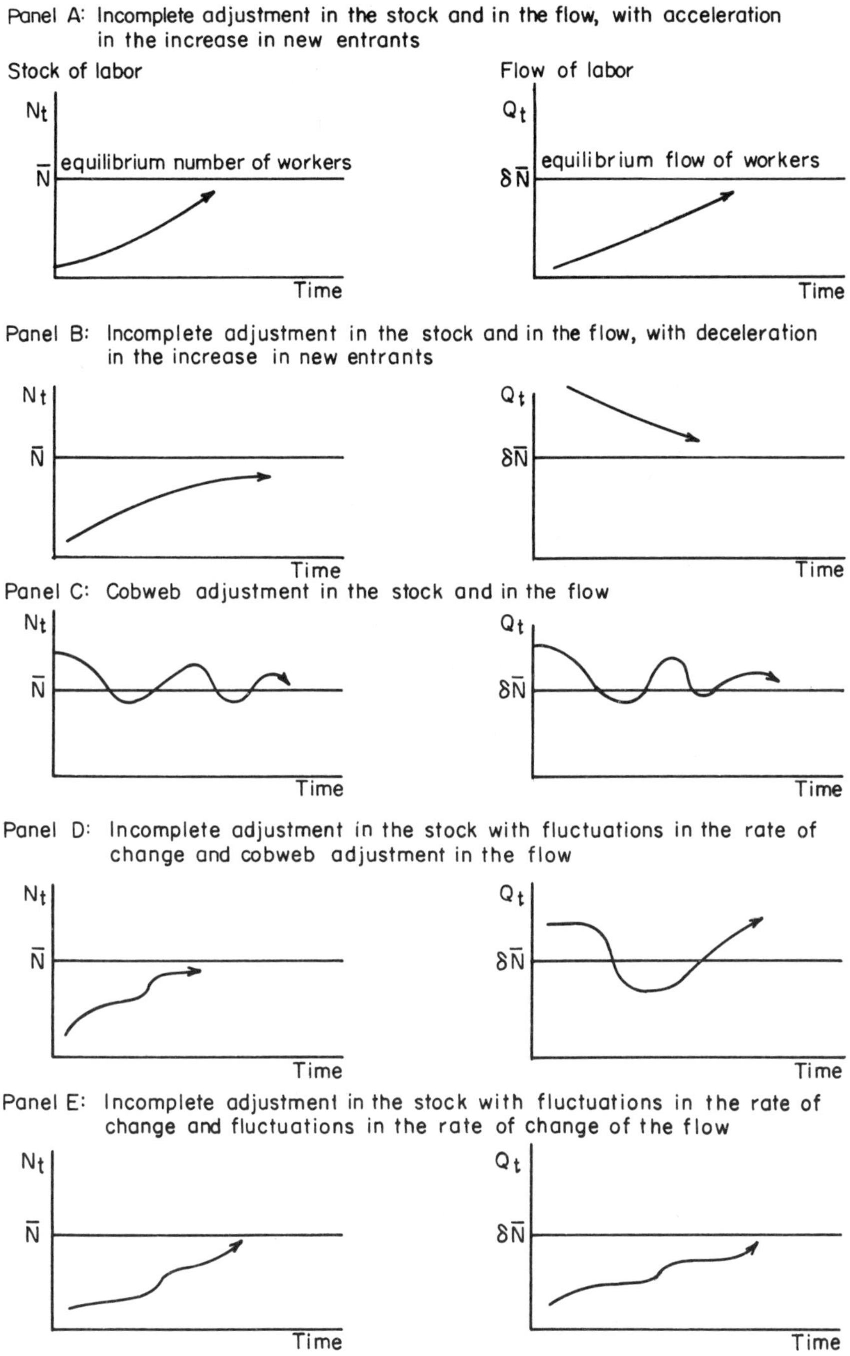

2.3 A comparison of paths to equilibrium in the market for new entrants with paths to equilibrium in the market for the stock of workers

3) The smaller the adaptive expectations coefficient (B_0), the more likely is incomplete adjustment. This is because limited response to current conditions is needed to undershoot equilibrium.*

4) The extrapolation coefficient (B_1) makes cobweb adjustment more likely by enhancing responsiveness to changes in wages.

An additional factor influencing the nature of adjustment, whose impact is not revealed in a *linear* model, is the extent of the initial change in market conditions. Because of likely nonlinear limits on supply and demand responsiveness, the greater the initial shift, the more probable is incomplete adjustment.†

Finally, the adjustment path observed in the market also depends on the time period under consideration. In the very short run, incomplete adjustment will be frequent, for overshooting is impossible. In the long run, cobweb adjustment is more likely.

Incomplete Adjustment and the Acceleration of Supply

Under incomplete adjustment and expectations rule (2a), changes in supply (ΔT_t) depend on changes in expectations and thus on the deviation between actual and expected income:

$$(8) \qquad \Delta T_t = \alpha_0 B_0(W_t - W_{t-1}^*) - \alpha_1 B_0(A_t - A_{t-1}^*).$$

Since expected income is generally unobservable, W_{t-1}^* (and A_{t-1}^*) must be eliminated from the equation for empirical implementation. One way to do this is to make use of the fact that in disequilibrium the equilibrium wage ($\overline{W}$) lies between expected and actual wages and replace W_{t-1}^* with a function of W_t and $\overline{W}$. For the linear model of equations (1)–(6) the result is a linear function dependent on the supply and demand parameters:[11]

$$(9) \qquad W_{t-1}^* = \overline{W}_t - (a_0/r\alpha_0)(W_t - \overline{W});$$

* The effect of B_0 on the time path to equilibrium is actually more complex than this, for small B_0 also extend the range of supply and demand parameters consistent with stable cobweb fluctuations and may produce a complex oscillatory solution to the difference equation. However, the length or periodicity of fluctuations increases as B_0 declines in value, so that small B_0 will be associated with incomplete adjustment for several time periods.

† Supply is likely to become less elastic as the number of "required" workers increases because of the necessity of attracting less able and less interested individuals and because of limitations on training facilities. Demand — in this case wages — will respond slowly to great changes because of information-decision lags and the danger of upsetting internal salary scales.

and similarly for A_{t-1}.* The deviation of W_{t-1}* from W can be estimated in cross-sectional calculations by differences in lifetime incomes or rates of return among occupations, possibly after correcting for the nonpecuniary value of work characteristics.

Alternatively, equation (1) can be substituted into (8), yielding a testable relation between changes in supply and income and past supply:

$$(10) \qquad \Delta T_t = \alpha_0 B_0 W_t - \alpha_1 B_0 A_t - B_0 T_{t-1}.$$

This relation differs from the usual equilibrium supply function or from a cobweb function in one fundamental way: it relates *changes* in supply to the *level* of wages (relative to equilibrium), rather than to changes in wages. Under incomplete adjustment, supply always tends toward equilibrium, with changes in wages governing the speed, not the direction, of movement:

$$(11) \qquad \Delta(\Delta T_t) = \alpha_0 B_0(\Delta W_t) - B_0 \Delta T_{t-1} - \alpha_1 B_0 \Delta A_t.$$

Greater changes in wages accelerate the adjustment process, while smaller changes retard it. Supply is thus expected to obey a "rule of acceleration" in markets with extended disequilibria. Conformance to the rule is evidence for the incomplete adjustment variant of the model.

Shortages and Surpluses[12]

Within the context of the basic model, the concepts of labor shortages or surpluses can be given a definite meaning. A shortage or surplus is obviously the difference between actual and equilibrium numbers of workers $(N_t - \overline{N})$. Since there is a one-to-one correspondence between quantity and wage, this definition is similar to the human capital identification of disequilibrium with rates of return different from those for other investments. It is more general than the rate-of-return concept because it explicitly allows for the effect of nonpecuniary factors, job characteristics, ability requirements, and changes in demand or supply on the equilibrium wage and quantity.

A further distinction can be made between the *cyclic* shortage or surplus associated with cobweb adjustment and the *continual* disequilibrium that accompanies incomplete adjustment for extended periods of time. By introducing lags into the wage equation, it is also possible to bring into the analysis "dynamic shortages" of the kind envisaged by Arrow and Capron.[13] Since supply generally lags behind demand, the dynamic shortage is a shorter-run concept than those described above.

2.3 Availability of Training Facilities

The supply of specialists is governed by individual career decisions only if the educational system offers adequate training facilities. What determines the availability of facilities in colleges and universities? How are the needs of the labor market transmitted to the educational system?

Labor and Education Markets

The most important linkages between the education and labor markets, the two mechanisms for allocating manpower in a modern economy, are described graphically in Figure 2.4. When the markets are properly

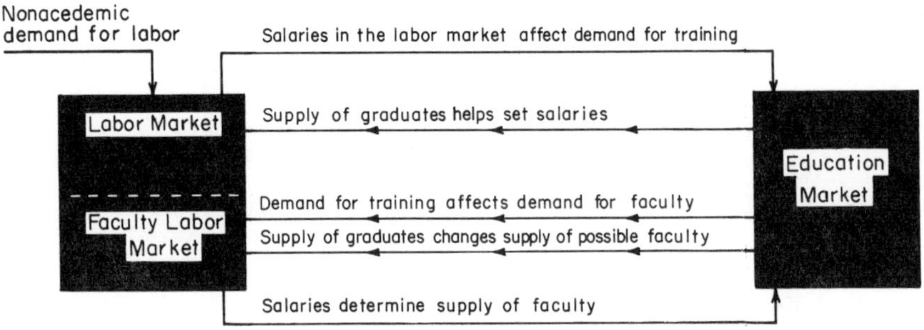

2.4 Linkages between the education and labor markets

coupled, changes in the number of graduates alleviate imbalances in the labor market and facilitate future adjustments in the education market by altering the supply of potential faculty. When the markets are improperly coupled, on the other hand, excess demand for specialists produces a "vicious training circle" of higher nonacademic salaries, fewer faculty, fewer places, and a reduction in graduates that raises salaries even further.

There are several ways in which imbalances can be equilibrated. Faced, say, with a sudden upsurge in demand, educational institutions can:

— raise tuition and fees, as is frequently done to finance higher costs throughout academia, though rarely to reduce applications to a curricula or to specific institutions;

— hire additional faculty, either by raising salaries to attract qualified specialists or by lowering hiring standards;

— admit all applicants, without increasing facilities, thereby reducing quality;

— ration places, as is common in high-quality universities and in medical schools.

The mix of adjustments used in the market depends on the decisions of university administrators and on the operation of the market for the principal input into higher education, the faculty.

University Decision-making

In the absence of knowledge of the weights placed by university decision-makers on diverse objectives, it is best to focus on the impact of the major constraints — educational production functions, budgets, applicants, and the labor market — on the decision process.

An educational production function has, for a variety of reasons, including the difficulty of measuring the quality of inputs or outputs and of interpreting input-output relations in nonprofit enterprises, yet to be satisfactorily identified.[14] Many models assume an especially simple production relation — fixed coefficients between faculty and students.[15] While administrators may have approximately fixed *desired* faculty: student ratios, the diversity of resources used in the education process (student and faculty time, textbooks, libraries, laboratory facilities, and the like), makes the fixed production limitation unrealistic. In this study I assume that the desired ratio is constant, but that the actual ratio will vary in response to changes in economic conditions. Adoption of a fixed ratio goal to guide decisions may be rational in the context of a nonprofit institution whose output is difficult to measure.

The budget and applicant constraints obviously limit the scale of operations. They are also likely to influence operating decisions indirectly, with the *source* of funds and students affecting the kind of education provided. Greater emphasis on the importance of teaching, for example, is to be expected when tuition accounts for the better part of budgets and greater emphasis on sciences when the population of students is limited (as in Europe).[16]

The labor market has a dual effect on university behavior: First, on the basis of nonacademic wages and job opportunities and the number of qualified specialists, the *external* market determines the supply of faculty available at given salaries. Second, the *internal* market, operating through the desire for an "equitable" internal salary scale, limits interspecialty salary variation. Narrow interspecialty differentials make recruitment of men in occupations with good nonacademic opportunities difficult and increases the use of nonpecuniary rewards.

Faculty Labor Market

The labor market for faculty is composed of three decision-making bodies: universities, nonacademic employers, and qualified specialists. Given the educational production function, university budgets, number of applicants, and the internal labor market, university administrators decide on how many faculty to hire at various levels. Nonacademic employers make a similar decision on the basis of the technology of production, demand for their output, and the prices of other inputs. Qualified specialists evaluate the pecuniary and nonpecuniary benefits of academic and nonacademic work and choose between them.

As a first approximation, the market can be represented by a "simultaneous equations" model in which the allocation of workers and salaries is jointly determined. Such a model should take account of several distinctive features of the faculty case: the nonprofit motivation of universities, which may make the demand for faculty different from other demand schedules; the role of nonpecuniary income in influencing supply decisions; and the way in which shifts in the demand for nonacademic specialists are transmitted to the demand for faculty through changes in enrollment. The following "simultaneous allocation" model allows for the first of these features; the others are dealt with in the empirical work reported in Chapter 9.

Simultaneous Allocation Model

The simultaneous determination of the salaries and employment of a fixed stock of workers between two sectors of work can be described with three behavioral and three balance equations. For purposes of this study the sectors are identified as (i) the university system and (ii) all other employers of specialized manpower. The model is set out first in logarithmic difference form to show the dynamic effect of a fixed desired faculty: student ratio on demand. With different specifications of the variables shifting the demand for specialists, the model can be applied to other markets.

Behavioral Equations

1) Demand for faculty is represented by a relation between the number of faculty and salaries, the budget of universities, student enrollment, and the difference between last period's faculty: student ratio and the desired ratio:

$$\Delta \ln F^d = \alpha_0 \Delta \ln E + \alpha_1 \Delta \ln B - \alpha_2 \Delta \ln W - \alpha_3[\ln (F/E)_{-1} - \ln (\overline{F/E})].$$

Increases in the number of students enrolled (E) and in the budget constraint (B) increase demand, while increases in wages and large faculty : student ratios relative to the fixed goal reduce it. The coefficient on enrollment is expected to be less than unity because tenure arrangements and investment in "specific" human capital make faculty a quasi-fixed factor of production for which immediate and complete adjustments are costly.[17]

2) Supply of faculty is a relation between the number of prospective teachers, academic and nonacademic salaries, and the stock of qualified specialists:

$$\Delta \ln F^s = \alpha_0 \Delta \ln W - \alpha_1 \Delta \ln A + \Delta \ln \overline{Q}.$$

3) The demand for nonacademic specialists links the number desired, salaries, and output in specialist-employing industries:

$$\Delta \ln G^d = -c_0 \Delta \ln A + c_1 \Delta \ln Y.$$

Balance Equations

4) An accounting identity relating nonacademic supply to the stock of qualified specialists and the supply of faculty. This equation must of necessity be a linear relation:

$$G^s = \overline{Q} - F^s$$

5) Market clearing in academic sector:

$$\Delta \ln F^d = \Delta \ln F^s.$$

6) Market clearing in nonacademic sector:

$$\Delta \ln G^d = \Delta \ln G^s.$$

Variables

F^s, F^d = number of faculty supplied and demanded, respectively;
E = enrollment;
$(F/E)_{-1}$ = faculty: student ratio, lagged one period;
$(\overline{F/E})$ = desired faculty: student ratio;
B = budget of universities;
W = faculty salary;
A = nonacademic salary;
G^s = the supply of specialists to nonacademic employers;
G^d = the demand by nonacademic employers for specialists;

Y = output in specialist-employing industries;
$\overline{Q}$ = stock of specialists

F^d, W, A, G^d, F^s, G^s are the endogenous variables.

This model has three complicating features. First, simultaneity rules out the use of ordinary least-squares in estimating the behavioral equations. Second, inclusion of the linear accounting identity in a system of logarithmic equations creates a mixed linear-log-linear structure, with additional problems of estimation. Third, our limited knowledge of university goals and the operation of the university sector make the entire model more tentative and exploratory than that developed in section 2.2. With additional information about university behavior, it might be possible to modify the postulated fixed desired faculty : student ratio and to make variables like university budgets endogenous. Development of a general model of the higher educational system is beyond the scope of this study.

Summary

The cobweb, incomplete adjustment, and simultaneous allocation models developed in this chapter provide the framework for ensuing empirical analysis. In the cobweb model, the recursive structure of the market for highly trained workers produces cyclic fluctuations. Changes in salaries alter the supply of specialists, thereby changing salaries several years later, and so on. In the incomplete adjustment model, the recursive structure produces relatively lengthy disequilibria. The market moves toward an equilibrium level of salaries and employment for extended periods of time, with no overshooting of the equilibrium. In the simultaneous allocation model the employment and salaries of a fixed stock of workers are jointly determined with respect to several types of employers.

3 Developments in the Market for Highly Specialized Workers after World War II

Can the models of Chapter 2 explain changes in the employment and education of highly specialized workers that followed the Second World War? How well does an economic theory of career choice account for the decisions of college students?

This chapter takes the first step toward answering these questions. It sets out the principal postwar developments that should be explained by a theory of the labor market and career choice. Since highly specialized workers are predominantly male, and female decision-making is based on more complex factors, the chapter focuses on the changed position of male workers.

3.1 Specialized Occupations

The professional, technical, and kindred (PTK) occupations that contain most of the highly specialized workers of an industrial economy employ a large and growing proportion of the male work force in the United States. In 1967 over 13 percent of American men were employed in PTK jobs — 3–4 percent in scientific fields, and an additional 2½ percent in related technical activities (Table 3.1). Although the relative number of PTK workers has been increasing since the beginning of the twentieth century, the rate of professionalization did not attain impressive dimensions until after World War II. From 1947 to 1967 the PTK share of male employment more than doubled — an increase two and a half times as great

Table 3.1 Proportion of Male Workers in Professional and Science-oriented Occupations, 1947–1967[a]

		Percent of Employed Males					
Year	*Employed Males (thousands)*	*Total Professional, Technical and Kindred*	*Engineers*	*Scientists*	*Technicians*	*Social Scientists*	*All Science-Oriented*
1947	41,535	5.6	—	—	—	—	—
1950	42,156	6.4	1.3	0.4	1.3	0.1	3.1
1954	42,420	8.4	1.5	0.5	—	—	—
1960	44,485	10.7	1.9	0.8	2.0	0.2	4.9
1967	47,479	13.0	2.3	1.0	2.4	0.3	6.0

SOURCES: *Manpower Report of the President*, 1968; *Scientific and Technical Manpower Resources*, National Science Foundation, 1964.

[a] The number of employees in engineering, science, and technical occupations includes a small number of females; the 1967 estimates in these cases are extrapolations of 1963 date.

as that in the preceding half-century. For the first time, census figures have shown the professions to be the fastest-growing group of occupations.

Other developed countries also report large and growing numbers of professional workers. In 1960, the PTK shares of the work force, including females, in West European countries ranged from .085 to .115, proportion roughly equivalent to those for the United States.[1] The number of professionals in these countries and in Japan has increased rapidly since World War II. Only in scientific and engineering fields does the United States have a manpower "advantage," though here the advantage disappears when technicians are included as part of the scientific population.

Specific Occupations

There are over sixty detailed occupations in the PTK group. What are their relative sizes? How important are college-trained workers in each? How has employment grown?

The largest single specialty in the PTK group is engineering, which contains one fifth of all male professionals. An additional fifth of the work force is employed in closely related drafting or technician jobs (Table 3.2, columns 1 and 2). Other large occupations, encompassing roughly 10 percent of professionals, are secondary school teaching, accounting and auditing, and, as a group, the traditionally independent practitioners of law, medicine, and dentistry. Natural scientists make up less than 5 percent of the PTK work force.[2]

Table 3.2 Employment and Education of Male Engineers, Scientists, and Other Professionals in 1960 and Changes in Employment and Education, 1950–1960

Occupational Group	(*1*) *Number* (*thousands*) (*1960*)	(*2*) *Percent of All Profes-sionals* (*1960*)	(*3*) *Percent with 4 or 4+ Years of College* (*1960*)	(*4*)[a] *Change in Percent with 4 or 4+ Years of College, 1950–60*	(*5*)[a] *Percent Rate of Growth of Employment 1950–60*
Total, experienced civilian labor force	45,686	—	9.7	+2.4	6.9
Total, professional, technical, and kindred (PTK)	4,543	100.0	55.8	—	50.2
Engineers, technical	880	19.4	55.5	1.9	63.4
Aeronautical	52	1.1	60.3	1.9	194.6
Chemical	41	0.9	86.0	3.7	26.1
Civil	157	3.5	53.8	−0.9	26.2
Electrical	184	4.0	58.4	4.1	72.8
Industrial	96	2.1	43.8	0.2	137.4
Mechanical	160	3.5	53.8	4.0	39.7
Metallurgical	18	0.4	63.3	4.8	51.0
Mining	12	0.3	74.2	8.4	−14.2
Sales	57	1.3	52.9	—	128.7
Natural Scientists	204	4.5	76.0	9.9	42.9
Agricultural	11	0.2	65.7	11.3	26.1
Biological-medical	23	0.5	85.1	2.4	69.9
Chemical	83	1.9	70.4	7.4	11.6
Geological	20	0.4	89.5	10.1	83.3
Mathematical	17	0.4	84.1	14.6	133.2
Physics	20	0.4	86.9	9.2	81.7
Social Scientists	55	1.2	70.5	12.8	75.7
Economists	21	0.4	66.8	—	126.5
Psychologists	16	0.4	96.8	—	202.5
Statisticians and actuaries	15	0.3	82.4	—	27.3
Other Professionals	3,404	74.9	54.9	—	48.5
Accountants & auditors	396	8.7	43.6	8.5	20.7
Architects	30	0.7	71.7	9.2	29.4
Clergymen	197	4.3	70.9	8.9	21.5
College presidents, professors and instructors, n.e.c.[b]	81	1.8	95.2	5.5	44.4
Dentists	81	1.8	91.8	1.5	10.6
Draftsmen	201	4.5	10.3	−3.8	61.8
Editors and reporters	65	1.4	51.7	6.7	42.2
Lawyers and judges	206	4.5	89.7	2.0	16.7
Physicians & surgeons	214	4.7	89.7	2.0	16.7
Teachers, elementary and secondary	478	10.8	86.7	11.5	49.0
Technicians (including medical)	313	6.9	10.7	−2.0	237.1

SOURCE: *U.S. Census of Population*, 1950 and 1960.

[a] Columns (4) and (5) refer to workers aged 25–64.

[b] College teachers are allocated to the occupation in which they specialize in Columns (1) and (2). In the remaining columns the data refer to all teachers, including those in engineering and the sciences.

Educational qualifications vary greatly among the professions according to the figures in column 3 of Table 3.2. A college degree is normally a prerequisite for work in the sciences, chemical engineering, medicine, law, and teaching, and of some significance in obtaining jobs in journalism, accounting, and the remaining branches of engineering. For technicians and draftsmen, on the other hand, college education is relatively unimportant. In addition, the level of the requisite degree differs from one field to another. As Table 3.3 shows, the B.S. suffices for most engineers, while the M.S. or Ph.D. is needed by natural and social scientists.

The proportion of specialists with college training increased in virtually all PTK occupations from 1950 to 1960 (Table 3.2, column 4). There were substantial gains in the educational qualifications of natural and social scientists, architects, and ministers. Degree recipients in engineering also increased relative to the total work force, reversing the decline in the average level of education in engineering observed by Blank and Stigler in the decade from 1940 to 1950.[3] Finally, an increasingly large number of business executives also held college degrees. The fraction of managers, officials, and proprietors with degrees doubled from 1950 to 1960. Leading firms hired the vast majority (80 percent) of young managers from the ranks of college men.[4]

The rates of growth of professional employment recorded in Table 3.2 show substantial differences in specific fields. Most striking is the shift in employment from the independent professions to scientific and academic specialties. In dentistry, medicine, and law, employment grew by only 15 percent compared to an average increase of 50 percent in the sciences and engineering. The job market also treated the different scientific fields very differently. Chemistry, agriculture, and three branches of engineering — mining, chemical, and civil — had very slight rates of growth.

Sectoral Distribution of Jobs

The distribution of jobs among types of employers, and consequently the freedom, responsibility, and risk of work, varies substantially among the professions. Some scientific specialists — engineers, chemists, geologists, statisticians and actuarians, and economists — are employed almost entirely by business firms, while others are concentrated in educational institutions (Table 3.4). With the advent of the computer, mathematicians who were previously employed exclusively by universities now find work in industry. From 1950 to 1960 the number of industrial mathematicians increased by a phenomenal 365 percent. Independent practitioners —

Table 3.3 Distribution of College-Trained Scientists and Engineers, by Degree, 1964–1966[a]

	Percentage Distribution		
Occupation	*B.S.*	*M.S.*	*Ph.D.*
Engineers	83.2	14.4	2.1
Aeronautical	71.5	25.1	3.0
Chemical	76.8	13.7	9.1
Civil	87.8	11.2	1.0
Electrical	81.2	16.4	1.5
Industrial	86.2	13.1	0.8
Mechanical	87.9	11.6	0.4
Metallurgical	74.0	17.1	8.5
Mining	94.4	5.7	0.4
Professors	16.1	53.4	30.5
Natural Scientists			
Agriculture	46.3	28.4	25.0
Biology[b]	11.8	18.6	69.6
Chemistry	44.3	19.0	35.9
Geology	45.2	33.2	20.4
Mathematics	28.9	43.9	27.1
Physics	29.1	31.7	39.2
Social Scientists			
Psychology	2.5	32.6	64.9
Economics	21.9	35.3	42.8
Sociology	2.4	16.2	81.7
Linguistics	12.5	31.3	56.2

SOURCES: National Science Foundation, *National Register of Scientific and Technical Personnel*, 1964; National Science Foundation, *Postcensal Survey of Professional and Technical Manpower*, 1966; National Engineers Register, *Engineering Manpower in Profile*.

[a] The data for aeronautical, chemical, mining, and metallurgical engineers are taken from *Engineering Manpower in Profile* and have been adjusted for comparability with the postcensal figures used for other occupations.

[b] The population of "doctorate" biologists includes those with an M.D. as well as those with the Ph.D. In 1964, 19.9% of all biological scientists were M.D.'s.

lawyers, doctors, architects, and the clergy — are generally employed in the noneducational service sector. School teachers are, of course, found in public education; accountants and journalists work for private business.

At the highest level of education the pattern of job opportunities is somewhat different. Doctorate chemists and engineers and many physicists work in industrial jobs. Other natural and social scientists, including economists, are employed almost exclusively by universities.

Table 3.4 Percentage of Male PTK Workers Employed in Business, Government, and Professional Services in 1960

Occupation	*Business*	*Government*	*Professional Services*	
			Noneducational	*Educational*
Total, male	87.8	5.3	4.0	2.9
Total, professional	49.2	7.7	25.2	17.9
Engineers	83.6	8.1	6.4	1.9
Aeronautical	94.2	4.6	0.7	0.5
Chemical	93.7	2.1	3.7	0.5
Civil	69.8	14.9	14.5	0.8
Electrical	89.6	5.9	4.5	1.0
Industrial	86.4	10.8	2.6	0.2
Mechanical	87.5	5.0	6.7	0.8
Metallurgical	99.5	0.2	0.2	0.1
Mining	89.4	5.2	5.2	0.2
Sales	98.0	—	2.0	—
Natural Scientists[a]	54.8	11.5	8.1	25.6
Agricultural	24.5	26.5	2.3	46.7
Biological-medical	17.2	18.9	15.0	48.9
Chemical	77.2	5.3	9.2	10.3
Geological	68.3	12.0	8.4	9.3
Mathematical	24.5	11.7	4.8	59.0
Physical	35.8	16.9	11.7	35.6
Social Scientists[a]	33.8	13.9	8.8	43.6
Economists	59.1	18.4	2.8	19.7
Psychologists	6.6	12.3	32.7	48.4
Statistician and actuary	68.7	19.3	8.5	3.5
Other Professionals	38.6	7.3	52.8	21.3
Accountant	50.7	12.9	25.7	0.7
Architects	11.1	4.1	83.1	1.7
Clergy	—	—	99.5	—
College teachers	—	—	0.0	100.0
Dentists	—	0.5	98.8	0.3
Editors and reporters	91.7	3.1	3.1	2.1
Lawyers	9.1	12.8	78.0	0.1
Physicians and surgeons	2.5	0.1	96.1	1.3
Teachers	2.0	1.6	0.9	95.5
Draftsmen	78.6	4.9	15.8	0.7
Technicians	71.0	9.0	11.0	9.0
All professionals except draftsmen and technicians	31.6	7.3		24.9

Source: U.S. Bureau of the Census, *U.S. Census of Population*, 1960.
[a] The figures for Natural Scientists and Social Scientists include teachers of those subjects.

3.2 Educational Qualifications

The truly singular feature of the U.S. labor market is the enormous number of young persons preparing for work in institutions of higher education — upward of 55 percent of 18–21-year-old males in 1968. It is significant, though not generally recognized, that more young persons seek work in the college labor market than in the unionized markets stressed by the labor economists.[5] In the near future the college graduate work force will exceed the blue-collar union work force, denoting an historic change in the nature of the labor market.

No other country has a system of higher education of comparable size. The United States typically graduates from four to five times as many college specialists relative to the number of 20–24-year-olds as Western Europe, an advantage not due to peculiar fields like hotel administration and physical education. In the hard sciences the United States exceeds Europe by ratios of 3 or 4 to 1 (Table 3.5).

Several factors can be offered to explain this extensive reliance on colleges and universities. Higher per capita income in the United States may lead to greater consumption of education. The total cost of university training may be lower than in Europe, and the demand for specialists greater. National goals and patterns of socio-economic mobility possibly make it easier for Americans to move up the job ladder.[6] In this study these comparisons are not pursued further;[7] we deal strictly with U.S. developments.

*Changes in the College Populace, 1950–1965**

The size and composition of the male college student population changed greatly in the years after World War II. The most significant developments were

a) a jump in the fraction of young men enrolled in degree programs from 34 to 55 percent of the 18–21-year-old population (1950–1968).

b) expansion of graduate education. In 1950, 19 percent of college degrees were awarded to postgraduates; in 1965, 28 percent.

c) a shift from professional to academic fields. As Figure 3.1 shows, law and medicine lost ground relative to doctorate and master's programs.

d) changes in the academic majors of students, often in different directions at different levels of education. The number of doctorate engineers, for example, increased, while the number of bachelor's engineers declined.

* Developments described here have continued in the period 1965–1970.

Table 3.5 Percentage of College-age Persons with College Training in U.S. and OECD Countries, 1959[a]

Country	*Percent Enrolled in College*	*Percent Receiving First Degrees*	*Percent Receiving First Degrees in Science*
United States	36.6	16.9	3.7
Canada	10.0	6.9	1.6
Sweden	7.1	4.3	1.3
Yugoslavia	6.1	4.3	1.2
France	5.4	3.4	1.4
Netherlands	4.7	1.7	0.6
Belgium	4.6	3.3	0.9
Austria	4.2	1.7	0.8
United Kingdom	4.1	3.4	1.4
Norway	4.0	2.8	1.2
Switzerland	3.8	4.7	1.1
Denmark	3.7	2.2	1.0
Italy	3.6	2.6	0.7
Spain	3.3	1.0	0.4
Germany, F.R.	3.1	2.7	0.8
Greece	3.0	3.0	0.4
Turkey	1.1	n.a.	0.2

SOURCE: *Resources of Scientific and Technical Personnel in the OECD Area* (Paris: Organisation for Economic Co-operation and Development, 1963).

[a] The OECD data are calculated on the basis of the age group that normally attends or graduates from college in each country. Thus, the relevant college-age span differs among countries.

Doctorate Degrees

Beginning at the top of the educational ladder, Table 3.6 presents figures on the relative number of doctorate recipients by field and on the percentage change in graduates from 1950 to 1965. Scientific fields, includ-

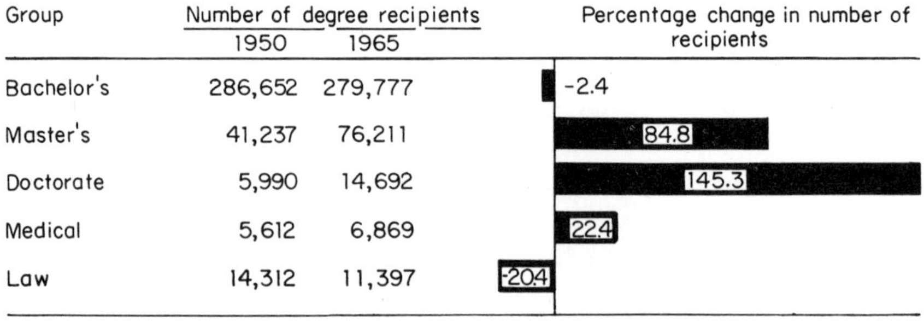
Group
Number of degree recipients
1950
1965
Percentage change in number of recipients
Bachelor's
286,652
279,777
-2.4
Master's
41,237
76,211
84.8
Doctorate
5,990
14,692
145.3
Medical
5,612
6,869
22.4
Law
14,312
11,397
-20.4

3.1 Percentage change in male degree recipients, 1950–1965

Table 3.6 Doctorate Degrees Awarded to Males, by Major, 1950–1965

	Number of Degrees		*Percentage Change,*	*Share of Ph.D. Degrees (in %)*		*Absolute Change in Share*
Field of Study	*1950*	*1965*	*1950–60*	*1950*	*1965*	*1950–1965*
All fields	5,990	14,692	145.3	100.0	100.0	—
Science (except social sciences and psychology)	2,925	7,559	158.4	48.8	51.5	2.7
Engineering	416	2,026	387.0	6.9	13.8	6.9
Aeronautical	23	91	295.7	0.4	0.6	0.2
Chemical	172	362	110.5	2.9	2.5	−0.4
Civil	28	250	792.9	0.5	1.7	1.2
Electrical	80	509	536.3	1.3	3.5	2.2
Industrial	n.a.	60	—	0.1	0.4	0.3
Mechanical	46	265	476.1	0.8	1.8	1.0
Metallurgical	n.a.	179	—	0.1	1.2	1.1
Mining	n.a.	24	—	0.1	0.2	0.1
Biological Sciences	543	1,698	212.7	9.1	11.6	2.5
Botany	116	205	76.7	1.9	1.4	−0.5
Zoology	102	209	104.9	1.7	1.4	−0.3
Microbiology	60	188	213.3	1.0	1.3	0.3
Biophysics	n.a.	38	—	—	0.3	—
Genetics	n.a.	78	—	—	0.5	—
Entomology	50	129	158.0	0.8	0.9	0.1
Pathology	n.a.	32	—	—	0.2	—
Pharmacology	n.a.	73	—	—	0.5	—
Biochemistry	99	247	149.5	1.7	1.7	—
Physics	30	105	250.0	0.5	0.7	0.2
Physical Sciences	1,451	2,886	85.1	24.2	18.3	−5.9
Chemistry	914	1,277	39.7	15.3	8.7	−6.6
Physics	353	922	161.2	5.9	6.3	0.4
Geology	110	251	128.2	1.8	1.7	−0.1
Mathematics	151	623	312.6	2.5	4.2	1.7
Agriculture	364	526	44.5	6.1	3.6	−2.5
Psychology	241	688	185.5	4.0	4.7	0.7
Social Sciences	742	1,806	143.4	12.4	12.3	−0.1
Sociology	107	194	81.3	1.8	1.3	−0.5
Economics	191	393	105.8	3.2	2.1	−0.5
History and Geography	282	591	109.6	4.7	4.0	−0.7
Political Science	117	318	171.8	2.0	2.2	0.2
Education	792	2,179	175.1	13.2	14.8	1.6
Arts and Humanities	205	611	198.0	3.4	4.2	0.8
Languages and Literature	338	870	157.4	5.6	5.9	0.3
Business and Commerce	52	241	363.5	0.9	1.6	0.7
Other	695	732	5.3	11.6	5.0	−6.6

SOURCE: Office of Education, *Earned Degrees Conferred* (1950, 1965).

ing the social sciences and engineering, account for nearly three fourths of the Ph.D.'s, with half of these degrees awarded in the natural sciences and engineering and a fifth in the social sciences and psychology (columns 1 and 2). The single largest specialty exclusive of education (where the Ed.D. is awarded) is engineering. Cultural fields — arts, humanities, languages — receive just one tenth of the doctorates.

The preeminent position of engineering as a doctorate specialty is a recent development and probably the most important change in the Ph.D. market in postwar years. Prior to World War II, fewer than 3 in 100 Ph.D.'s were awarded in engineering, compared to 15 in 100 in the late 1960's. Civil, electrical, and mechanical engineering had the most phenomenal growth, while chemical engineering, where the Ph.D. was common in prewar years, expanded modestly. The increase in engineering degrees is probably related to the relative decline in the number of Ph.D.'s in chemistry, which was the largest doctorate field until the 1960's. Chemistry and engineering are industry-oriented sciences likely to attract persons with similar abilities and interests.

The most rapidly expanding field after engineering was mathematics, with an increase in degrees exceeding 300 percent. In other sciences, physics had a slight relative gain in degrees; biology a more rapid gain, concentrated in areas like microbiology and physiology. Biological specialties involving classification work — zoology and botany — grew relatively slowly. As a group, the social sciences maintained a stable proportion of Ph.D.'s, while the related area of business and commerce (D.B.A.) recorded a sizable gain, though from a small base.[8]

*Master's Degrees**

The distribution and expansion of master's degrees by specialty differs considerably from that of the doctorate (Table 3.7). First, only mathematics and engineering receive roughly equal shares of M.A. and Ph.D. degrees. Professional occupations — business and commerce, education — are far more important at the master's level, accounting for 40 percent of degrees, and the sciences less important. Second, the increase in the number of

* Because of the peculiar position of the master's degree — as a predoctorate award or consolation prize — the changes described in the text are not as meaningful as those at the doctorate level. However, although some of the trends may be influenced by possible changes in use of the master's degree as a way station for Ph.D. candidates, the substantial difference in the size of the degree categories (the master's population outnumbers doctorates by 9 to 1) assures us that the dominant influence is the wish to attain master's competence.

Table 3.7 Master's Degrees Awarded to Males, by Major, 1950–1965

Field of Study	Number of Degrees 1950	Number of Degrees 1965	Percentage Change	Share of M.A. Degrees (in %) 1950	Share of M.A. Degrees (in %) 1965	Absolute Change in Share
All fields	41,237	76,211	84.8	100.0	100.0	—
Science fields	11,429	23,718	107.5	27.7	31.1	3.4
Engineering	4,481	12,012	168.1	10.9	15.7	4.8
Aeronautical	372	693	86.3	0.9	0.9	—
Chemical	698	803	15.0	1.7	1.1	−0.6
Civil	686	1,681	145.0	1.7	2.2	0.5
Electrical	1,055	3,498	231.6	2.6	4.6	2.0
Industrial	246	1,010	310.6	0.6	1.3	0.7
Mechanical	781	2,031	160.1	1.9	2.7	0.8
Metallurgical	180	363	101.7	0.4	0.5	0.1
Mining	32	84	162.5	0.1	0.1	0.0
Biological Sciences	1,738	2,629	51.3	4.2	3.4	−0.8
Botany	234	506	116.2	0.6	0.7	0.1
Zoology	435	425	−2.3	1.1	0.6	−0.5
Microbiology	297	217	−26.9	0.7	0.3	−0.4
Biochemistry	114	164	43.9	0.3	0.2	−0.1
Entomology	80	144	80.0	0.2	0.2	0.0
Genetics	n.a.	53	—	—	0.1	—
pathology	n.a.	35	—	—	0.0	—
pharmacology	n.a.	50	—	—	0.1	—
physiology	126	83	−34.1	0.3	0.1	−0.2
Physical Sciences	2,934	4,405	50.1	7.1	5.8	−1.3
Chemistry	1,368	1,362	−0.4	3.3	1.8	−1.5
Physics	888	1,826	105.6	2.2	2.4	0.2
Geology	477	452	−5.2	1.2	0.6	−0.6
Mathematics	784	3,342	326.3	1.9	4.4	2.5
Agriculture	1,492	1,330	−10.9	3.6	1.7	−1.9
Psychology	948	1,509	59.2	2.3	2.0	−0.3
Social Sciences	3,150	5,930	188.3	7.6	7.8	0.2
Sociology	373	792	112.3	0.9	1.0	0.1
Economics	807	1,118	38.5	1.9	1.5	−0.4
History	1,373	2,258	64.5	3.3	3.0	−0.3
Political Science & Public Administration	597	1,762	195.1	1.5	2.3	0.8
Education	11,679	22,976	96.7	28.3	30.1	1.8
Arts and Humanities	2,191	3,134	43.0	5.3	4.1	−1.2
Language and Literature	2,120	3,817	80.0	5.1	5.0	−0.1
Business and Commerce	4,006	7,344	83.3	9.7	9.6	−0.1
Other	5,714	7,783	36.2	13.8	10.2	−3.6

Source: Office of Education, *Earned Degrees Conferred.*

degrees diverges noticeably in some fields. The share of master's degrees awarded in biology and psychology, for example, fell, while the share of Ph.D.'s in these specialties rose. In engineering, the rate of increase was much slower at the master's level and centered in different branches. The fastest-growing doctorate specialty, civil engineering, was only a moderately growing master's specialty.

In other areas of study, the pattern of change was similar for both post-graduate degrees. Social sciences kept a stable share of degrees; business and commerce and education had increasing shares; chemistry, agriculture, and geology had declining shares. In chemistry and agriculture there was an absolute decline in the number of master's graduates from 1950 to 1965.

Bachelor's Degrees

Although specialization is less intense at the bachelor's level, degrees are still a meaningful indicator of occupational interest. In some specialties — engineering, accounting, chemistry — the B.A. or B.S. is the first professional degree, often leading directly to employment. In others, the bachelor's degree is the first step toward further study in the field or to law or business school.

In contrast to the master's and doctorate, baccalaureate degrees are more frequent in social science and business administration. These fields account for one third of all graduates (Table 3.8). The number of students concentrating in education is much smaller at this level of training, and in the natural sciences and engineering moderately smaller.

The change in the number of baccalaureates in the 1950–1965 period differed from the change in Ph.D.'s and master's in three ways: (1) the Bachelor of Science degree in engineering showed a sharp decline, partly for cyclic reasons (see Chapter 4); (2) business administration also lost ground; (3) the social sciences increased their fraction of degrees. In other areas the pattern mirrors that at the graduate level. Chemistry, agriculture, and geology grew slowly; mathematics grew rapidly. The cultural fields — the humanities, literature, languages — expanded their share of baccalaureate degrees, as they did of doctorate but not of master's degrees.

Explanation of Changes in Fields of Study

The patterns of change in degrees described above — differing trends for bachelors, master's, and doctorate degrees in some fields and similar

Table 3.8 Bachelor's Degrees Awarded to Males, by Major, 1950–1965[a]

Field of Study	Number of Degrees 1950	Number of Degrees 1965	Percentage Change, 1950–1965	Share of B.A. & B.S. Degrees (in %) 1950	Share of B.A. & B.S. Degrees (in %) 1965	Absolute Change in Share
All fields	273,621	279,777	2.2	100.0	100.0	—
Science fields	101,574	89,233	−12.1	37.1	31.8	5.3
Engineering	52,071	36,161	−30.6	19.0	12.9	−6.1
Aeronautical	1,698	1,709	0.6	0.6	0.6	0.0
Chemical	4,474	3,050	−31.8	1.6	1.1	−0.5
Civil	7,761	5,187	−33.2	2.8	1.9	−0.9
Electrical	13,231	11,694	−11.6	4.8	4.2	−0.6
Industrial	3,369	2,230	−33.8	1.2	0.8	−0.4
Mechanical	14,414	8,019	−44.4	5.3	2.9	−2.4
Metallurgical	469	864	84.2	0.2	0.3	0.1
Mining	483	152	−68.5	0.2	0.1	−0.1
Biological Sciences	13,182	17,902	35.8	4.8	6.4	1.6
Physical Sciences	16,538	15,238	−7.9	6.0	5.4	−0.6
Chemistry	9,134	8,111	−11.2	3.3	2.9	−0.4
Physics	3,287	4,708	43.2	1.2	1.7	0.5
Geology	2,934	986	−66.4	1.1	0.4	−0.7
Mathematics	4,946	13,132	165.5	1.8	4.7	2.9
Agriculture	14,837	6,800	−54.2	5.4	2.4	−3.0
Psychology	6,058	8,688	43.4	2.2	3.1	0.9
Social Sciences	39,940	56,978	42.7	14.6	20.4	5.8
Sociology	4,034	5,123	27.0	1.5	1.8	0.3
Economics	13,471	9,856	−26.8	4.9	3.5	−1.4
History & Geography	11,464	18,138	58.2	4.2	6.5	2.3
Political Science	6,232	10,655	71.0	2.3	3.8	1.5
Education	27,539	28,147	2.2	10.1	10.1	0.0
Business Administration	65,911	57,901	−12.2	24.1	20.7	−3.4
Accounting	13,031	13,969	7.2	4.8	5.0	0.2
Arts & Humanities	10,361	13,492	30.2	3.8	4.8	1.0
Languages & Literature	14,297	18,205	27.3	5.2	6.5	1.3
Other	7,941	7,133	−10.2	2.9	2.5	−0.4

SOURCE: Office of Education, *Earned Degrees Conferred.*
[a] These data exclude first professional degrees.

trends in others — can be explained by the simultaneous operation of two distinct adjustment mechanisms: an *occupational adjustment* that shifts students among specialties until changes are equalized on the margin for all careers; and an *educational adjustment* that alters the educational attainment of specialists within an occupation until present values of income are equalized for each level of education. Either or both mechanisms may be functioning at any moment of time. The work force could be appropriately distributed among careers but not among levels of education, or vice versa.

The dual adjustment mechanism accounts for the observed pattern of change in a relatively direct way. In fields where all degree levels exhibit similar patterns of change (chemistry, agriculture, geology, mathematics) the hypothesis directs attention to the occupational adjustment. In fields where growth differs by level of education the hypothesis suggests that the educational adjustment dominates. The market is presumably moving toward an equilibrium occupational distribution in the former case and toward an equilibrium educational structure in the other. The validity of this interpretation is examined in succeeding chapters.

3.3 The Relation between Education and Occupation

Fields of study in higher education are linked to types of work in the labor market. The relation between education and occupation can be summarized in an Education-Occupation Matrix, in which the rows of the matrix denote fields of study and the columns, occupations. An element in the matrix (a_{ij}) tells the number of persons educated in field i working in occupation j.

Shape of the Education-Occupation Matrix

A typical education-occupation matrix is rectangular with several nonzero elements in each column and row. The matrix deviates from a one-to-one correspondence of field with occupation because of the possibility of training for a job in several ways and of entering careers removed from the area of college specialization. Several factors determine the degree of divergence or similarity relative to an identity matrix:

a) The vocational content of education: When a field of study offers very specific training, it approaches apprenticeship. Row coefficients will thus be clustered about a limited group of occupations. The medical, engineering, and accounting majors fit into this category. They supply job-oriented training, with most graduates seeking work in the related occupation.

b) The existence of alternative training routes: When an occupation can be reached by several methods of preparation — on-the-job training, experience, alternative college majors — many column coefficients will be nonzero. Managerial work, which often does not require a specific kind of education, is the best example of this type of career. Men with business, humanities, or science degrees are found in management.

c) Licensing restrictions: Governmental regulation of occupations like medicine restricts the ways in which persons can enter these fields. Column coefficients are zero except in the row of the approved curriculum and licensing program.

d) State of the labor market: When the labor market is in disequilibrium, incentives will exist for persons to change their area of specialization. As a result, an especially large number are likely to choose occupations removed from their principal area of study. Both row and column coefficients will be dispersed.[9]

e) The time dimension: The longer the period after entrance into the labor market the greater are the opportunities for changing jobs. Occupational mobility and the dispersion of matrix coefficients for a graduating class thus increase as time proceeds.

For a labor market analysis of the selection of fields of study to be fruitful, education-occupation matrices must be well-defined and stable, with students choosing majors at least partly for vocational reasons and occupations requiring specialized training.

Education-Occupation Matrix: the Class of 1958

That actual matrices have a definite, economically sensible shape is evident from the coefficients summarized in Tables 3.9–3.11. For ease in presentation, the tables deal with "structural row coefficients," the fraction of students in particular majors electing the specified occupations.

Table 3.9 examines the occupations of natural science, engineering, and professional school graduates. It shows the relation of field of study to the most frequently chosen occupations (columns 1–3), to major alternative occupations (columns 4–5), and — for the sciences — to work in a science- or engineering-related job (column 6).[10]

Engineering holds a unique position in the table. As a field of study it is the only bachelor's specialty with a close link to the related occupation: 80 percent of B.S. engineering majors obtain jobs as engineers, while most other B.S. majors work outside their major field, though in some scientific area. Even at the master's level, where specifications and careers are more closely related, engineering has the tightest link to the major occupation. As a career, engineering is also exceptional, being the principal alternative

Table 3.9 1960 Occupations of June 1958 Male College Graduates, By Field of Study

Field	(1) *Major Occupation*	(2) *Percent Employed in Major Occupation*	(3) *Percent Employed in Major and Related Occupations*[a]	(4) *Major Alternative Occupations*	(5) *Percent Employed in Major Alternatives*	(6) *Percent Employed in All Science Occupations*
Natural Sciences and Engineering						
Agriculture						
B.S.	Agric. Scientist	28.1	41.9	Farmer	10.8	49.1
M.S.	Agric. Scientist	54.1	66.0	Biological Scientist	8.2	87.1
Biology						
B.S.	Biolog. Scientist	9.5				
	teacher, secondary	29.8	47.8	Service worker	7.5	60.2
M.S.	Biolog. Scientist	33.3	79.5	Other Nat. Science	10.3	89.8
Biological Sciences						
B.S.	Biolog. Scientist	20.5	53.0	Agric. Scientist	7.4	69.4
M.S.	Biolog. Scientist	42.3	65.0	Agric. Scientist	11.3	86.5
				Chemist	9.3	—
Chemistry						
B.S.	Chemist	44.3	69.2	Engineer	6.0	81.8
M.S.	Chemist	75.3	86.4	Chem. Engineer	3.7	90.1
Earth Sciences						
B.S.	Earth Scientist	32.2	45.3	Engineer	10.3	60.4
M.S.	Geologist	59.1	69.3	Nat. Scientist	10.2	86.3
Mathematics						
B.S.	Teacher, secondary	32.4				
	Mathematician	26.3	61.4	Engineer	12.5	79.0

M.S.	Mathematician	60.4	79.2	Engineer	8.5	86.3
Physics						
B.S.	Physicist	32.6	48.7	Engineer	34.3	87.4
M.S.	Physicist	60.4	79.2	Engineer	15.4	96.5
				Electrical engineer	7.2	
Engineering						
B.S.	Engineer	81.3	83.6	Business executive	3.0	86.7
M.S.	Engineer	85.4	88.6	Business executive	4.9	91.2
Education and Business						
Education						
B.A.	Teacher	77.8	79.5	Social welfare worker	1.6	—
M.A.T.	Teacher, high school	62.1	87.8	(Scattered)	—	—
	Teacher, college	9.6	—			
Business						
B.A.	Businessman & Salesman	78.6	78.6	Teachers	4.0	—
M.B.A.	Businessman & Salesman	66.5	66.5	Engineer	10.7	—
Professional Degrees						
LL.B.	Lawyer	77.6	77.6	Accountant	2.9	—
M.D.	Physician & Surgeon	95.7	95.7	Scientist	2.0	—
D.D.S.	Dentist	96.7	96.7	(Scattered)	—	—
D.V.M.	Veterinarian	96.3	96.3	(Scattered)	—	—
B.D.	Clergyman	89.4	89.4	College teacher	2.6	—

SOURCE: *Two Years After the College Degree* (NSF No. 63-56), 1963.

[a] Related occupations refer to teaching, research, or other work obviously closely linked to the major field. Because there are no closely related fields for business or professional majors, I have not adjusted these data.

Table 3.10 1960 Occupations of June 1958 Male Graduates: Social Sciences, Psychology, Humanities Majors

		Percentage of Graduates				Other Alternatives	
Field	*Occupation Most Closely Related to Field of Study* (1)	*Most Closely Related Occupation*[a] (2)	*H.S. Teaching Same or Related Subject* (3)	*Management* (4)	*Sales* (5)	*Occupation* (6)	*Percent Employed in (6)* (7)
Social Science							
Economics							
B.A.	Economist	6.3	1.2	33.1	19.2	Accountant	4.0
M.A.	Economist	42.3	4.2	25.4	—	Officials	5.6
						Mathematician	4.2
History							
B.A.	Historian	3.0	20.2	14.0	6.3	Clergy	8.2
M.A.	Historian	31.0	32.3	—	7.8	Teacher, non-history	7.8
Political Science							
B.A.	Political Scientist	2.0	7.0	19.0	12.6	Service worker	5.3
M.A.	Political Scientist	26.1	7.2	14.6	—	Clerical worker	5.3
						Public official	14.6
Sociology and Anthropology							
B.A.	Sociologist	5.1	4.8	11.5	7.9	Social welfare worker	16.2
M.A.	Sociologist	60.1	6.2	18.8	—	Social welfare worker	12.5
Psychology							
B.A.	Psychologist	18.4	1.9	12.3	10.3	High school teacher, natural science	5.2
M.A.	Psychologist	61.2	4.1	11.2	—	College teacher, non-psychology	7.1

Humanities							
English							
B.A.	Secondary teacher	30.8	—	13.9	9.3	Clergy	6.3
M.A.	College teacher	43.8	20.6	4.7	1.9	Writer	7.5
Foreign Languages							
B.A.	Secondary teacher	45.6	—	10.4	2.4	College teacher	12.8
M.A.	College teacher	47.5	30.0	—	—	teacher, other fields	7.5
Fine Arts							
B.A.	Artist	19.1	—	12.9	4.8	High school teacher	23.0
M.A.	College teacher	27.7	26.3	—	—	College teacher, other fields	11.5

SOURCE: N.S.F., *Two Years After the College Degree* (N.S.F. No. 63-56).
[a] Including college teaching in the field and work as research assistant.

Table 3.11 Percentage of Doctorate Recipients Remaining in the Same Field from Baccalaureate to Doctorate and Doctorate to Job

Field	*Percent with Baccalaureate in Same Field as Doctorate*	*Percent with Job in Same Field as Doctorate*
Mathematics	70	91
Physics and Astronomy	75	90
Chemistry	85	84
Earth sciences	74	93
Engineering	89	92
Agriculture and Forestry	75	73
Health sciences	52	78
Biochem., Biophys., Physiol., Biostatis.	—	70
Anat., Cytol., Entomol., Genet.	—	47
Botany, Zoology, General Biology	71	51
Psychology	64	90
Anthropology and Archeology	42	—
Sociology	43	79
Economics and Econometrics	51	76
Political Science, Int. Relations	51	81
History	66	85
English and Amer. Lang. and Lit.	77	} 83 (English, Modern Foreign, Classical)
Modern Foreign Lang. and Lit.	59	
Classical Lang. and Lit.	59	
Philosophy	58	} 70 (Philosophy, Speech, Fine Arts)
Speech and Dramatic Arts	52	
Fine Arts and Music	72	
Business Administration	55	} 73 (Business, Religion)
Religion and Theology	19	
Education	43	81

SOURCE: National Research Council, Office of Scientific Personnel, Doctorate Records File and *Profiles of Ph.D.'s in the Sciences*, Publ. No. 1293, p. 116.

occupation of most natural science students. Physics majors, in particular, evince a strong bent for engineering: one third of the 1958 graduating class were working as engineers three years later.

As for the other fields, in mathematics and biology secondary school teaching rather than "scientific work" is the most common occupation. In professional fields there is a close relation between area of study and occupation, with most graduates obtaining jobs in their major. Only law graduates tend to work in other occupations, probably because legal training is good preparation for business and government bureaucracies.

The row coefficients for social science and humanities are scattered among many occupations, meriting the changed format of Table 3.10. This table records the proportion of baccalaureate and master's majors working in the occupation most closely related to a field, and in teaching, management, sales, and other significant alternatives. There is a marked difference in coefficients between the social sciences and humanities, with social science majors finding jobs in a wider variety of occupations. Many social science graduates work as managers or salesmen, some as teachers in secondary school (history majors, for example), but few as social scientists in their special field of study. Even at the master's level, only in sociology and psychology is work as a social scientist common. In the humanities, on the other hand, graduates are concentrated in teaching jobs. Bachelor's graduates are employed primarily in secondary schools, master's graduates in colleges and universities.

Although training in the social sciences is not linked to any single occupation making "direct use" of the field, it appears to have some vocational value. Approximately 60 percent of B.A. social science graduates report using their major in their current jobs. This figure is below that for the average college graduate (82 percent) but still constitutes a substantial majority of the students.[11]

The path from baccalaureate to doctorate training and from the Ph.D. to work is considered in Table 3.11. Column 1 of the table records the percentage of doctorate students whose first degrees were in the same field as the Ph.D. It shows that students in the social sciences and humanities come from many undergraduate curriculums, while those in science and engineering are drawn from a limited set of undergraduate fields. Upon receipt of the Ph.D., including those in the social sciences, most specialists remain in the area of their major (column 2). Only the detailed breakdown of biology produces a scattering of row coefficients at this level of education.

The education-occupation matrix can be reorganized to show the proportion of specialists in each occupation trained in various curricula. These figures (for the sake of simplicity not presented here) describe a coherent and a priori sensible pattern. As might be expected, work in the natural sciences and engineering "requires" graduates with science or engineering degrees. Ninety percent of the B.S. engineers, for example, were engineering majors in 1958. Nonscientific occupations, on the other hand, have less rigid entry conditions: management draws on men with economics, engineering, sociology, or business administration training. Secondary school teachers also come from a diverse set of majors. Even the most specialized — those in the sciences — are as likely to have majored outside the sciences as not. Accounting is the only nonscientific occupation with a one-to-one correspondence between the occupation and the major.

Conclusion

The factual material of this chapter complements the theoretical discussion of Chapters 1 and 2. These three chapters have developed the analytic and empirical foundation for the remainder of the study. In succeeding chapters the theory and models are used to explain the principal developments following World War II. The investigation is both a test of the theoretical framework and an empirical analysis of the phenomena described in this chapter.

4 The Cobweb Pattern: The Bachelor of Science in Engineering

This chapter uses the cobweb variant of the basic labor market model to explain postwar developments in the largest scientific profession, engineering. It focuses on fluctuations in the number of B.S. engineering students and in starting salaries. The chapter is divided into five parts: the first presents background information on the engineering work force; the second a cobweb model that can be tested with available data; the third and fourth contain estimates respectively of supply and demand equations.* The final section is a general interpretation of cobweb adjustment in the labor market.

4.1 Employment and Training of Engineers

The engineering work force differs in industrial and educational composition from other scientific occupations. Jobs are concentrated in industry rather than in universities. Non-degree preparation for work is common, and post-bachelor's training is infrequent.

Employment

Table 4.1 presents the principal facts about the industrial composition of engineering employment in the post-World War II period. Throughout

* In this discussion and throughout the book I describe statistical findings by recording the estimated parameter and the t-statistic. The t-statistic is always written in parentheses below the parameter estimate. Regression fits are described by the R^2-statistic. The Durbin-Watson (D.W.) statistic summarizes the serial correlation properties of the regression.

Table 4.1 Distribution of Employment of Engineers, by Major Industry, 1950–1966

Industry	Percentage Distribution of Employment by Industry		
	1950	*1960*	*1966*
	100.0	100.0	100.0
Private Industry	78.4	82.6	81.5
Manufacturing	46.4	54.3	54.0
Durable Goods	36.2	44.8	45.5
Ordnance	.5	3.8	5.2
Primary metals	2.8	2.5	2.1
Fabricated metals	3.5	2.9	2.8
Machinery	7.7	7.3	7.5
Electrical equipment	10.0	13.8	13.6
Motor vehicles	2.9	1.9	2.2
Aircraft	4.0	8.6	7.7
Other transportation equipment	.7	.6	.5
Professional and scientific instruments	2.2	2.8	3.0
Miscellaneous manufacturing	.9	.6	.5
Non-durables	10.2	9.5	8.5
Food	.9	.7	.5
Textiles and apparel	.5	.4	.4
Lumber and furniture	.5	.4	.4
Paper	1.1	1.1	1.0
Chemicals	4.9	4.0	4.1
Petroleum refining	1.5	1.3	1.0
Rubber	.8	.7	.8
Stone, clay, and glass	1.0	1.0	.9
Nonmanufacturing	32.0	28.3	27.5
Mining	2.6	2.1	1.7
Petroleum extraction	1.5	1.5	1.2
Other mining	1.1	.6	.6
Construction	6.0	5.6	5.1
Transportation, communications, and public utilities	6.5	5.5	5.3
Railroads	1.3	.6	.4
Other transportation	.8	.6	.5
Telecommunications	1.5	1.1	1.2
Radio and TV	.4	.6	.5
Public utilities	2.5	2.6	2.6
Other industries	16.9	15.1	15.4
Miscellaneous business service	4.0	3.8	3.6
Engineering and architectural services	10.0	9.2	9.0
Other nonmanufacturing	2.8	2.1	2.8
Government	18.6	14.1	14.5
Federal	9.6	7.4	8.0
State	4.7	3.8	3.6
Local	4.4	3.0	2.8
Universities and colleges	2.8	2.9	3.5
Nonprofit institutions	.2	.3	.5

Source: *U.S. Census of Population,* 1950 and 1960; Bureau of Labor Statistics, 1966.

the period the chief industries of employment were durable goods manufacturing, particularly the machinery and equipment sectors, and construction. In 1966 nearly 60 percent of engineering jobs were found in these industries. Employment expanded greatly in the 1950–1966 interval, though with a declining rate relative to the rate of expansion of total employment. From 1950 to 1960 the number of engineers increased in percentage terms 13 times as fast as the total number of male employees. From 1960 to 1966 the increase in engineering was just 2.5 times the average. The growth of engineering employment was accompanied by a shift in the industrial composition of jobs. Aircraft and ordinance, fabricated metals, and electrical machinery increased their share of engineers at the expense of transportation, utilities, and nondurable manufacturing.

The figures in Table 4.1 can be used to examine some of the factors underlying the rapid increase in engineering jobs. In particular, by weighting the growth of total employment by industry with the distribution of engineering employment in a base year, we can partition the increase in the number of engineers into two factors: that due to growth of industrial employment and that due to changes in the ratio of engineers to all employees within individual industries.

Such an analysis tells an interesting story. From 1950 to 1960 the growth of engineer-employing industries explains only a relatively small fraction of the increase in the number employed. On the basis of industrial shifts, the number of engineers would have grown at 25.7 percent compared to an actual rate of growth of 63.9 percent. In this period, therefore, the increased use of engineers within industry is the critical element in the change in the number of jobs. By contrast, in the 1960–1966 period almost all of the growth of engineering can be attributed to the growth of total employment by industry. The rate of increase expected as the basis of industrial expansion is 20.2 percent compared to an actual rate of 24.5 percent. The substantial drop in the intra-industrial component of the change in employment suggests that the fraction of workers in engineering may be approaching an "equilibrium" level within most industries. If this is the case, the over-all expansion of the field will level off considerably in the future.

Education and Training

Engineers prepare for work through formal college programs leading to a degree or through a combination of on-the-job training and non-degree courses in technical institutes, junior colleges, and correspondence or special schools. The college-trained specialists constitute over half the profession, earn 15 to 30 percent more than non-degree engineers of the same age, and account for about 60 percent of the engineering wage bill. In recent years the qualifications of graduate engineers have improved markedly: in 1947 nearly all (90 percent) were B.S. graduates; in 1967, 30 percent of degree recipients obtained an M.S. and 10 percent a Ph.D. At the same time, the ratio between new graduates and the stock of engineers fell from 0.09 to 0.03.[1] This is approximately equal to the outflow of workers from the profession due to occupational mobility, retirement, and the like. At 1967 stock-flow ratios, growth in engineering would cease were the profession to rely solely on college graduates.

Non-degree specialists also prepare for work by *formal study* in educational institutions. The majority spend one to three years taking academic courses, supplemented by considerable on-the-job training and work experience. The importance of experience can be seen in Census of Population statistics, which show a sharp increase in the number of technicians attaining engineer status over the working life. In the 25–34 cohort of 1950, for example, the number of non-degree engineers doubled from 1950 to 1960. Not until the non-degree engineer reaches age 40, however, does he attain earnings and presumably skill equality with the starting B.S. graduate. This suggests that 20 years' experience is needed to match a 4–5-year degree program and that the bachelor in engineering is therefore a highly profitable investment in human capital (see Chapter 5).

4.2 The Cobweb Model in B.S. Engineering

The cobweb model used to explain developments in the engineering market is specified in equations (1)–(3) below. To reduce problems of multicollinearity, the equations are in first (logarithmic) difference form:

(1) Supply of freshmen engineers:

$$\Delta\ln \text{ENR}_i = a_0\,\Delta\ln \text{FRSH}_t + a_1\,\Delta\ln \text{ESAL}_t - a_2\,\Delta\ln \text{PSAL}_t + a_3\,\Delta\ln \text{VET}_t - a_4 \ln(\text{ENR/FRSH})_{t-1};$$

(2) Supply of graduates:

$$\Delta\ln \text{GRD}_{t+4} = b_0\,\Delta\ln \text{ENR}_t + b_1\,\Delta\ln(\text{ESAL}_{t+2}) + b_1\,\Delta\ln \text{ESAL}_{t+1} - b_2\,\Delta\ln(\text{PSAL}_{t+2}) - b_2\,\Delta\ln + \text{PSAL}_{t+1} + b_3\,\Delta\ln \text{CVET}_{t+4} - b_4 \ln(\text{ENR/FRSH})_t;$$

(3) Salary determination:

$$\Delta\ln \text{ESAL}_t = -c_0 \Delta\ln \text{GRD}_t + c_1 \Delta\ln \text{RD}_t + c_2 \Delta\ln \text{DUR}_t;$$

where

ENR_t = number of first-year enrollments in B.S. engineering programs throughout the United States;
FRSH_t = number of male freshmen enrolling in four-year educational institutions;
ESAL_t = starting salaries of B.S. engineers;
PSAL_t = annual earnings of professional workers;
GRD_t = number of engineers graduating with B.S. degrees;
$(\text{ENR/FRSH})_t$ = proportion of the freshman class enrolled in engineering;
VET_t = number of veterans enrolled as freshmen;
CVET_t = number of veterans enrolled as sophomores or upperclassmen;
RD_t = annual expenditure for research and development;
DUR_t = output in durable goods industries.

The endogenous variables are ENR, GRD, and ESAL.

The Supply Relations

The model contains two supply equations, one determining the number of freshmen enrolling in the major, the other the number of enrollees graduating four years later. For empirical convenience the theory of occupational choice is simplified in both cases. First, the incentive of engineering is measured by starting salaries, not by discounted lifetime incomes. As long as age–earnings curves are relatively stable over time this simplification causes no problem, for with stable curves initial salaries will be good indicators of lifetime opportunities. In support of the overall validity of this assumption, a recent study of engineers found that "large differentials in the starting salaries of different specialties play a major role in maintaining the long-term rank order of salaries associated with specialties." [2] Second, alternatives to engineering are represented by annual male professional earnings — a plausible but crude measure of the opportunities facing potential engineers. This measure is dictated by the absence of annual salary statistics for college men, a major gap in manpower information. Third, the lag structure in both supply equations is simple: in equation (1), only current salaries affect the initial enrollment decision (that is, expected income equals current income, $W_t^* = W_t$); in equation (2), salaries prevailing in the market during the freshman-sophomore years taken together influence the decision to complete a program. The former specification is relaxed in empirical calculations; the latter is justified by the fact that most field-switching occurs prior to the junior years.[3]

The remaining supply variables specify the population of prospective engineers. In equation (1) the number of male freshmen is chosen as the relevant population of first-year engineering students because almost all American engineers are male.[4] If the model is properly specified, the coefficient in this term will be unity in regression calculations. The next variable, the number of veterans enrolled in college, is designed to test a hypothesis advanced by the Committee for the Analysis of Engineering Enrollment that the pattern of demobilization is the main cause of fluctuations in enrollment. Demobilization is important because of an alleged special propensity of veterans for the engineering major.[5] The last variable in equation (1), the proportion of freshmen in engineering in the preceding year, is expected to reduce the rate of growth. There are three reasons for this: first, large classes reduce future job opportunities and thus deter some from engineering; second, capacity of engineering schools may be strained by substantial enrollment; third, supply elasticity is expected to decline as an increasingly large fraction of a cohort chooses a field.

In equation (2) the population variables are the number of initial enrollees in engineering, the number of veterans with pre-military training,* and the percentage of freshmen choosing engineering. The number of veterans is introduced to catch the distorted enrollment-graduation sequence of students who interrupt college for military service. The percentage of freshmen choosing the field is expected to reduce the rate of graduation because relatively large classes are likely to contain many less qualified persons.

The supply behavior to be explained by the equations is depicted in Figures 4.1 and 4.2. Figure 4.1 shows that the fraction of male freshmen choosing engineering varied greatly in the years following World War II, jumping from 14 percent in 1950, for example, to 24 percent in 1957 and back to 14 percent five years later. Underlying the fluctuations is enormous variability in the rate of growth of engineering enrollment, which has a

* According to the Veterans Administration, a large number of veterans in college have previous experience in institutions of higher education. In the 1948–1966 period, one in four enrolled veterans reported one to three years of premilitary college training.

coefficient of variation of 13.2 compared to a coefficient of just 2.1 for the rate of change of all male freshmen.

The figure also indicates that changes in the fraction of freshmen in engineering are closely related to changes in engineering starting salaries, suggesting an economic explanation of the fluctuations. Correlation analysis provides further evidence of economic behavior, revealing an extremely

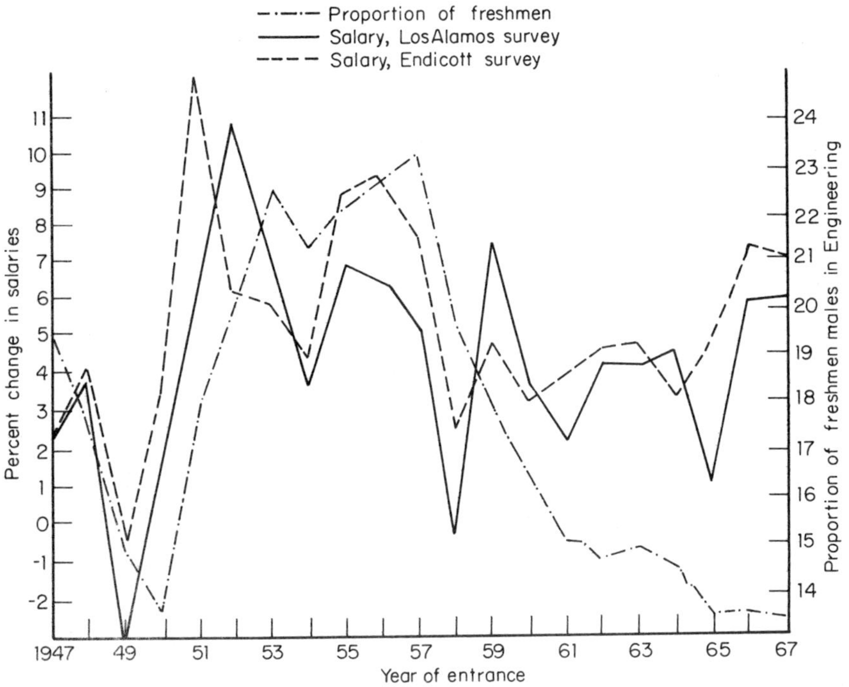

4.1 Proportion of freshmen in engineering and changes in engineering salaries, 1947–1967

close connection between *changes* in enrollment and *changes* in engineering starting salaries ($r = 0.71$, where the 1 percent significance level is 0.55).[6]

Figure 4.2 shows a similar variability in the fraction of first-year students eventually graduating with a B.S. degree. In this case, the portion of a class completing a degree program ranges from 65 percent of the men entering in 1947 to 45 percent of those in the class of 1957. The attrition rate in engineering is clearly not constant, as often assumed in manpower projections.

Demand for Engineers

The demand side of the market is represented in equation (3) as a relation between salaries and number of graduates, R & D spending, and output in durable manufacturing. Salary is the appropriate dependent variable since the number of graduates is predetermined by past supply decisions. The R & D activity of engineers and the importance of durable goods industries in employment motivate these explanatory variables.

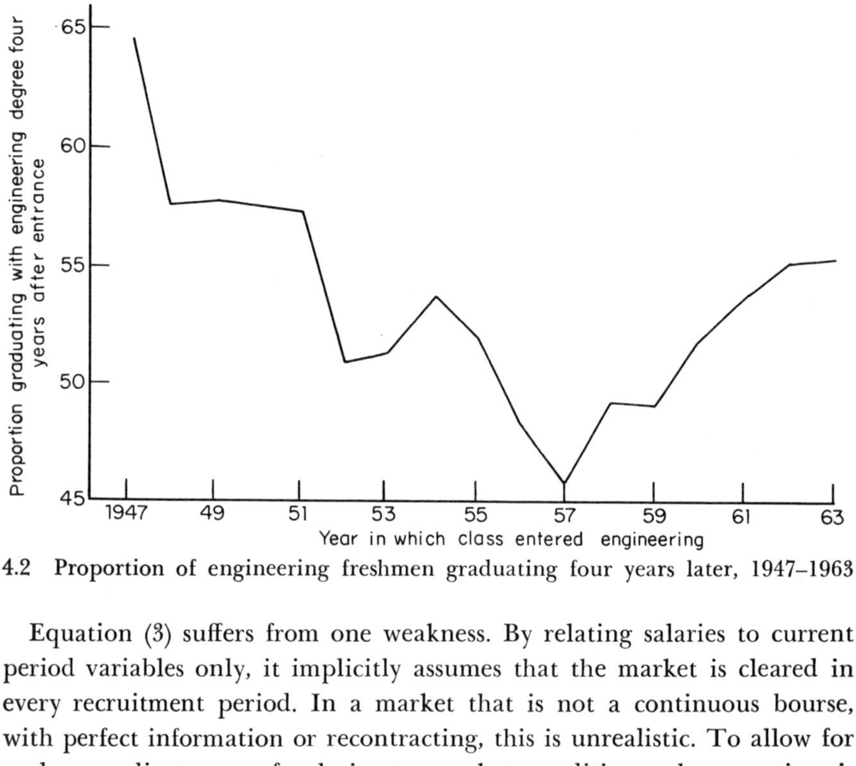

4.2 Proportion of engineering freshmen graduating four years later, 1947–1963

Equation (3) suffers from one weakness. By relating salaries to current period variables only, it implicitly assumes that the market is cleared in every recruitment period. In a market that is not a continuous bourse, with perfect information or recontracting, this is unrealistic. To allow for a slower adjustment of salaries to market conditions, the equation is modified by a two-step procedure:

First, salaries are assumed to depend on the *initial salary* plans of firms as well as on the current state of the market. According to the Endicott survey of engineer-employing firms, many large enterprises plan their salary offers in the winter preceding the spring recruitment period,[7] presumably on the basis of expected market conditions. The observed market salary is thus a weighted average of initial plans and the market-clearing or equilibrium salary, with the weight dependent on the speed with which firms adjust to unexpected conditions:

$$(4) \qquad \ln \text{ESAL} = (1 - w) \ln \text{ESAL}^p + w \ln \text{ESAL}^e,$$

where

$$\begin{aligned} \text{ESAL} &= \text{actual salary;} \\ \text{ESAL}^p &= \text{planned salary;} \\ \text{ESAL}^e &= \text{equilibrium salary; and} \\ w &= \text{adjustment coefficient} \quad (0 \leq w \leq 1). \end{aligned}$$

Second, planned salaries are assumed to result from the intersection of the demand curve and an *expected supply function.* Firms are aware of their demand for engineers but may misconstrue future supply because of changes in the number of graduates and demand elsewhere in the market. Whenever firms have faulty expectations of the supply of engineers, their planned salary will deviate from the equilibrium set by the intersection of demand with the true supply schedule. Equations (5) and (6) present the postulated planned and equilibrium salary equations:

$$(5) \qquad \ln \text{ESAL}^p = -c_0 \ln \text{GRD}^p + \text{demand shift variables,}$$

where GRD^p = planned or expected supply; and

$$(6) \qquad \ln \text{ESAL}^e = -c_0 \ln \text{GRD} + \text{demand shift variables.}$$

Substituting (5) and (6) into equation (4), yields a relation for actual salaries

$$(7) \quad \ln \text{ESAL} = -wc_0 \ln \text{GRD} - (1 - w)c_0 \ln \text{GRD}^p + \text{Demand shift variables.}$$

To complete the model, expected supply must be related to observable phenomena. There are several ways to do this. The simplest is to assume that firms expect supply to equal last period's supply

$$(8) \qquad \text{GRD}_t^p = \text{GRD}_{t-1}.$$

Figure 4.3 depicts the operation of the market in this case. Panel A shows the adjustment of a firm to an exogenous increase in demand. The firm plans its salary offer on the basis of the new demand curve and the previous (i.e. expected) supply schedule, leading to planned salaries in excess of equilibrium and actual salaries between the two extremes. In Panel B, adjustment in the entire market is illustrated. Since aggregate supply is predetermined, the actual salary–employment point lies to the right of the demand curve, producing a surplus of engineers.

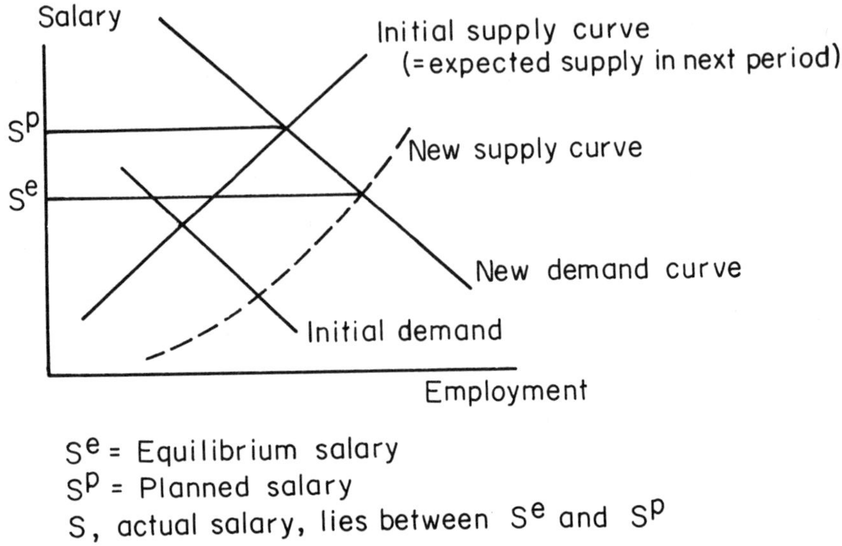

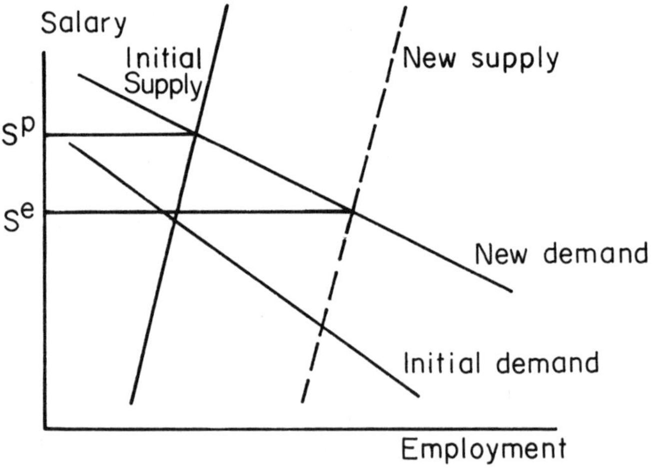

4.3 Lagged adjustment of salaries to shifts in supply when firms expect supply to equal last period's

A more complex theory of expected supply allows firms to extrapolate past changes into the future:

$$\text{(9)} \qquad \begin{aligned} \ln \mathrm{GRD}_t^p &= \ln \mathrm{GRD}_{t-1} + \ln(\mathrm{GRD}_{t-1}/\mathrm{GRD}_{t-2}) \\ &= 2(\ln \mathrm{GRD}_{t-1}) - \ln \mathrm{GRD}_{t-2} \end{aligned}$$

Finally, if firms take account of past errors in expected supply, we obtain a third approximation to the formation of salary plans:

$$(10) \qquad \ln \mathrm{GRD}_t^p = 2(\ln \mathrm{GRD}_{t-1}) - \ln \mathrm{GRD}_{t-2} + c \ln (\mathrm{GRD}_{t-1}/\mathrm{GRD}_{t-1}^p);$$

where c is a correction coefficient ($0 \leq c \leq 1$). Substitution yields:

$$\ln \mathrm{GRD}_t^p \approx (2 + c) \ln \mathrm{GRD}_{t+1} - (1 + 2c) \ln \mathrm{GRD}_{t-2} - c \ln \mathrm{GRD}_{t-1},$$

where terms involving higher orders of c are omitted for simplicity.

When equation (8), (9), or (10) is entered into the salary equation, the result is a testable relation between salaries and current and lagged supply. The coefficients on the lagged supply terms are linear transformations of the structural parameters. Overidentification permits an internal check on the consistency of the postulated structure in the case of (10).

Empirical evidence regarding the salary determination process is presented in Table 4.2. The significant correlations of salaries with R & D spending and durable goods output and between salaries and current and *lagged* numbers of graduates suggest that the modified salary equation is a reasonable representation of market phenomena. The absence of lags between demand-shift variables and salaries supports the hypothesis that lagged salary determination is due primarily to slow adjustment to unexpected supply conditions.

4.3 Supply of B.S Engineers

Since the cobweb model is recursive, the supply equations are estimated by ordinary least-squares. Two series of engineering salaries are used— one from the Endicott placement survey and the other from the Los Alamos Scientific Laboratory.[8] Differences in the salaries reported in the surveys due to the sample and period covered were relatively minor and do not substantially affect the statistical findings.

The Enrollment Decision

Estimates of the enrollment equation contained in Table 4.3 provide strong evidence of economically rational supply behavior on the part of freshmen considering engineering. First, the postulated structure explains most of the variation in enrollment in a sensible way, with independent variables obtaining coefficients with appropriate signs and, in most cases, high statistical significance. The overall ability of the equation to explain the fluctuations described earlier is illustrated graphically in Figure 4.4.

Table 4.2 Correlation Evidence of the Lagged Effect on Starting Salaries of the Number of Engineering Graduates, 1949–1967[a]

A. THE CORRELATION OF THE LOG CHANGE IN ENGINEERING STARTING SALARIES WITH THE NUMBER OF B.S. GRADUATES SEEKING WORK

Log Change in the Number of Graduates	*Simple Correlation Coefficient*[b]	*Correlation Coefficient with Changes in R & D Spending Held Fixed*[c]
Current period	−0.642	−0.732
Lagged one period	−0.646	−0.690
Lagged two periods	−0.348	−0.279
Lagged three periods	−0.026	0.144

B. THE CORRELATION OF THE LOG CHANGE IN ENGINEERING STARTING SALARIES WITH CHANGES IN THE DEMAND FOR ENGINEERS

Log Change of Measures of Demand	*Simple Correlation Coefficient*[b]	*Correlation Coefficient with Changes in Number of Graduates Held Fixed*[c]
R & D spending	0.481	0.625
R & D spending, lagged one period	0.123	0.265
Output in durable manufacturing	0.525	0.513
Output in durable manufacturing lagged one period	0.067	−0.010

[a] This table uses the starting salaries of the Los Alamos Survey; analogous results are obtained with use of the Endicott Survey data.

[b] The level of significance for the simple correlation coefficients are 1%, 0.590; 5%, 0.468.

[c] For the multiple correlations, the levels of significance are 1%, 0.606; 5%, 0.482.

Second, the chief explanatory variable is engineering starting salaries, which by itself accounts for over half of the variance in $\Delta \ln$ ENR. Most of the salary effect occurs in a single time interval, the remainder within a year (equation 2). The estimated elasticity of supply is quite substantial — on the order of 2½ to 3.[9] The alternative income variable, on the other hand, performs less satisfactorily,[10] probably because professional earnings are only a crude indicator of nonengineering work opportunities.* Experimentation with other measures of alternatives yields similiar results.[11]

The remaining variables are accorded proper signs and significance.

* Since engineering salaries are likely to be correlated with alternative income opportunities, incorrect measurement or specification of alternatives biases the estimated supply coefficient. Note 10 discusses the likely bias in detail.

Table 4.3 Supply of First-Year Students to Engineering, 1948–1967
(The dependent variable is Δln ENR, the log change of enrollment of freshmen in engineering)

	Regression Coefficients and t-Statistics[a]								
Equation Number	*Constant*	Δln FRSH	Δln ESAL	Δln PROF	Δln VET	Δln SHR_{-1}	Δln $ESAL_{-1}$	R^2	*D.W.*[b]
(1)[a,c]	−0.11	0.76	2.70	−0.47				0.75	1.64
	(3.67)	(3.80)	(5.19)	(1.47)					
(2)[a,c]	−0.72	0.70	2.48	−0.42	0.17	−0.35	1.30	0.87	1.26
	(3.43)	(3.68)	(5.90)	(1.62)	(1.89)	(2.69)	(2.50)		
(3)[a,d]	−0.16	0.92	2.86	−0.31	0.20			0.89	1.61
	(5.33)	(6.57)	(7.15)	(1.41)	(3.36)				
(4)[a,d]	−0.36	0.96	2.86	−0.28	0.22	−0.16	0.19	0.93	1.68
	(3.27)	(6.40)	(6.98)	(1.23)	(3.69)	(3.20)	(.69)		

[a] The levels of significance for the *t*-statistics are:

	1%	5%
Equation (1)	2.95	2.13
Equation (2)	3.06	2.18
Equation (3)	2.98	2.15
Equation (4)	3.06	2.18

[b] D.W. represents the Durbin-Watson statistic.
[c] Uses Los Alamos salaries series to measure ESAL.
[d] Uses Endicott salary series to measure ESAL.

Male freshmen has the proportional impact on enrollment required of a well-specified model: in some equations its coefficient is nearly 1, in others a standard deviation away. The enrollment of veterans increases the number of first-year engineering students, but with a coefficient sufficiently small to reject decisively the demobilization explanation of postwar developments.[12] Finally, the lagged fraction of freshmen in engineering has the expected negative impact on growth of enrollment.

Non-econometric evidence corroborates the regression findings of responsive supply behavior in the engineering market. First, the survey results described in Chapters 10 and 11 show that students have the information about starting salaries, life-cycle earnings, and relative incomes needed for rational supply behavior. Engineering majors, in particular, report sensible income expectations and accurate knowledge of job opportunities — which is perhaps not surprising in view of the publicity given the profession and the large number of engineers in the United States. Second, a study of California high school seniors shows that students respond to perceptions of salaries in an economically rational way. The vast majority (80 percent)

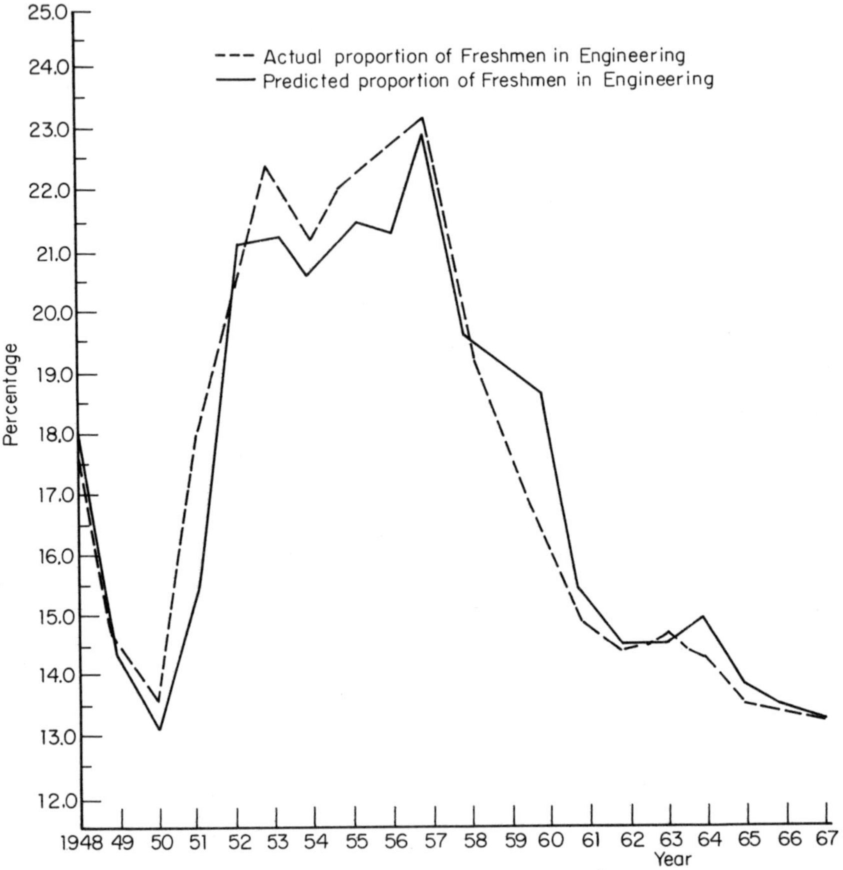

4.4 The proportion of freshmen in engineering compared to the proportion predicted by the cobweb supply equation, 1948–1967

of male seniors rating engineering first in income relative to other college-level careers express the intention of entering the field. By contrast, just one fourth of those ranking engineering low in salary plan on engineering careers.[13] Third, another survey has found engineering majors to be exceptionally vocationally oriented and thus presumably responsive to economic incentives.[14]

The Completion Decision

Regression estimates of equation (2), which deals with the decision to complete an engineering program, indicate that responsive supply behavior is not limited to the initial selection of a major. Salaries prevailing during the freshman–sophomore years have, according to the calculations in Table 4.4, a unit elastic impact on the number of graduates (regressions 2–4). The elasticity is below that for the initial supply decision because of the cost of switching fields after several years of study.

Table 4.4 Supply of Engineering Graduates, 1951–1967
(The dependent variable is Δln GRD, the log change in number of engineering graduates seeking work)[a]

		Regression Coefficients and t-Statistics[b]						
Equation Number	*Con-stant*	Δln $FRSH_{t-4}$	Δln $ESAL_{t-2}$ + Δln $ESAL_{t-3}$	Δln CVET	(ENR/ $FRSH_{t-4}$)	Δln $PROF_{t-2}$ + Δln $PROF_{t-3}$	R^2	*D.W.*
(1)	—	0.72	0.56				0.794	1.59
		(5.60)	(1.22)					
(2)	—	0.40	0.85	0.0087			.920	1.56
		(3.53)	(2.77)	(4.14)				
(3)	—	0.51	0.97	0.0088	−0.28		.940	2.20
		(4.31)	(3.41)	(4.52)	(1.86)			
(4)	—	0.45	1.29	0.0079	−0.29	−0.005	.948	1.88
		(4.27)	(3.36)	(4.51)	(1.84)	(0.056)		

[a] To close the model, the dependent variable in these calculations is the log change in the number of graduates seeking work, not the number actually graduating. Regressions with the total number of graduates yield similar results. The computations in the table are based on the data from the Los Alamos survey. Results of equations of the Endicott Placement data depict a similar picture of supply responsiveness.

[b] The levels of significance for the *t*-statistics are 1%: 2.95, 2.98, 3.01, 3.06, 3.11; 5%: 2.13, 2.15, 2.16, 2.18, for the four equations respectively.

The estimated role of the other variables of equation (2) supports the general validity of the model. Necessarily, most of the variation in the number of graduates is attributable to the number of freshmen engineers four years earlier. In the first equation this term has a coefficient that does not differ significantly from unity, suggesting that the model is reasonably specified. The number of veterans in college (CVET) has a positive effect on graduates because many of the veterans graduate after an interruption in the normal four-year college sequence. Inclusion of this term reduces the size of the coefficient on the number of freshmen. In equation (3) the proportion of freshmen choosing engineering in a given class also helps explain the change in the number of graduates: the higher the proportion the greater is the dropout rate and the smaller the change in graduates.

Finally, professional earnings are insignificantly related to the supply of graduates, though with the appropriate negative sign (equation 4).

4.4 Demand for B.S. Engineers

Salary determination equations for actual and planned salaries were estimated under several specifications of the formation of expected supply. Planned salaries are measured by the plans of firms in the winter prior to recruitment, as reported in the Endicott survey; actual salaries are measured by June starting salaries in the Los Alamos survey.

Actual Salary Determination

Table 4.5 summarizes the results of a multiple regression analysis of starting salaries for the period 1948–1967. Overall, the regressions support

Table 4.5 Determination of Changes in Engineering Starting Salaries, 1948–1967 (The dependent variable is Δln ESAL, the log change in the starting salary of B.S. engineers, as reported in the Los Alamos Survey.)

	Regression Coefficients and t-Statistics[a]								
Equation Number	*Constant*	Δln RD	Δln DUR	Δln GRD	Δln GRD_{t-1}	Δln GRD_{t-2}	Δln GRD_{t-3}	R^2	D.W.
(1)	0.001	0.323	0.102	−0.095				0.805	3.27
		(3.97)	(3.31)	(4.44)					
(2)	0.005	0.302	0.107	−0.051	−0.047			.860	3.03
		(4.17)	(3.92)	(1.83)	(2.15)				
(3)	−0.003	0.356	0.101	−0.002	−0.149	0.075		.945	2.53
		(7.23)	(5.56)	(0.08)	(5.20)	(4.11)			
(4)	0.000	0.335	0.116	−0.026	−0.150	0.116	−0.043	.961	2.30
		(7.41)	(6.49)	(1.07)	(5.91)	(4.43)	(1.99)		

[a] The levels of significance for the *t*-statistics are 1%: 2.98, 3.01, 3.06, 3.11; 5%: 2.15, 2.16, 2.18, 2.20 for the four equations, respectively.

the salary equation of the cobweb model, explaining most of the variation in the log-change of salaries by shifts in demand due to R & D and durable goods spending and movements along the demand curve due to the changing number of graduates seeking work.* With the simplest specification

* Because many B.S. graduates enroll for graduate education, supply is adjusted to reflect the number actually seeking work.[15] Experiments with unadjusted figures and with alternative adjustments show that the statistical results do *not* depend on the precise measurement of supply.

of salary determination — that of immediate market clearing — the current number of graduates has a pronounced negative effect on salaries, and an estimated flexibility coefficient of one tenth (equation 1). Serial correlation of the errors suggests, however, that the equation is not correctly specified.

Addition of lagged supply variables to improve the specification leads to better statistical results. On the assumption that expected supply equals last period's, the R^2 increases and serial correlation diminishes (equation 2). In this case the lagged and current number of graduates obtain roughly equal coefficients, indicating an adjustment coefficient of one half. The flexibility of salaries remains on the order of one tenth. With the addition of graduates lagged two periods to represent extrapolation of supply, there is a further improvement in the statistical fit and a decrease in serial correlation (equation 3). More important, the size and sign of the estimated coefficients support the extrapolation hypothesis: the double lagged term has a positive coefficient approximately half that on the graduates lagged one period.* The drop in significance of current supply suggests slow adjustment to new conditions. Equation (4) describes salary determination with a correction for errors in expectations. Again, the statistical results are improved and coefficients receive the appropriate size and sign.†

Although measurement and specification error make any single regression finding highly tentative, it seems safe to conclude from this exercise that salaries respond to changes in supply with a lag.[16] Certainly the market does not clear in a single recruitment period.

Planned Salary Determination

Analysis of the factors determining planned salaries provides further support for the lagged salary model. Planned salaries are, as predicted in the model, affected by demand at the time plans are formulated and by past supply conditions. Supply in the period to which salaries refer, on the

* Recall that in the extrapolation model $\ln(\mathrm{GRD})_t = 2\ln(\mathrm{GRD})_{t-1} - \ln(\mathrm{GRD})_{t-2}$ so that the $t-1$ term has a coefficient opposite in sign and twice the absolute value of the $t-2$ term.

† Solving the first three coefficients for the structural parameters yields the following estimates:

$a = 0.09$ (flexibility of salaries)
$w = 0.70$ (speed of adjustment)
$c = 0.45$ (correction coefficient)

According to the model, the coefficient on the number of graduates lagged three periods should equal the product of these parameters (awc). In fact, the coefficient is -0.03, which is within a standard deviation of the estimate (-0.04).

other hand, has no effect on plans. In the case of simple extrapolation of past changes in supply, for example, we obtain the following statistically "good" explanation of planned salaries.

$$\Delta\ln(\text{ESAL})^p = \underset{}{-0.096} + \underset{(5.02)}{0.253}\,\Delta\ln \text{RD} + \underset{(3.93)}{0.306}\,\Delta\ln \text{DUR}$$

$$\underset{(5.35)}{-0.125}\,\Delta\ln \text{GRD}_{-1} + \underset{(3.15)}{0.096}\,\Delta\ln \text{GRD}_{-2} - \underset{(2.71)}{0.051}\,\Delta\ln \text{GRD}_{-3}$$

$$R^2 = 0.869$$
$$\text{D.W.} = 2.32$$

An additional test of the planned salary process is possible for the period since 1953, when the Endicott survey began gathering actual as well as planned salary figures. In this test the difference between planned and previous salaries is regressed on changes in demand and lagged changes in supply, under the hypothesis that firms react to current demand, and, through expectations, past supply.

$$\ln(\text{ESAL})_t^p - \ln(\text{ESAL})_{t-1} = \underset{(1.78)}{0.017} + \underset{(1.62)}{0.115}\,\Delta\ln \text{RD} + \underset{(1.57)}{0.050}\,\Delta\ln \text{DUR}$$

$$\underset{(2.84)}{-0.142}\,\Delta\ln \text{GRD}_{t-1}$$

$$R^2 = .63$$
$$\text{D.W.} = 1.99$$

Both equations support the postulated structure and present a picture of salary determination consistent with that of the actual salary regressions. Traditional market forces — shifts in supply and demand — explain changes in engineering starting salaries, though with a lag due to sluggish adjustment to unexpected supply conditions.

4.5 The Cobweb Mechanism

The stability of the cobweb structure and the time required to attain equilibrium after an exogenous disturbance can be determined from the estimated supply and demand parameters. In the first case, it is evident that the cobweb fluctuations generated by the model are extremely stable. The product of the supply and salary coefficients is on the order of 0.30, fulfilling the usual criterion for stability that the product be less than unity. Stability is enhanced, moreover, by the negative impact of a large entering class on ensuing growth and on the fraction of enrollees earning a degree four years later. It is also apparent that the market restores equilibrium rapidly when faced with sudden disturbances. A one-period rise in salaries by 10 percent followed by a return to the previous level will, for example, increase the number of freshmen by 30 percent and the number of graduates by at most 20 percent. Since the salary coefficient is about one tenth, the disturbance results in salaries just 2 percent below equilibrium four years later. Approximately 80 percent of the disturbance is eliminated in a single training period. Allowance for more complex supply and salary behavior does not change the picture of a rapid return to equilibrium. Barring extraordinary or recurrent disturbances, the market for engineers will be close to the equilibrium salary and number of entrants.

A Job Opportunities Interpretation

By substituting the salary equation (3) into the enrollment equation (2), the entire cobweb system can be summarized with a single equation relating enrollment to endogenous nonsalary and exogenous variables. In the case of a simple nonlagged salary function, this yields:

$$(11)\quad \Delta\ln \mathrm{ENR}_t = a_0\,\Delta\ln \mathrm{FRSH}_t - a_1c_0\,\Delta\ln \mathrm{GRD}_t + a_1c_1\,\Delta\ln \mathrm{RD}_t + a_1c_2\,\Delta\ln \mathrm{DUR}_t - a_2\,\Delta\ln \mathrm{PSAL}_t + a_3\,\Delta\ln \mathrm{VET}_t.$$

Conceptually this "cobweb equation" shows that a large graduating class reduces freshman enrollment in a given year (which decreases the number of graduates and increases the number of first-year enrollees four years later).

The elimination of engineering salaries from the model (and the possible analogous elimination of alternative salaries) suggests a "non-price" interpretation of the cobweb mechanism. Specifically, equation (11) may be regarded as a relation between supply and job opportunities, where opportunities depend, reasonably enough, on the number of graduates seeking work relative to demand. According to this theory, students respond to such labor market incentives as job vacancies, existence of attractive openings, and other measures of opportunity, as well as, or instead of, to "pure" salary incentive.

Statistically, estimates of the cobweb equation presented below show that it explains enrollment in the 1948–1967 period as accurately as the supply equations of section 4.3. The coefficient of determination is sizable, variables are significant, and the number of current graduates has an especially significant effect on enrollment, as required by the model. By itself, the change in graduates is extraordinarily well correlated with the change in freshman enrollment in the same year ($r = -0.80$). The cobweb dynamics posited at the beginning of the chapter is thus strongly confirmed in these calculations.

Table 4.6 "Cobweb Equation" for Supply of First-Year Students to Engineering, 1948–1967

(Δln ENR is the dependent variable)

	Regression Coefficients and t-Statistics[a]							
Equation Number	*Constant*	Δln FRSH	Δln GRD	Δln RD	Δln DUR	Δln SHR	R^2	D.W.
(1)	−0.70	0.57	−0.50	0.60	0.14		0.862	1.57
	(2.52)	(3.08)	(5.72)	(2.68)	(1.25)			
(2)	0.014	0.64	−0.47	0.77	0.29	−0.23	0.902	2.17
	(0.80)	(4.59)	(5.29)	(3.56)	(2.37)	(2.69)		

[a] The levels of significance of the t-statistics are 1%: 3.01, 3.06; and 5%: 2.16, 2.18 for equations (1) and (2) respectively.

Shortages and Surpluses

Recurring public concern over shortages or surpluses of engineering manpower is partially explained by the cobweb structure of the market. First, cobweb fluctuation in the number of graduates — which in postwar years ranged from increases of 50 percent to decreases of 50 percent within the span of three years — would seem to be sufficient cause for concern over shortages or surpluses, especially if cyclic phenomena are misinterpreted as trends. Second, the lagged adjustment of salaries, which produces job vacancies when supply is less than anticipated and surpluses when it is greater, is likely to exacerbate the impact of fluctuations on firms. These phenomena would seem to explain the uproar over shortages in the mid-1950s when the number of graduates fell from its 1951 peak.[17]

Summary

1) The supply of college students to B.S. engineering responds to economic incentive, with freshmen and undergraduate majors taking account of labor market conditions in their career plans.

2) The incentive in the market may be represented by salaries or employment opportunities.

3) Starting salaries are determined by classical labor market forces — shifts in supply and demand — with a lag due to slow adjustment to changed supply.

4) The market for engineers is well described by the cobweb variant of the basic labor market model, with stable highly dampened fluctuations.

5 The Income of Doctorate Specialists

The labor market for doctorate workers sustained an unprecedented boom after World War II. Salaries increased more rapidly than ever before; the number of Ph.D. graduates grew dramatically; stipend support became more prevalent and remunerative. These and related developments in the vibrant doctorate market are examined in the next three chapters. After a brief look at the characteristic features of the market, I analyze the income position of doctorate specialists (chapter 5), subsidization of graduate students (chapter 6), and the determinants of the supply of graduates (chapter 7).

5.1 Doctorate Labor Market

How does the doctorate market differ from those usually studied by labor economists? In broad perspective the supply and demand for doctorate workers is distinguished by:

a) A large investment in human capital. The substantial investment of the doctorate worker in his career creates lengthy commitments to the specialty and reduces occupational mobility. It also provides great incentive to search for information before making a career decision[1] and so is likely to produce an especially well-informed body of decision makers.

b) Subsidization of graduate training. By offering financial aid to some students, the government and private organizations bifurcate the market for investment in doctorate education. Persons with stipend support receive low-cost financing while those without awards must pay high rates for loans or other nonsubsidized funds. The number of stipends determines the relative importance of the segments[2] and, in conjunction with other factors, the occupational choice of prospective Ph.D.'s.

c) Nonpecuniary income differentials. Differences in the work offered by universities, industries, and government create especially large nonpecuniary income differentials in the doctorate market. As a result, equilibrating wage differentials can be confused with the disequilibrium differentials that motivate mobility.[3] Low salaries in biology, for example, can reflect low real income or the nonmonetary income associated with pleasant work in a university setting.

d) Research and development activities. Research and development work obfuscates the significance of market earnings. When R & D is successful, it yields ideas or information which either cannot be appropriated by firms or become patented monopolies. As Kenneth Arrow puts it:

> Information (produced by research or other means) is by definition an indivisible commodity . . . [and] . . . in the absence of special legal protection, the owner cannot simply sell information on the open market (since) any one purchaser . . . can reproduce the information at little or no cost.[4]

If the research is nonappropriable, it will not be undertaken in a competitive economy; if it is patented or guarded by secrecy, it will be diffused slowly throughout the economy and possibly be needlessly duplicated. In either case the amount and type of research may be nonoptimal and the salaries of researchers different from their social marginal product.[5]

From this brief examination it appears that the market for doctorate workers operates differently from many other labor markets and for this reason deserves special attention in analysis and in public policy.

5.2 Changes in Income, 1935–1965

From the 1930s to the mid-1950s the relative income position of doctorate workers deteriorated, with increases below the economy-wide average. In 1957 or thereabouts, this trend was broken and Ph.D. salaries began increasing exceptionally rapidly.

Long-term Decline

The long-run change in doctorate earnings is described in Table 5.1, which compares Ph.D. starting salaries with other incomes and with gen-

Table 5.1 Percentage Change in Starting Salaries of Doctorate Graduates and in General Economic Conditions, by Quinquennium, 1935–1960

	Percentage Change					*Percentage Change Entire Period*
	1935–40	*1940–45*	*1945–50*	*1950–55*	*1955–60*	*1935–60*
Ph.D. starting salary (Current dollars)	10.7	45.6	29.7	19.4	25.0	212.0
Ph.D. starting salary (1958 Dollars)	6.5	14.8	1.6	8.1	14.5	45.3
Wages in manufacturing (1958 dollars)	23.9	15.0	6.8	15.7	10.1	93.8
Wages and salaries (1958 dollars)	13.3	26.7	13.4	14.8	10.7	88.9
Gross National Product (Current dollars)	43.7	87.3	35.6	39.7	26.6	545.9
Gross National Product (1958 dollars)	36.9	34.4	6.3	23.3	11.4	169.6
Consumer Price Index	4.2	30.8	28.1	11.3	10.5	114.8
Research & development spending	76.0	100.0	88.9	88.3	115.9	—
Number of Ph.D. graduates	25.7	−49.8	237.8	36.6	12.4	287.4
Number of persons enrolled in colleges	16.2	19.4	37.3	28.0	26.4	208.4

SOURCE: National Academy of Sciences-National Research Council study for *Profiles of the Ph.D.*, for doctorate salaries. L. S. Silk, *The Research Revolution*, for research and development figures. *Statistical Abstract*, for other data.

eral economic conditions for the period of 1935–1960.* Columns 1–5 record percentage changes by five-year intervals; Column 6 shows the changes over the entire quarter-century. The historic decline in the relative earnings of the Ph.D. is evident, with doctorate starting salaries increasing by only 45 percent over the entire period — half the rate for other workers. In only one specialty — mathematics — was the increase in Ph.D. salaries greater than the increase in manufacturing wages.

The story is similar when doctorate earnings are compared to the income of college graduates who have not attained the Ph.D. From 1939 to

* I deal with starting salaries because they are the longest income series currently available. As the Survey of the National Academy of Science-National Research Council does not go beyond 1960, Table 5.1 terminates in that year. Post-1960 developments are consistent with the picture revealed in the NAS-NRC statistics.

1958 the mean income of graduates advanced approximately twice as fast as doctorate starting salaries in the comparable 1940–1960 period.

To obtain some notion of how economic conditions affect starting salaries, I examined the relation between those salaries, R & D, number of graduates, GNP, and enrollment across the five periods distinguished in the table. The principal empirical regularities are:

1) in periods with great increases in the number of graduates, the rate of increase in salaries is especially low (The Spearman rank correlation coefficient is −0.90);
2) When R & D spending increases greatly, salaries tend to increase greatly (a rank correlation of 0.50).

No clear relations between changes in salary and changes in college enrollment or in real GNP are revealed in Table 5.1.

From these calculations it appears that the supply of doctorate graduates and the demand for research workers are the principal determinants of doctoral starting rates. Together, these two variables explain the pattern of salary variation in the five periods: changes in the ratio of R & D to graduates, a composite measure of supply and demand shifts, is perfectly rank-correlated with changes in salary, by period. Given the crude data and the peculiarities of the time intervals, however, this is a highly tentative finding.

The Break in Trend

A reversal of the long-term relative decline of doctorate income in the mid-1950s is documented in a variety of income statistics. In Table 5.2 it will be seen that the 1955–1960 period is the *only* five-year interval during which Ph.D. salaries advanced more rapidly than other earnings. For the first time a majority of specialties (16 of 23) outdistanced manufacturing workers in wage gains. In Table 5.3 comparisons of income for the interval 1948–1967 also point toward a break in trend. From 1948 to 1957 doctorate scientists had relatively small percentage gains in income, and from 1957 to 1967, abnormally large gains. Ph.D.'s were the only group of workers enjoying a more rapid gain in the latter period.

A similar pattern is found for doctorate specialists in industry. Prior to 1957, starting Ph.D.'s registered annual increases of 4.9 percent, slightly below those of other workers; after 1957, their gain of 5 percent per year was

Table 5.2 Changes in Doctorate Salaries by Field Compared to Changes in Manufacturing Wages, 1935–1960

	Number of Ph.D. Fields					
	1935–40	*1940–45*	*1945–50*	*1950–55*	*1955–60*	*1935–60*
Fields with increases in salaries above increases in wages	0	7	7	5	16	1
Fields with increases in salaries below increases in wages	23	15	16	17	7	22

Source: Unpublished NAS-NRC survey data.

Table 5.3 Compound Annual Changes in Salaries and Wages, 1948–1957 and 1957–1967

	1948–1957	*1957–1967*
All Ph.D. scientists and engineers	4.5	4.7
Manufacturing workers	5.0	3.3
Construction workers	5.3	3.5
Personal income per capita	4.8	4.4
All professionals	4.6	2.9
Consumer Price Index	1.8	0.8

Source: Bureau of Labor Statistics and Los Alamos Scientific Laboratory.

nearly twice the average. Within specific industries, also, doctorate scientists did best after 1957 (Table 5.4). From 1948 to 1957, Ph.D. salaries fell relative to the wages of production workers and to the salaries of bachelor's graduates in most industries. Afterward, both starting and experienced Ph.D.'s obtained exceptionally large increases.

Overall, the rapid increase in Ph.D. salaries after the 1955–1957 interval produced a substantial gain in the relative economic status of doctorate specialists in the entire postwar period. The annual compound rate of increase in doctorate income from 1948 to 1967 was 4.6 percent compared to an increase of 4.3 percent for manufacturing workers and 3.9 percent for all male professionals.

Changes in Income, by Doctorate Field

The rate of change in doctorate salaries varies greatly across the main specialties (see column 1 of Table 5.5). In some fields the rate of increase

Table 5.4 Monthly Earnings of Nonsupervisory Scientists, Average Hourly Earnings of Production Workers and Changes in Earnings, by Industry, 1949–1965

	Monthly and Hourly Earnings			Percentage Change in Earnings	Percentage Change of Earnings Relative to Increase for Production Workers[b]	
Industry	*1949*	*1957*	*1965*	*1949–65*	*1949–57*	*1957–65*
Chemicals						
Starting Ph.D.	$465	$700	$1053	126.5	92.0	160.8
Experienced Ph.D.[a]	652	875	1217	86.7	62.3	124.5
Starting B.S.	282	458	660	134.0	113.7	140.4
Production workers	1.42	2.20	2.89	103.5	100.0	100.0
Petroleum						
Starting Ph.D.	486	720	1067	119.5	89.2	262.0
Experienced Ph.D.	648	896	1249	92.7	71.1	214.1
Starting B.S.	315	499	662	110.2	108.3	177.7
Production workers	1.80	2.77	3.28	82.2	100.0	100.0
Instruments						
Starting Ph.D.	489	825	1125	130.1	136.3	134.3
Experienced Ph.D.	591	975	1254	112.2	129.0	105.5
Starting B.S.	315	496	708	125.5	115.1	157.6
Production workers	1.37	2.06	2.62	91.2	100.0	100.0
Aeronautical						
Starting Ph.D.	490	833	1165	137.8	138.3	118.8
Experienced Ph.D.	793	970	1357	71.1	44.1	118.8
Starting B.S.	292	488	685	134.6	79.8	120.2
Production workers	1.56	2.35	3.14	101.3	100.0	100.0
Machinery						
Starting Ph.D.	542	725	1171	116.1	66.6	209.9
Experienced Ph.D.	584	808	1225	109.8	75.9	176.1
Starting B.S.	313	475	696	122.4	102.2	158.7
Production workers	1.52	2.29	2.96	94.7	100.0	100.0
Rubber						
Starting Ph.D.	432	725	1031	138.7	136.7	178.1
Experienced Ph.D.	572	820	1175	105.4	87.5	182.3
Starting B.S.	273	460	668	144.7	138.1	190.7
Production workers	1.41	2.11	2.61	85.1	100.0	100.0
Food						
Starting Ph.D.	445	645	1036	138.7	84.9	191.1
Experienced Ph.D.	624	742	1308	109.6	35.7	243.0
Starting B.S.	258	428	651	152.3	124.6	165.9
Production workers	1.21	1.85	2.43	100.8	100.0	100.0
Biology and Pharmaceutical						
Starting Ph.D.	455	699	1045	129.7	108.1	146.9
Experienced Ph.D.	613	871	1286	109.8	84.8	141.2
Starting B.S.	242	424	610	152.1	51.6	130.3
Production workers	1.31	1.96	2.62	100.0	100.0	100.0

Source: Los Alamos Scientific Laboratory; Bureau of Labor Statistics.

[a] Experienced Ph.D.'s are men with 15 years work experience.

[b] These figures are calculated by dividing the percentage change in the earnings of scientists in each industry by percentage change for production workers in that industry.

Table 5.5 Percentage Change in Doctorate Starting Salaries, 1935–1960 and 1950–1960

	Percentage Change in Salaries	
Field	*1935–60*	*1950–60*
Medical Science[a]	42.7	0.8
Engineering	68.6	35.8
Chemistry	80.2	22.4
Education	47.3	23.1
Mathematics	105.7	48.0
Economics	37.9	49.5
Physics	65.8	27.4
Pharmacology	42.0	6.5
Microbiology	58.6	21.4
Psychology	45.2	11.1
Political Science	54.2	20.0
Genetics	48.3	25.8
Agriculture	35.3	22.4
Physiology	49.7	38.8
Sociology	32.3	20.1
Geology	43.0	16.3
Biochemistry	45.3	7.6
Zoology	39.4	18.1
Language & Literature	32.4	31.0
Botany	32.4	7.2
Arts & Humanities	30.6	27.2
History & Geography	21.5	25.7

SOURCE: National Academy of Sciences — National Research Council.
[a] The starting salaries for medical sciences jump around, probably because of the different number of M.D.'s included in the group, so that the figures here are unreliable.

from 1935 to 1960 was 1.5 to 2.0 times the average rate. In others, such as agriculture, history, botany, sociology, the arts and humanities, salaries grew at barely half the average. The most remarkable change in salaries occurred in mathematics, which jumped from the bottom position in the 1935 array of fields by salary to fifth position in the 1960 array. Physics also enjoyed especially large gains, rising in the salary structure in the 1940–1945 quinquennium when the atomic bomb and other wartime devices were developed. As a result of the changes in salaries, the structure of doctorate rates has been substantially altered. The rank correlation of 1935 rates by specialty with the 1960 rates is only 0.51, a figure much below those obtained for industrial wage structures.[6] The flexibility of Ph.D.

salaries may reflect great shifts in demand, extraordinary responsiveness of starting rates to new conditions, or the absence of technological and institutional rigidities in occupational salary structures.

In postwar years the increase in Ph.D. salaries also varied greatly among fields. According to Table 5.6, physics, mathematics, and linguistics experienced relatively large increases from 1948 to 1966, while agriculture, earth sciences, and statistics did relatively poorly. In the social sciences, economics and sociology recorded sizable advances, sociology doing better in terms of average income and economics better when incomes are adjusted for age composition of the fields.* The ranking of fields by salary change is, interestingly enough, positively correlated with the growth of degrees among specialties, indicating that the change in salaries has an impact on the allocation of manpower.[7]

Table 5.6 Salary and Annual Changes in Salary of Doctorate Scientists, by Field of Specialization, 1948 to 1966

	Median Annual Salary								*Compound Annual Percent Change*
Field	*1948*	*1951–52*	*1954*	*1957*	*1960*	*1962*	*1964*	*1966*	*1948–1966*
All Ph.D. Scientists	5720	—	7111	8567	10,000	11,000	12,000	13,200	4.8
Physical Sciences									
Mathematics	4920	6200	7410	7924	10,000	11,000	12,000	13,000	5.6
Physics	5840	—	7750	9421	11,000	13,000	13,500	14,400	5.2
Biology	4940	6200	6940	7400	9,000	10,000	11,200	12,500	5.3
Chemistry	6030	6900	6850	9670	11,000	12,000	13,000	14,000	4.8
Agriculture	5660	6300	7650	7911	9,000	10,000	11,300	12,800	4.5
Earth Sciences	5710	7200	7570	8667	10,000	10,000	11,000	12,000	4.2
Psychology	5320	—	6600	7414	9,000	10,000	11,000	12,100	4.6
Social Sciences									
Economics	—	7200	—	—	—	—	12,100	13,500	4.6
Sociology	—	5800	—	—	—	—	10,400	11,800	5.2
Statistics	—	7500	—	—	—	—	12,000	13,800	4.5
Linguistics	—	5300	—	—	—	—	10,000	11,000	5.3

SOURCES: National Science Foundation and Bureau of Labor Statistics.
[a] For all of the social sciences the compound changes are taken over the period 1952–1966.

* With this exception, age composition did not affect the ranking of fields by change in salaries.

A more detailed picture of postwar developments is given in the NAS-NRC data for 23 detailed doctorate specialties in column (2) of Table 5.5.[8] In these tabulations the greatest gains in salary in the 1950–1960 decade are found in mathematics and economics, followed by engineering and sociology. Increases in salaries were especially slight in botany, chemistry, and psychology. The structure of salaries was altered considerably in this period: the mean unweighted logarithmic increase in salaries was 0.412 while the standard deviation of the change was 0.214, yielding a coefficient of variation in excess of 50 percent. By contrast, the variation of changes in the wages of production workers in two-digit manufacturing industries was on the order of 0.20.[9] It seems safe to conclude that in the long and short run the doctorate salary structure is exceedingly flexible.

Income by Sector

Because of nonpecuniary income differentials associated with place of work, doctorate salaries differ by sector of employment as well as by area of specialisation (Table 5.7). In all cases, industry pays more than government agencies and the latter more than educational institutions. A Ph.D. scientist in industry in 1964, for example, earned 43 percent more than his colleague in education and 20 percent more than the governmental employee. The advantage of industry increases over the life cycle as specialists in education or government trade off income for tenure and job security. The steep age–earnings curve in industry is also partly due to the large return to work experience in the business world.

The effect of sector on salaries differs among fields. First, there is wide variation in the size of sectoral differentials. At one extreme, industrial economists earn 72 percent more than academic economists; at the other, agricultural scientists do just 8 percent better in industry than in the universities. Second, sector of work affects the extent to which salaries differ among fields. In industry, salaries ranged from $18,700 in economics to $12,000 in agriculture, while in education the differential was much less, from $11,000 to $9,000. Similarly, the rate of change in salaries varies widely among fields in the industrial sector and narrowly in education, probably because of the internal labor market described in Chapter II. The coefficient of variation of the mean logarithmic change in salary by specialty was 0.109 in education, 0.147 in government, and 0.201 in industry. Overall, earnings grew most rapidly in education in the postwar period, thereby narrowing sectoral differentials.

Notwithstanding the sectoral influence, however, occupation is the key

Table 5.7 Salary and Changes in Salary of Doctorate Workers in Industry, Government, and Education, and the Salary Advantage of Industry, 1948–1964

Field	*Median Annual Salary* 1948 (1)	1964 (2)	*Percentage Change in Salary, 1948–64* (3)	*Industrial Salaries Relative to Other Salaries*[a] 1948 (4)	1964 (5)	*Changes to the Advantage of Industry, 1948–64, Col. (5) – (4)* (6)
Agriculture						
Education	5390	11,100	105.9	1.22	1.08	−0.14
Industry	6670	12,000	79.9	1.00	1.00	
Government	5980	11,500	92.3	1.12	1.04	−0.08
Biology						
Education	4610	10,500	127.7	1.36	13.3	−0.03
Industry	6250	14,000	124.0	1.00	1.00	
Government	5480	11,900	117.1	1.14	1.18	+0.04
Earth Science						
Education	5200	9,900	90.4	1.50	1.36	−0.14
Industry	7780	13,500	73.5	1.00	1.00	
Government	6120	11,700	91.1	1.27	1.15	−0.12
Mathematics						
Education	4760	10,300	116.3	1.57	1.65	+0.08
Industry	7350	17,000	131.2	1.00	1.00	
Government	6830	15,100	121.0	1.08	1.13	+0.05
Chemistry						
Education	4670	10,000	114.1	1.47	1.40	−0.07
Industry	6880	14,000	103.4	1.00	1.00	
Government	6290	12,700	101.9	1.09	1.10	+0.01
Physics						
Education	5040	11,000	118.2	1.46	1.45	−0.01
Industry	7350	16,000	117.6	1.00	1.00	
Government	7400	13,800	86.4	0.99	1.16	+0.17
Psychology						
Education	4920	10,000	103.2	1.61	1.59	−0.02
Industry	7940	15,900	100.2	1.00	1.00	
Government	6180	11,500	86.0	1.28	1.38	+0.10

SOURCE: National Scientific Register.

[a] These figures are calculated by dividing industrial salaries in each field by the salaries for education, industry, and government respectively. Thus, in every case the data report the ratio of industrial to other salaries. Of necessity, industrial salaries = 1.00 in both columns (4) and (5).

determinant of changes in salaries. Rapid increases for individuals in the same specialty are found in every sector, while *intra*sectoral variation for different specialties is considerable. A nonparametric analysis of variance substantiates this observation. According to the Kendall coefficient of concordance, changes in salaries by specialty are correlated at the 1 percent level of significance across sectors, while changes in the salaries of different specialties within sectors occur randomly.

5.3 Discounted Lifetime Income

The principal variable in the human capital model of career choice is discounted lifetime income (DLI). We examine in this section the way in which discounted income can be used in labor market analysis and the variation of DLI's by doctorate specialty and between the doctorate and other degrees.

Analysis with Discounted Lifetime

Discounted lifetime incomes may be employed in the investigation of the operation of labor markets in two ways. First, under the assumption that equilibrium requires equal returns to training in alternative possibilities, differences in DLI's can be used to measure the divergence of incomes from equilibrium. Comparisons of rates of return among levels of education or occupations so as to identify "shortages" or "surpluses" exemplify this methodology. As long as there are no great differences in the nonmonetary value of job characteristics among the alternatives, differences in DLI's will reflect disequilibrium, as posited. For some problems, such as the analysis of educational adjustments within similar occupations, this condition is roughly fulfilled, so that comparisons of rates of return or DLI's are meaningful.

Analysis of occupational decision-making, on the other hand, is likely to require a more complex methodology. Occupations differ greatly in their job characteristics. Differences in money income needed to balance out the nonpecuniary advantage or disadvantage of characteristics may be confused with differences in real income. For a proper analysis of decision-making, it is necessary to adjust for nonpecuniary factors. One way of doing this is to introduce the discounted incomes or rates of return into supply equations. If individuals respond to differences in DLI's, the differences must reflect disequilibrium in the market. If they do not respond, the differentials are, *ceteris paribus,* equilibrating differentials. The correspondence of differentials with disequilibrium or equilibrating levels of income can be tested by applying the estimates from one set of data or one period to another.

A second way to take account of nonpecuniary factors is to correct money income for the value of nonmonetary job characteristics. This involves estimation of the "shadow price" of characteristics, possibly by regression analysis of incomes on measures of characteristics. Once the shadow price is calculated, money incomes can be "purged" of the value of characteristics. Calculations of this type are reported below.

Discounted Lifetime Income by Specialty

The principal evidence on the lifetime income of doctorate workers — cross-sectional DLI's in 22 specialities in 1960 — is presented in Table 5.8. The estimates are based on geometric mean incomes for graduates in the classes of 1935, 1940, 1945, 1950, 1955, and 1960. They use several discount factors and are unadjusted for mortality or for the expected secular growth of real income.[10] Mortality adjustments are unneccessary if interest rates already take account of life expectancies; growth adjustments are unnecessary because for reasonable rates the discount factor adjusted for growth is approximately one over the interest charge minus the growth rate.[11] For example, a discount factor based on a 6 percent rate of interest can be regarded as an 8 percent rate with a 2 percent growth factor or a 10 percent rate with 4 percent growth factor and so on.

At all rates there are substantial interfield differences in the DLIs, the highest paying field having a 60 percent advantage over the lowest. The coefficient of variation of incomes about the unweighted mean for the fields is 0.15. Because specialties have similar age–earnings curves, however, differences in interest rates do not affect the ordering of fields by DLI. Selecting an appropriate rate is *not critical* in analyzing occupational adjustments at the doctorate level.

To correct for the value of nonpecuniary characteristics, the discounted incomes are regressed on measures of job characteristics in Table 5.9. The characteristics relate to the type of employers and work activities common to a specialty in 1960: EDUC measures the fraction of Ph.D.'s with university employment; IND is the percentage in business; TEACH is the percentage teaching; RES, the percentage doing research.

The calculations summarized in Table 5.9 show that from 50 to 60 per-

Table 5.8 Lifetime Income of Doctorate Workers, Discounted to the Time of Graduation at Varying Rates of Interest, by Specialty, 1960

	Lifetime Income in Thousands of 1957–59 Dollars Discounted with a Rate of Interest of:				
Field	*.00*	*.02*	*.06*	*.10*	*.16*
Engineering	539.7	356.4	197.9	122.9	83.7
Physics	509.6	334.4	184.9	113.5	77.5
Medical Sciences	474.3	313.0	178.4	113.5	79.6
Chemistry	467.0	309.5	172.3	107.6	73.3
Economics	457.6	301.7	168.0	105.3	71.9
Mathematics	455.1	298.5	165.5	103.8	70.7
Pharmacology	433.5	291.8	165.0	103.7	71.6
Geology	449.7	293.0	159.8	97.3	64.9
Psychology	419.9	276.7	153.7	95.8	65.2
Political Science	418.9	271.5	148.4	92.0	61.7
Biochemistry	414.6	269.9	147.0	89.8	59.8
Education	371.7	251.7	144.3	94.3	66.3
Agriculture	393.3	259.4	144.0	90.9	61.2
Microbiology	391.5	258.4	143.3	89.9	61.1
Physiology	372.9	246.5	137.3	87.0	59.4
Sociology	363.0	240.1	133.8	84.2	56.3
Genetics	364.5	241.1	133.3	83.5	56.3
Botany	341.7	232.3	129.0	80.6	54.5
History — Geography	339.8	224.2	124.6	77.5	52.9
Arts and Humanities	349.2	226.7	123.6	76.1	50.9
Zoology	321.1	213.8	119.6	75.5	51.8
Language and Literature	310.8	207.7	117.0	74.0	51.1
All Ph.D. (weighted average)	413.4	272.7	151.3	94.4	64.2

SOURCE: NAS-NRC, unpublished data from survey of Ph.D. recipients.

cent of the variations in DLIs is attributable to differences in the job characteristics. The proportion of Ph.D.'s in educational employment "explains," for example, 50 percent of the interfield differential in discounted income (equation 1). Each percentage point of employment in education reduces money income by $1000 (discounted at 6 percent). Analagously, industrial employment raises income, presumably because of the nonpecuniary disadvantage of such work. Teaching and research reduce money income (equations 3 and 4), while administrative work (the third possible activity) raises it.

Finally, changes in lifetime income from 1955 to 1960 (Δln DLI) was

Table 5.9 Estimates of Compensating Income Differentials in the Doctorate Market, 1960

(The dependent variable is lifetime income in 1960, discounted with a 6% interest rate)

Equation Number	*Constant*	*Regression Coefficients and t-Statistic*	R^2
(1)	211,700	−1047 EDUC (5.21)	0.533
(2)	129,100	+1135 IND (5.54)	.565
(3)	231,300	−2157 TEACH−1385 RES (5.98) (4.15)	.600
(4)	191,900	−1122 EDUC + 1759 Δln DLI (6.60) (3.11)	.674
(5)	206,600	−2232 TEACH − 1416 RES (7.47) (5.15) +.1246 Δln DLI (3.15)	.727

Source: Table 5.8, for discounted lifetime incomes; NAS-NRC, *Profile of the Ph.D.*, for distribution of employment.

introduced into equations (4) and (5) to see whether interfield differentials are affected by relatively recent changes in the market, to which supply had not yet adjusted adequately. The significant positive coefficient on the term supports this contention. Part of the 1960 pattern of differentials seems to have arisen in the preceding five years, presumably as a result of transitory disequilibrium.

If the regressions in Table 5.8 provide tolerably good estimates of equilibrating income differentials, the difference between observed and calculated incomes reflects market disequilibrium. Fields with incomes in excess of expected income (that is, positive regression residuals) face a *relative* shortage of manpower; those with incomes below the estimates, a surplus. The position of the 22 specialties according to the residuals from regression equation (1) is depicted in Figure 5.1. In this figure occupations with a surplus of workers lie above the regression line and occupations with a shortage of workers lie below the line.* By this criterion, mathematics, engineering, physics, and medical sciences are the principal fields showing a great need for additional workers. Chemistry, biochemis-

* Estimates of disequilibrium using equations (2)–(5) of Table 5.9 present a similar, though not identical, picture of the doctorate market. Experiments with different equation forms also confirm the general validity of the categorization described in the text.

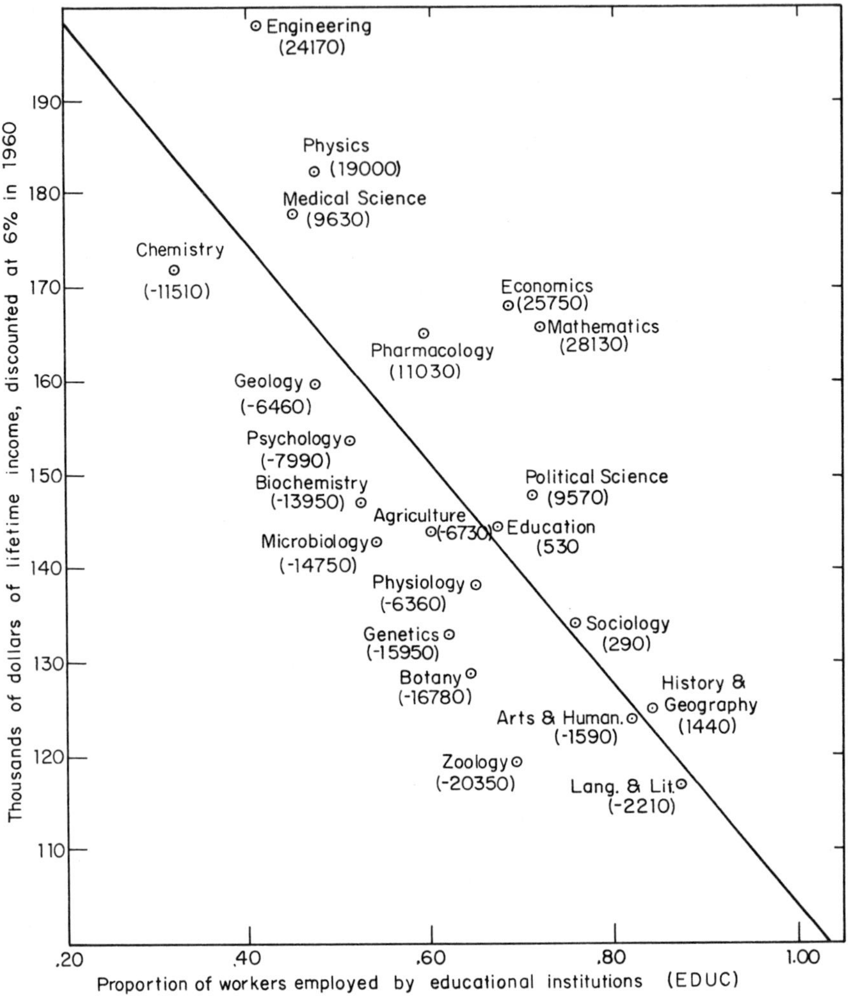

5.1 Disequilibrium in the doctorate labor market in 1960, as indicated by the deviations of expected from actual discounted lifetime income

try, botany, and zoology show the least need. This categorization of supply–demand imbalances is reasonable for 1960 and, in the absence of a more sophisticated treatment of nonmonetary factors, is used in ensuing explanations of supply behavior.

Discounted Income by Level of Education

Is the doctorate a profitable investment in human capital? How does it compare in capital value with the bachelor's or master's degree?

With the 6 percent discount factor used in preceding computations, the Ph.D. clearly pays off. At this rate, in 1960 the degree was worth $151,300 in discounted future income upon receipt at age 27, exclusive of earnings obtained during the years spent in graduate school. Addition of stipend and summer earnings and substraction of schooling expenses raise the figure to $169,300.[12] By comparison, the baccalaureate degree had a value of $144,700 in 1960, according to Census median income figures[13] — 15 percent below the DLI of the Ph.D. When incomes are measured by mean figures, the results are similar: the Ph.D. has an estimated value of $184,-400 and the bachelor's degree a value of $168,200. The differential is 10 percent in this case.[14] Further calculations pinpoint the discount rate equating the value of the two degrees. At 10 percent the DLIs based on mean incomes are virtually the same; at 11 percent, those based on median figures are equalized. As a first approximation, then, the rate of return of the doctorate is in the area of 10–11 percent.

Greater education is not, however, the sole cause of differences in income between Ph.D.s and less educated workers. Typically, the Ph.D. specialist has more ability and is engaged in different kinds of work than bachelor's or master's graduates. The estimated value of doctorate training can be improved by taking account of these factors.

Adjustment for Differences in Abilities

As Table 5.10 indicates, doctorate graduates tend to be more able than bachelor's graduates. The average Ph.D. has a higher I.Q. and a higher rank in his high school class than the typical B.S. or B.A. and thus might be expected to earn more than the bachelor's graduate even without the additional years of schooling. The higher ability of the Ph.D. biases upward the estimated rates of return to the degree.

The measures of differential ability recorded in Table 5.10 indicate, however, that the bias is relatively small. By each criterion the differences between a Ph.D. and a baccalaureate worker is *considerably less* than the differences between the B.A. and the high school graduate, suggesting a smaller effect of differential ability on the return to the Ph.D. than on the return to the baccalaureate. Moreover, whereas the average bachelor's graduate comes from a higher social stratum than the high school graduate and is thus likely to enjoy an advantage in "contacts, tastes, and knowledge of better paying occupations," [15] the family background of the Ph.D. is similar to that of the B.S. or B.A. (column 4).

In view of the comparatively small differences between Ph.D. and bachelor's graduates, it seems reasonable to use estimates of the size of the ability bias in the bachelor's case as an upper bound on its potential impact on the calculated return to the Ph.D. Gary Becker has estimated that the ability bias for the baccalaureate is about 12 percent of the computed rate of return.[16] To account for the ability advantage of the Ph.D., the return has been reduced by 10–12 percent, yielding a rate of 9–10 percent.

Table 5.10 Comparison of Ability of the B.A., the Ph.D., and the High School Student and Effect of Ability on Rates of Return to Education

Education	*I.Q.*	*Percentage with I.Q. over 120*	*Average Percentile Rank in High School*	*Percentage with Fathers in Professional, Semi-professional and Managerial Jobs*	*Estimated Effect of Ability on Rates of Return to Education*
High school graduate	106.8	20.8	44	22	
					+12%
College graduate	120.5	50.0	68	45	
					+10–12%
Ph.D. graduate	130.8	74.8	85	46	

Sources: Gary Becker, *Human Capital* (New York: National Bureau of Economic Research, 1964); L. Harmon, "High School Ability Patterns," Scientific Manpower Report No. 6 (NAS-NRC, Office of Scientific Personnel, August 1965); L. Harmon *Profiles of Ph.D.'s in Sciences*, NAS-NRC Publication No. 1293, Washington, D. C. 1965, Table 18.

Adjustment for Place of Work

Because doctorate workers are employed preponderantly in the university system, much of their real income is in the form of nonmonetary benefits, whose omission from discounted lifetime incomes biases the estimated value of the Ph.D. downward. To adjust for this bias, DLI's inclusive of nonpecuniary income were calculated by estimating the return to persons in the industrial sector, where both baccalaureate and doctorate workers are employed in large numbers. The rate of return to doctorate training in industry far exceeds the rate calculated earlier. A Ph.D. in industry earns 50–60 percent more than a B.S. with equivalent experience. At rates of pay prevalent in 1968, the absolute differential is approximately $5000 per year. To obtain this advantage the Ph.D. must forego five years of working life, which in 1968 also amounted to about $5000 per year (a graduate student netted $3000 per year; a B.S. graduate, $8000).[17] At a 10 percent rate of interest the benefits of the Ph.D. are $48,500: the costs, just $30,500. Not until the discount factor reaches 14 percent are the earnings streams equalized in present value. The "real" return to the Ph.D. is thus 35–40 percent more than the monetary return. Adjusted for nonmonetary income and ability, the rate is approximately 12.5 percent.

Return to the Doctorate by Occupation

Because of differences in the state of the labor market for particular skills, the Ph.D. is highly profitable in some sciences or in some branches of engineering and only moderately valuable in others. Tables 5.11 and 5.12 A and B summarize evidence regarding the differential value of doctorate, master's, baccalaureate, and nondegree training in several fields, with incomes discounted at 6 percent.

For all but one of the occupations listed in Table 5.11 the Ph.D. is a very profitable investment at 6 percent. Its capital value exceeds that of the baccalaureate by 20–25 percent on the average. The exceptional field is social science, where bachelor's graduates working in industry are higher paid than doctorate faculty. Master's degree training, by contrast, is only marginally profitable at 6 percent. The discounted lifetime income of M.S. mathematicians, biological scientists, and professors of engineering barely exceeds that of their B.S. counterparts. Master's graduates earn less over the life cycle than recipients of the bachelor's degree in the social sciences and in mechanical and civil engineering. In engineering specialties where nongraduate preparation is possible, the B.S. degree appears to have a high rate of return. At 6 percent, the discounted lifetime earnings of the B.S. graduate exceeds that of the nondegree engineer by 20–25 percent. Both the B.S. and Ph.D. degrees appear to be very profitable investments in human capital while the M.S. is only moderately remunerative.

The incomes reported by scientists in the National Scientific Register generally corroborate these results (Table 5.12A). In the natural and biological sciences where employment is concentrated in universities, doctorate training pays off handsomely at 6 percent, while the M.S. is only marginally profitable. In fields where most bachelor's graduates work in industry and doctor's graduates in education, however, the capital value of the Ph.D. is less than that of the B.A. or B.S. Economics, mathematics, statistics, and geology fit this pattern. Over 70 percent of doctorate mathematicians, for example, are university employees compared to 11 percent

Table 5.11 Lifetime Income of Scientists and Engineers in 1962, Discounted to Present Value at Age 26 with a 6% Rate of Interest

	Income in Thousands of Dollars, Unadjusted for Cost of Education and Earnings during Years of School				*Income Adjusted for Net Earnings during the Years of School[a] and Income Advantage of Additional Education (in parenthesis)*		
	Ph.D.	*M.S.*	*B.S.*	*No Degree*	*Ph.D.*	*M.S.*	*B.S.*
Engineering							
Teachers	176.6	152.5	157.4	142.8	186.4	156.1	154.5
					(30.3)	(1.6)	(11.7)
Civil	209.6	179.2	187.6	153.7	220.4	183.7	185.1
					(36.7)	(−1.4)	(32.6)
Electrical	230.3	223.1	208.4	164.9	239.8	226.2	204.5
					(13.6)	(20.8)	(40.5)
Industrial	228.9	194.3	192.0	161.2	237.7	198.1	190.2
					(39.6)	(7.9)	(29.0)
Mechanical	235.4	190.4	200.6	166.3	245.5	194.8	198.4
					(49.7)	(−3.6)	(32.1)
Other	211.7	204.5	205.5	170.6	224.8	212.1	203.4
					(12.6)	(8.7)	(32.8)
Science							
Physical	189.0	168.2	166.7	—	200.9	173.0	163.0
					(27.9)	(10.0)	—
Biological	146.2	128.6	130.8	—	158.6	133.7	127.9
					(24.9)	(5.8)	—
Agricultural	163.8	147.9	133.2	—	174.7	152.1	130.4
					(22.6)	(21.7)	—
Mathematics	176.0	158.0	161.3	—	185.6	161.8	158.4
					(23.8)	(3.4)	—
Psychology	155.6	141.5	—	—	163.5	143.7	—
					(19.8)	—	—
Other Social Science	149.3	141.6	162.3	—	158.0	144.7	159.3
					(13.3)	(−14.6)	—

SOURCE: *Postcensal Survey of Professional and Technical Manpower* (1966), for income figures. National Opinion Research Center, *Graduate Student Finances* (1963) for scholarship figures. Office of Education, *Financial Assistance for College Students* (1962), for schooling costs and subsidies.

[a] Adjustment for earnings during school follows the procedure set by Gary Becker, *Human Capital*, with students assumed to earn one-fourth the annual earnings of persons of the same age in the work force.

Table 5.12A Lifetime Income of Scientists in the National Register, Discounted to Present Value with a 6% Rate of Interest, 1964[a]

	Discounted Lifetime Income (in Thousands of Dollars)		
	Ph.D.	*M.S.*	*B.S.*
All Scientists	183.2	170.7	183.7
Agriculture	170.3	147.4	148.1
Biology	172.1	136.2	138.9
Chemistry	202.7	179.4	168.4
Earth Sciences	167.1	170.2	179.2
Geology	168.8	173.6	184.2
Meteorology	205.4	179.4	168.4
Economics	179.0	185.0	218.0
Geography	145.4	n.a.	n.a.
Linguistics	149.0	n.a.	n.a.
Mathematics	180.1	179.0	228.2
Statistics	190.6	191.8	193.1
Physics	211.6	188.7	202.8
Astronomy	188.5	n.a.	n.a.
Psychology	166.1	150.2	165.3
Sociology	155.1	n.a.	n.a.

of B.S. mathematicians, with the result that the Ph.D.'s average $180,000 in discounted lifetime income and the B.S.'s $228,000 (Table 5.12A). As long as there is nonpecuniary advantage to university employment, the return to the Ph.D. is biased downward by the sectoral distribution of jobs.

The capital value of the degree can be corrected for the bias by two-stage procedure. First, the value of academic work is estimated by regressing DLIs on the fraction of specialists employed in higher education. At each degree level, a percentage point of employment in education reduces income by $750 to $1000.[18] This suggests that educational employment is marginally worth $750 to $1000 in nonpecuniary income. These values are then multiplied by the fraction of specialists in universities and added to the actual DLI of each field. The result is an estimate of "real capital values" of the degrees.

For the Ph.D. and M.S. the real values are considerably greater than the uncorrected discounted incomes (Tables 5.12B). The lifetime earnings of Ph.D. economists are increased by 28 percent, for example, when university employment is valued at $750 percentage point in education and by 38 percent when it is valued at $1000. The capital worth of the bache-

Table 5.12B Discounted Lifetime Income Adjusted for the Nonpecuniary Value of Working in Educational Institutions, 1964[a]

	Income Adjusted by the Addition of $1000 per Percentage Point Employment in Education (in Thousands of Dollars)			*Income Adjusted by the Addition of $750 per Percentage Point Employment in Education (in Thousands of Dollars)*		
Field	*Ph.D.*	*M.S.*	*B.S.*	*Ph.D.*	*M.S.*	*B.S.*
Agriculture	235	192	156	219	178	154
Biology	238	195	183	221	173	171
Chemistry	1237	200	180	228	195	177
Earth Sciences	221	193	188	208	182	185
Economics	1247	219	224	230	211	223
Mathematics	250	224	239	233	213	236
Statistics	253	214	211	237	208	207
Physics	264	235	233	251	223	240
Psychology	220	190	193	206	180	181

SOURCE: *National Register of Scientific and Technical Personnel* (1964).

[a] The calculations assume the following working lives: Ph.D., 25–65; M.S., 22–65; B.S., 26–65; and are adjusted for the net income during the years of school.

lor's degree, on the other hand, is only modestly raised by this computation. As a result, the income advantage of postgraduate workers increases substantially. With discounted incomes corrected for the value of educational employment, the Ph.D. earns on the average 25 percent more than a B.S. in the same field. The rate of return on the doctorate implicit in this calculation exceeds 20 percent.

While the adjustments add to the income of master's graduates, however, the M.S. remains barely profitable at 6 percent. The DLIs presented in Table 5.12B show that the capital value of the M.S. is approximately equal to that of the B.S. in six of nine fields, and exceeds it by less than 10 percent in biology and chemistry. The M.S. pays off relatively well only in agriculture. On the average, the return to the M.S. appears to be in the area of 6–8 percent, which clearly makes it a less profitable investment in human capital than the doctorate.

Risk and Variability of Doctorate Earnings

Since the risk or variability of an investment in doctorate education may affect career decisions, I examine next two aspects of risk: the length of time needed for an investment in the Ph.D. to pay off and the variation of incomes about the mean. The longer the payoff period, the more in-

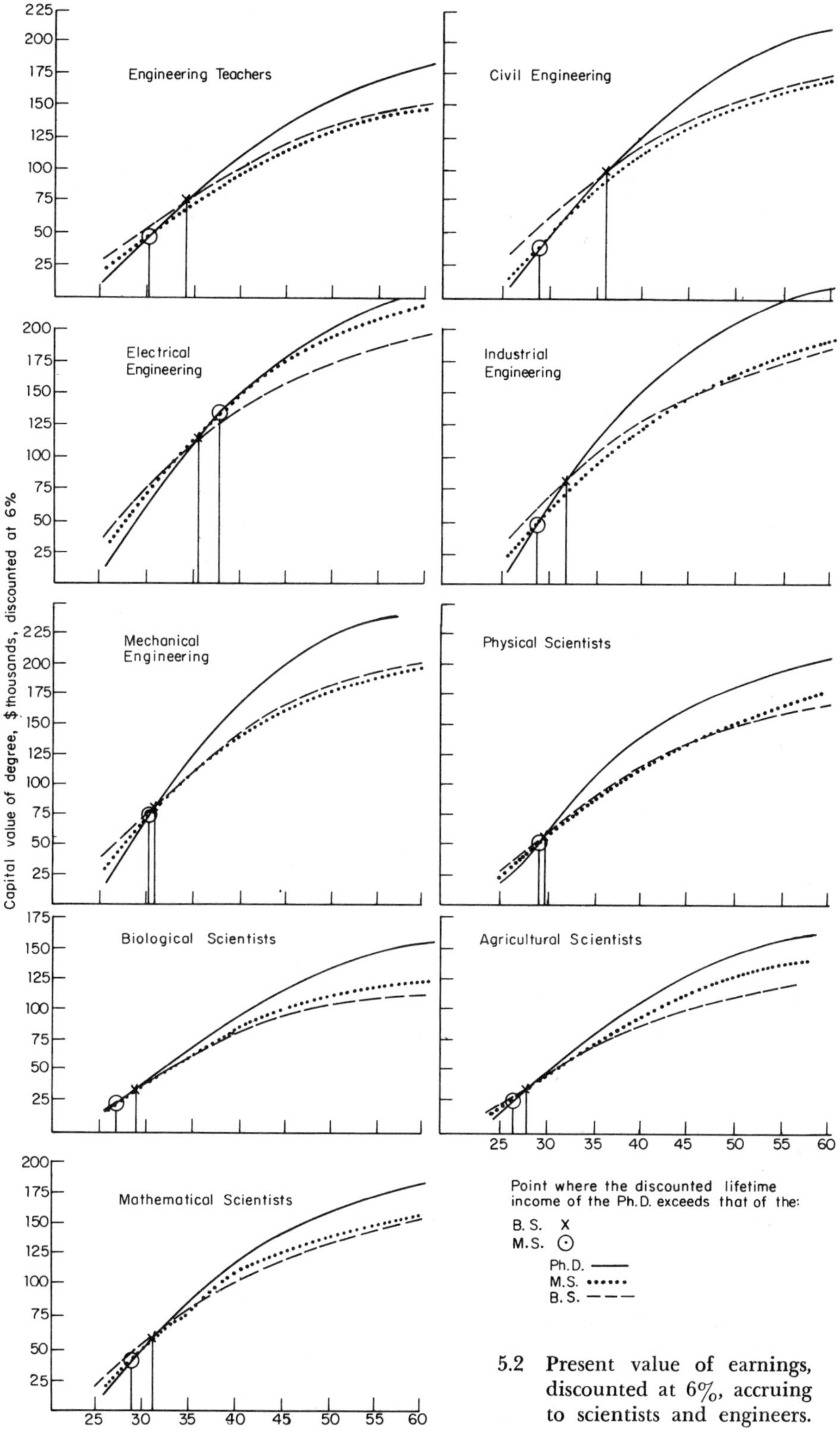

5.2 Present value of earnings, discounted at 6%, accruing to scientists and engineers.

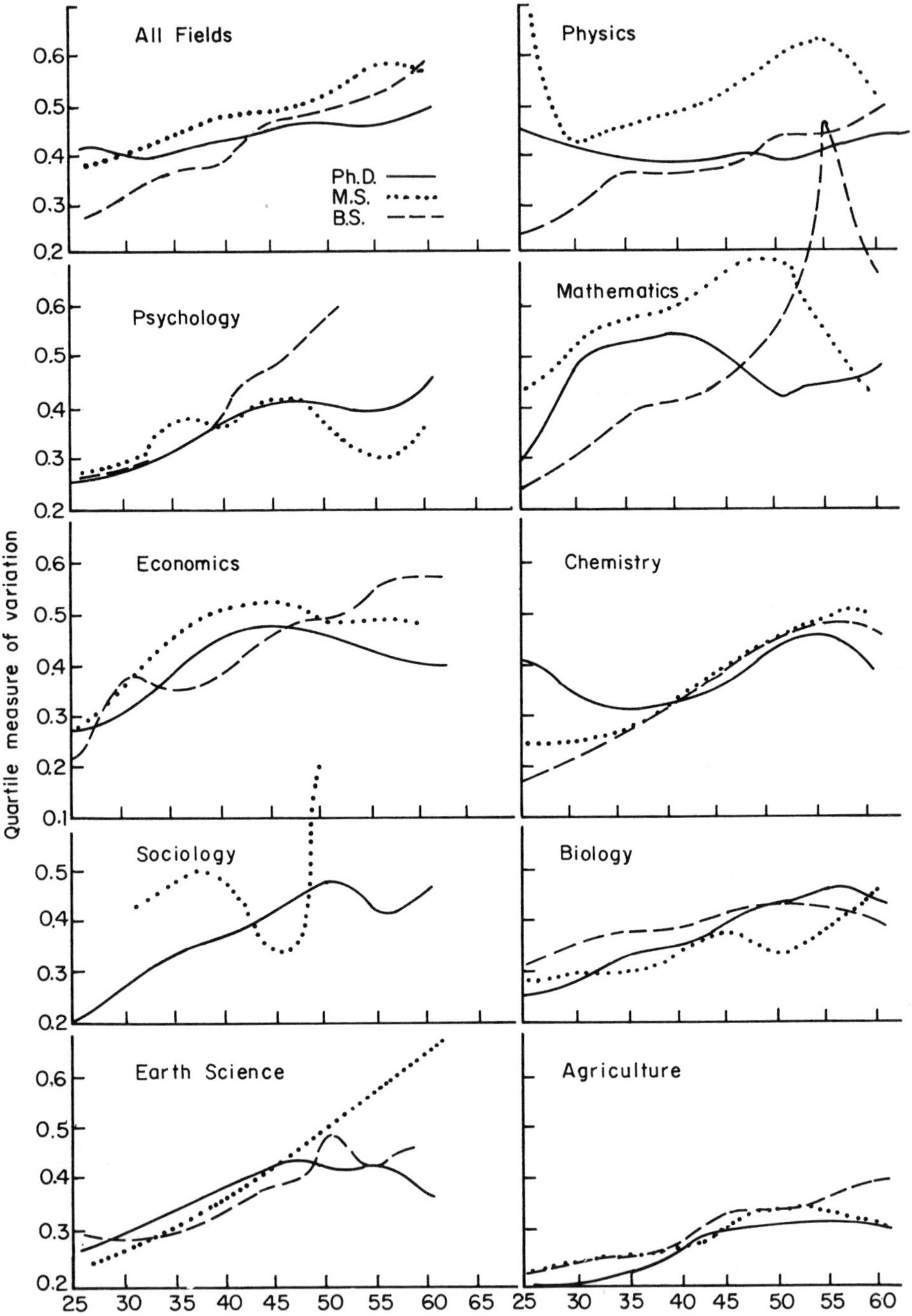

5.3 Variation in the cross-sectional earning of scientists, by degree, field, and age in 1964, as measured by the interquartile range of earnings divided by the median

formation is required about the distant future and the greater is the uncertainty and risk. Similarly, the more variation of income in a cross section, the greater is the risk of not attaining the average.

Figure 5.2 presents evidence regarding the length of payoff periods for Ph.D. and master's training. The figure shows the accrued capital value of each degree, discounted at 6 percent, over the life cycle. Since additional years of work add to earnings, the accrued incomes rise monotonically. The crossover points indicate the approximate time at which the income accruing to the Ph.D. surpasses that of other workers.

In all fields, relatively few years of work are required for the present value of the Ph.D. to overtake the accrued value of the M.S. or B.S. At the 6 percent discount rate crossing over occurs within five years in most cases.* In civil engineering the Ph.D. obtains a greater DLI than the M.S. within three years which offers one explanation for the rapid growth of Ph.D. degrees in that field. Overall, the short payoff periods suggest that the risk or uncertainty associated with future returns is not a major consideration in the decision to enroll for doctorate training.

The data on cross-sectional variations of income summarized in Figure 5.3 also point to a modest role for risk in the doctorate decision. In these figures there appears to be little difference in the variation of income among the Ph.D., M.S., and B.S. workers in the same field. The ratio of the interquartile range of income to the median rises over the life cycle everywhere with no degree having definitely higher or lower variation. At the upper age brackets doctorate incomes are somewhat less dispersed than M.S. or B.S. incomes, but not at the lower or middle portions of the life cycle. Since the degrees have roughly equal income variability, there is no reason for Ph.D. candidates to be exceptionally concerned with the variation of income opportunities.

In sum, the relatively short "payoff period" to doctorate training and the moderate variability of earnings indicates that risk is not a major factor in determining the supply of Ph.D.'s.

* At higher rates of discount, the number of years required for the Ph.D. to earn more than the B.S. or M.S. graduate increases. Even at rates of 10–12 percent, however, the payoff period does not extend beyond ten years in most specialties.

6 Stipend Income and Educational Subsidies

The lifetime income of college-trained specialists consists of stipends and financial aid received during the school years in addition to salaries from professional work. Stipends and subsidies are important policy tools for directing human capital to desired alternatives. This chapter is concerned with the ways in which stipends alter the financial return to college studies and influence the career decisions of doctorate students.

6.1 Subsidization of Graduate Students

How are students supported in the United States? Which fields receive the most stipend awards? How do awards affect the economic status of graduate students? How has support changed in the years since World War II?

Methods of Subsidization

Higher education can be subsidized through direct financial support of students or indirectly with below-cost tuition and fees. There are three broad categories of direct aid: non-duty stipends, consisting of fellowships and scholarships that do *not* require work by recipients; duty stipends such as teaching and research; and educational loans, with low interest and special repayment conditions.[1] Non-duty awards are the least market-oriented form of aid and are inappropriate in an economy where salaries reflect social marginal products and where loans for education are readily available; their extensive use is evidence of the difficulty of financing education and of the widespread belief in its external benefits. Duty awards, on the other hand, can be viewed as an exchange of money for work that differs from the usual labor market exchange by being limited to students. The low pay of research or teaching assistants is partly due to the fact that they receive general training for research or academic work. Educational loans help alleviate imperfections in the market for borrowing to invest in human capital.

The amount of subsidization varies greatly by curriculum. Throughout the 1960's direct support was extensive at the graduate level. In 1963 approximately three fourths of the graduate students in academic specialties received stipend support totaling $218 million. The average award was on the order of $2500 (Table 6.1). Graduate science students were likely

Table 6.1 Direct Subsidization of Students, 1963–1965

Curriculum	*Number Receiving Stipend Support, Including Educational Loans*	*Percentage of All Students Supported*	*Median Value of Stipend*	*Total Stipends Awarded (in $ Million)*
Graduate, excluding education and professional fields (NORC, 1963)	90,575	73	$2410	218.7
Graduate, including education and professional fields (Office of Education, 1965)	206,891	43	2170	449.2
Undergraduate (1963)	888,966	18	373	331.4
Medical (1963)	19,200	60	975	18.7

SOURCES: Graduate students: National Opinion Research Center, *Graduate Student Finances, 1963*, and Office of Education, *The Academic and Financial Status of Graduate Students, Spring 1965*. Undergraduates: Office of Education, *Financial Assistance for College Students* 1963.

to receive fellowships or research assistantships; those in the humanities obtained teaching assistant positions.

In professional fields loans rather than stipends are the prevailing form of aid. At Harvard University, for instance, business, law, and medical students rely extensively on educational loans (see Table 6.2). Professional school students are induced to borrow for their education by the "push" of relatively few fellowships and the "pull" of substantial future income.

At the undergraduate level, the principal mode of subsidization is below-cost tuition and fees, with student fees accounting for just one third of the income of the higher educational system, the remainder coming

Table 6.2 Educational Loans and Fellowships at Harvard University

	Percentage of Students at Harvard:	
Curriculum	*With Loans*	*With Fellowships or Scholarships*
Business	36	4
Law	33	29
Medicine	46	41

SOURCE: Harvard University, Report of the President (1964–1965)

from governmental, endowment, or philanthropic sources. Stipend awards to undergraduates are relatively infrequent and averaged less than $400 per student in 1963 (Table 6.1). Below-cost tuition also greatly benefits graduate students in curricula which require costly equipment or substantial inputs of professional time.

Stipend Support in Academic Fields

The proportion of students supported and the value of stipends vary among graduate specialties. As Table 6.3 shows, stipends constitute a large fraction of lifetime income in biological fields and only a small fraction in the arts and humanities. The variation in the value of awards far exceeds the variation in lifetime earnings among doctorate fields. The range of stipend income to the median, for example, is 1.7, while the range of lifetime income to the median among the various fields is 0.5.

Despite differences in the extent of stipend support there is no discernible relation between stipend income and the total income of graduate students (Table 6.4). Students in fields with substantial support often report less total income than those in other fields. In 1963, for example, students in biochemistry averaged $3800 over the year; English students $4600. There are three reasons for this anomolous situation: First, a minimum level of income is required for living and educational expenses. Persons without stipends make use of savings, loans, earnings of spouses, and part-time work to attain this level.[2] Second, because it is often possible to earn more from work than from awards, many older men with family responsibilities elect part-time or full-time work rather than full-time study. At current levels of support, these men would refuse aid if it were offered to them.[3] Third, family responsibilities aside, some reject stipends because of the attraction of employment. High starting salaries in engineering probably explain the frequency of part-time study and large student incomes in that field.

Table 6.3 Value of Stipend Income in 1960, Compounded at 6%

Field	*Mean Value of 4-Year Stipend Compounded to Year of Graduation at 6% (in Thousands of Dollars)*	*Discounted Lifetime Income, Including Stipends, At Year of Graduation (in Thousands of Dollars)*	*Stipend as Percentage of Income*
Engineering	6.7	204.6	3.3
Physics	9.1	194.0	4.7
Chemistry	8.8	181.1	4.9
Pharmacology	12.1	177.1	6.8
Economics	7.2	175.2	4.1
Mathematics	6.8	172.3	3.9
Geology	7.7	167.5	4.6
Psychology	6.3	160.0	3.9
Political Science	5.2	153.6	3.4
Biochemistry	11.8	158.8	7.4
Agriculture	9.9	153.9	6.4
Microbiology	9.3	152.6	6.1
Physiology	11.4	148.7	7.7
Genetics	12.1	145.4	8.3
Education	0.0	144.3	0.0
Sociology	6.6	140.4	4.7
Botany	9.7	138.7	7.0
History–Geography	3.7	128.3	2.9
Zoology	8.9	128.5	6.9
Arts and Humanities	1.9	125.5	1.5
Languages and Literature	3.7	120.7	3.1

SOURCES: Stipend income: National Opinion Research Center, *Graduate Student Finance*, 1963; Lifetime income, Table 5.8.

The availability and value of stipends increased greatly in the late 1950s, partly in response to *Sputnik* (1957). After a five-year period of near-constancy the mean value of fellowships at Harvard jumped 80 percent in the 1957–1965 period.[4] Nationally, there was a doubling in the average value of an award from 1954 to 1965. By comparison, manufacturing wages went up by 42 percent in the same period.

The increase in stipend spending reversed a long-term deterioration in the value of awards relative to wage or salary income. From 1920 to the early fifties the ratio of stipend to wage income fell; from 1957 to 1965 the ratio rose by enough to restore the initial 1920 relation.[5] The value of fellowships also increased in comparison to doctorate starting salaries. In 1935 stipends average 23 percent of starting salaries; in 1950, 15 percent; in 1960 the percentage reached a peak of 28 percent.

Table 6.4 Contribution of Stipend Income to the Median Total Income of Graduate Students in 1963

Field	*Percentage Receiving Stipends* (1)	*Median Value of Stipends* (2)	*Average Value* (1) × (2) (3)	*Median Total Income* (4)	*Stipend as Percentage of Total Income* (3) ÷ (4) (5)
Physical Sciences					
Astronomy	85	$2700	$2300	$4400	52
Chemistry	81	2500	2000	4200	48
Physics	76	2700	2100	4600	46
Geology	72	2400	1700	4200	41
Oceanography	87	3000	2600	4800	54
Meteorology	81	2500	2000	6400	31
Mathematics	67	2300	1500	4900	31
Agriculture	80	2800	2200	4000	55
Engineering					
Civil Engineering	66	2600	1700	5600	30
Metallurgy	61	2800	1700	7500	23
Chemical Engineering	71	2700	1900	5000	38
Electrical Engineering	56	2000	1100	7200	15
Mechanical Engineering	60	1800	1100	7200	15
All other	71	2500	1800	7300	25
Biological Sciences					
Anatomy	84	3200	2700	4400	61
Biological Science, general	71	2900	2100	4500	47
Biochemistry	92	2800	2600	3800	68
Botany	87	2500	2200	3700	59
Biophysics	91	3400	3100	4600	67
Genetics	91	3000	2700	4100	66
Microbiology	87	2400	2100	3900	54
Pathology	75	4500	3400	7100	48
Physiology	86	3000	2600	4700	55
Zoology	84	2400	2000	3800	53
All other	84	2800	2400	4200	57
Pharmacology	88	3100	2700	4900	55
Social Sciences and Business					
Geography	61	2100	1300	4900	27
Psychology	64	2400	1500	4600	33
Anthropology	66	2500	1700	4200	40
Economics	65	2500	1600	4500	36
Sociology	62	2400	1500	4600	33
Business and Commerce	31	400	—	—	—
Education and Library Science					
Elementary Education	14	200	—	—	—
Secondary Education	18	700	—	—	—
Educational Administration	16	1500	—	—	—
Counseling and Guidance	22	1400	—	—	—
Other Educational Fields	28	1400	—	—	—
Library Science	27	500	—	—	—

Table 6.4 (*Continued*)

Field	*Percentage Receiving Stipends* (1)	*Median Value of Stipends* (2)	*Average Value* (1) × (2) (3)	*Median Total Income* (4)	*Stipend as Percentage of Total Income* (3) ÷ (4) (5)
Humanities					
English	46	2000	—	—	—
History	46	1800	—	—	—
Fine Arts	40	1700	—	—	—
Foreign Languages	59	2300	—	—	—
Philosophy	62	1600	—	—	—
Religion	61	500	—	—	—

SOURCE: National Opinion Research Center, *Graudate Student Finances*, 1963; Office of Education, *The Academic and Financial Status of Graduate Students*, Spring 1965.

Federal Support of Graduate Education

Both the cross-sectional variation of stipend support among fields and the change in support over time are traceable to the policies of the federal government. Through agencies like the National Science Foundation, Public Health Service, Atomic Energy Commission, and so forth, the government supports nearly all students in selected sciences while providing little aid to those in cultural or humanities fields (Table 6.5). For example, 80 percent of biophysics majors receive federal stipends and just 10 percent of English majors. Overall, the total pattern of awards is set by federal policy, with the fraction of students obtaining a stipend and the average value of stipends significantly correlated across fields with the degree of federal support (the rank coefficients for the specialties listed in Table 6.5 are 0.57 and 0.69, respectively).[6]

Aside from the obvious criterion of field of study, a rationale for the pattern of awards is hard to come by. Support is not, for example, related to "excess demand" for specialists, as reflected in items like salaries, increases in salary, and so on. Perhaps the government supports the biological and natural sciences because of the belief that they offer exceptional external benefits to society. Perhaps the fact that the government employs, directly or indirectly, a large fraction of the scientific and engineering community determines the pattern of awards.[7]

Much of the postwar increase in stipend spending also resulted from the expansion of federal fellowship programs during the mid-1950s and early 1960s. In some fields federal awards were responsible for the entire rise in the fraction of students obtaining support. The relatively greater

Table 6.5 Proportion of Graduate Students Supported by Federal Agencies in 1963

						Office of Educ.		*Public Health Serv.*				
Field of Study	*Atomic Energy Commission*	*Department of Defense*	*National Science Foundation*	*Veterans Administration*	*Natl. Aeronautics and Space Admn.*	*Natl. Defense Education Act*	*Other*	*Natl. Inst. of Health Fellowship Program*	*NIH training*	*Other Public Health Service*	*Other Federal Government*	*Subtotal Federal Government*
Life Sciences												
All other biology	1	—	12	—	0	5	0	4	6	3	3	35
Anatomy	0	1	3	1	0	1	1	9	0	2	3	65
General biology	1	0	38	0	0	1	—	5	8	2	1	56
Biochemistry	1	—	7	—	0	2	—	18	25	8	1	63
Botany	1	0	18	0	—	4	0	2	1	2	2	30
Biophysics	9	2	12	0	1	0	0	20	30	7	1	80
Genetics	2	0	15	0	0	4	—	4	17	2	3	47
Microbiology	—	2	18	—	0	1	—	8	21	3	2	55
Pathology	1	2	0	1	0	0	0	20	30	5	8	68
Pharmacology	0	1	2	0	0	1	0	16	49	3	0	71
Physiology	2	2	3	1	1	2	0	17	29	3	2	61
Zoology	1	—	11	—	0	5	0	5	8	3	1	34
Agriculture	2	1	2	0	0	5	0	1	3	2	5	20
Forestry	2	0	7	0	0	2	0	1	1	—	11	25
Behavioral Sciences												
Psychology	—	1	6	3	—	2	2	13	11	6	4	47
Anthropology	—	—	9	—	0	15	1	8	2	1	1	37
Economics	0	2	3	—	—	10	0	0	0	—	6	21
Sociology	—	2	1	0	0	10	1	5	5	3	2	28
Humanities												
English	0	—	0	0	0	9	0	0	0	0	0	9
History	0	1	0	0	0	7	0	—	0	0	1	10
Social Work												
Social work	0	—	—	3	0	—	2	7	13	2	7	35
Physical Sciences												
Gen. phys. sci.	4	0	81	0	0	0	0	0	0	0	0	85
All other earth and phys. sci.	5	16	13	0	1	2	0	2	0	1	4	43
Astronomy	2	10	16	0	7	6	0	0	0	0	4	44
Chemistry	8	3	10	0	—	2	0	4	2	2	2	34
Physics	14	8	17	0	2	2	0	0	1	1	3	49
Geography	0	2	3	0	1	7	0	0	0	—	1	12
Geology and geophysics	1	3	12	—	—	5	0	0	—	0	2	24
Oceanography	6	12	11	0	0	7	0	1	2	3	18	59
Metallurgy	15	8	5	0	7	2	0	0	0	0	2	40
Meteorology	1	35	10	0	3	3	0	0	0	0	19	71
Mathematics	1	3	22	—	—	5	0	0	1	0	2	35
Engineering												
All other engineering	6	10	6	—	2	2	0	1	1	1	4	35
Civil engineering	—	6	7	—	0	3	0	1	3	5	3	28
Chemical engineering	4	1	12	0	3	7	1	1	—	1	3	33
Electrical engineering	—	7	6	—	4	1	0	0	—	0	3	22
Mechanical engineering	3	8	6	—	6	2	0	0	0	0	2	27

SOURCE: National Opinion Research Center, *Graduate Student Finances* (1963).

support of social science majors in 1963 than in 1954, for example, resulted wholly from an increase in the number of federal awards per enrollee. In other fields, notably biology, the increased fraction with federal support exceeded the overall rise in the fraction of students with fellowships, which suggests a substitution of federal for other stipends. As a consequence, federal support of the sciences may have freed funds for nonscience students and thus indirectly aided the humanities programs.

6.2 Stipends and Labor Supply

Stipend support of graduate students can be expected to affect the labor market in three ways:

1) By making study in supported fields highly remunerative, stipends will influence career decisions.

2) Stipends will induce persons to undertake full-time study and so may reduce the chronological time spent acquiring a Ph.D.*

3) By increasing the supply of specialists, stipends will lower the prevailing salary.

Stipends and Career Choice

Table 6.6 presents regression evidence of the effect of stipends on the choice of a doctorate specialty.[8] For 52 detailed Ph.D. fields the log change of degrees for 1959–1964 is regressed on 1959 stipend support, as reflected in the value and number of fellowships per Ph.D.† The computations reveal a substantial and well-defined stipend effect, explaining 25–32 percent of the differential growth of fields. Statistically, the best results occur with the total value of awards or with value decomposed into number and average income as the explanatory variables (equations 1 and 2). Since total value measures the entire incentive of stipends while other variables — the number of awards or degree of government support — are only partial indicators, the regressions favor the argument that stipends influence behavior primarily by altering incentives.

The estimated parameters present a plausible picture of supply responsiveness. A 1 percent change in stipend spending has a 0.23 percent

* The term "may" is used in the text because of the possibility that high-paying stipends induce persons to choose a student's life as opposed to working. With current limitations on the dollar value and tenure of stipends, however, it is more likely that they speed up the educational process, all else being the same.

† Stipend *per* Ph.D. was chosen as the independent variable to measure incentive to the individual. Since the number of degrees in 1959 is also in each equation, however, the coefficient is identical to that obtained without deflating by Ph.D.'s.[9]

Table 6.6 Effect of Stipend Support in 1959 on Growth of Ph.D. Degrees, 1959–1964

(The dependent variable is the log change in the number of degrees, 1959–1964)

Equation Number	*Constant*		*Regression Coefficients and t-Statistic*[a]	R^2
1	−1.39 (1.51)	+	0.18 ln FELDOL − 0.07 ln GRD_0 (2.84) (2.16)	0.32
2	−1.76 (1.38)	+	.23 ln FVAL + 0.18 ln FNUM − .07 ln GRD_0 (1.74) (2.83) (2.11)	.32
3	0.36 (.89)	+	.12 ln FNUM − 0.09 ln GRD_0 (2.20) (2.63)	.27
4	0.82 (3.22)	+	.03 ln GOVDOL − 0.13 ln GRD_0 (1.83) (4.00)	.25
5	0.94 (4.61)	+	.05 ln GNUM − 0.15 ln GRD_0 (2.04) (4.21)	.27

SOURCE: For degree data: Office of Education, *Earned Degrees Conferred*; for fellowship data: John L. Chase, *Doctorate Study* (Washington, D. C.: U.S. Government Printing Office, 1961).

[a] The variables are defined as:

FELDOL = Total dollars of fellowship support per Ph.D. granted in 1959
FVAL = Average value of fellowship in 1959
FNUM = Number of fellowships granted per Ph.D. in 1959
GRD_0 = Number of Ph.D. graduates in 1959
GOVDOL = Total dollars of federal government fellowships per Ph.D. in 1959
GNUM = Number of federal government awards per Ph.D. in 1959

The levels of significance for the *t*-statistic are 1%, 2.58; 5%, 1.96.

effect on the number of graduates (equation 1), while a 1 percent change in the number of awards has a smaller (0.12 percent) impact (equation 3). Extrapolation of these figures to aggregate behavior over time provides a rough notion of the stipend cost of an additional Ph.D.* With $35 million of fellowship expenditure and 9000 Ph.D.'s in 1959, a 1 percent increase in spending would produce 21 additional Ph.D.'s at a cost of $17,000 per degree. As many students study without awards and others drop out of programs, this is a reasonable estimate of the marginal effect of stipend funds.

Stipends and Years of Study

The proposition that stipends reduce the chronological time spent ac-

* The fellowship figures relate to awards for *all* students and thus are a rough indicator of support for an entire academic career. Hence, the elasticities relate to the response to anticipated support for an entire 4–5 year program.

quiring a graduate degree is supported by survey and regression calculations. Surveys show that students with awards graduate earlier than those without. In 1963, for example, a National Opinion Research Center Survey reported that 80 percent of students lacking support experienced "delays" in educational advancement compared to 50 percent of those with stipends. Fellowship recipients were delayed the least, followed by research and teaching assistants.[10] Another survey reports that federally supported students, usually recipients of the most lucrative awards, earn their degree especially quickly.[11]

Statistical analysis of the mean time lapse from B.A. to Ph.D. in 22 doctorate fields also points to a significant stipend effect. Interfield differences in the time spent in school are closely related to two variables: the availability of fellowships, as measured by the fraction of students with awards (FEL), and the economic advantage of early completion of studies, as reflected in the ratio of the earnings of experienced specialists to starting salaries (EXP). When work experience is valuable in a profession, the age–earnings curve is likely to be steep. Students will be motivated to complete their studies quickly to acquire experience. As indicated below, both variables significantly influence the mean B.A.-to-Ph.D. time lapse (TIME):

$$\text{TIME} = 17.0 - \underset{(6.81)}{7.50\,\text{FEL}} - \underset{(2.24)}{6.69\,\text{EXP}} \qquad R^2 = 0.771$$

(The *t*-statistics reported in parentheses are significant at 1% and 5% respectively.)

The shorter time in school made possible by stipends adds to the economic incentive of graduate study in two ways. First, it hastens the period of full-time earnings and extends the working life, thereby significantly increasing discounted lifetime earnings. The biology major who earns a degree in 4–5 years, for example, obtains 15 percent more income, discounted at 6 percent, than the English major taking four years longer. Second, it diminishes the length of payoff periods and thus lowers the risk and uncertainty of future earnings.

Longterm Effects

In the long run, stipend-induced increases in the supply of labor reduce salaries and thereby lower the incentive to enter supported fields. As a result the ultimate effect of awards on the equilibrium stock of labor is limited. The following stipend model is designed to analyze the differential impact of awards in the short and long run:

(1) Supply $Q_t^s = aW_t^* + bS_t - cA_t^*;$
(2) Wage expectations $W_t^* = W_{t-1};\ A_t^* - A_{t-1};$
(3) Demand $W_t = (1/\alpha)N_t + \beta y_t;$
(4) Stock $N_t = (1 - \delta)N_{t-1} + Q_t;$

where the variables are defined as follows:

Q_t^s = number of new entrants;
W_t^*, A_t^* = expected lifetime income in the occupation and in alternative fields, respectively;
W_t, A_t = actual lifetime income in the occupation and in alternative fields, respectively;
S_t = stipend income;
Y_t = output in industries employing specialists;
N_t = stock of specialists;
δ = rate of depreciation of stock.

Stipend income is distinguished in this model by (1) being set by nonmarket forces, independent by demand; (2) referring to actual rather than expected future income; and (3) altering supply differently from other incomes.*

The immediate effect of stipends on supply is measured by the b coefficient of equation (1). The long-term effect of awards is found by solving the system for the equilibrium value of supply and differentiating with respect to stipends. This yields

$$\partial \bar{N}/\partial S = b[(\delta + a)/\alpha] \quad \text{where } \bar{N} = \text{equilibrium stock},$$

which differs from the immediate effect of awards, b, by a factor that depends on the supply and demand parameters and the depreciation of stock. The more responsive the supply and the more flexible the wages, the smaller is the long-term impact of stipends compared to the short-term impact. Part of stipend spending is dissipated in lower salaries for experienced workers and a "twisted" age–earnings curve.

The path to equilibrium may also be altered by stipends. Depending on the time at which they are made, awards can lengthen or shorten the

* It is difficult to determine a priori the direction of the difference in supply responsiveness. If variables are measured in nondiscounted dollars, the elasticity of stipends will be high because stipend dollars are received earlier in life. If incomes are discounted, however, there are several possibilities. On the one hand, imperfect loan markets and the lower risk associated with stipends received immediately suggest a large effect. On the other, salary dollars may be more effective — at least in the short run — because of possible extrapolation to future earnings.

period of incomplete adjustment and initiate or ameliorate cobweb fluctuations.

The implications of the model with regard to the long-term effect of stipends appear to be supported by postwar experiences. First, fields with substantial stipend support generally report lower discounted lifetime incomes than comparable fields receiving less support. The fraction of students obtaining fellowships is negatively correlated with disequilibrium income among specialties, with a Spearman coefficient for 21 Ph.D. specialties of −0.79, significant at 1 percent.* Second, despite a continual stipend advantage, biology and other natural sciences have not expanded greatly relative to all other fields. In physics, enrollment jumped from 1954 to 1959, probably in response to the post-*Sputnik* increase in NSF awards, but declined relative to total enrollment thereafter. In biology the rate of increase of degrees has been falling despite continuous high levels of support. Thus stipends appear to reduce income later in life and to lose effectiveness in the long run, as predicted by the model.

6.3 Financing Higher Education

Graduate and undergraduate training can be financed in several ways. This section examines the methods of financing prevalent in the United States and the way in which the cost of higher education is shared between students or their families and the general public. The feasibility of alternative ways of paying for college training is also explored.

Educational Finance in the 1960s

Throughout the period following the Second World War higher education has been financed by the contributions of[12]

— state and local governments, who account for approximately 40 percent of college and university income, generally by support of low-tuition public institutions;

— the federal government, which paid roughly 7 percent of educational expenditures in the late sixties, exclusive of research and development purchases;

— gifts and endowments, which accounted for 25 percent of the income

* Disequilibrium income is measured by deviations from expected income according to the calculations of Chapter 5. The comparison excludes education because many Ed.D. graduates are older men. With education included, the correlation is −0.50, still good at 1 percent.

of private institutions and 11 percent of the budget for the entire higher educational system; and

— students and their families, who contributed about one third of the direct cost of college.

The principal change in the mode of financing in the 1960s was the advent of federal support of higher education with the passage of the Higher Education Acts of 1963 and 1966 and various supplementary bills. By 1968 the federal government was budgeting $3 billion in direct expenditures and $3¼ billion in loans to colleges and students.[13] Approximately 40 percent of all full-time graduate students and nearly 20 percent of all undergraduates received direct federal assistance.

Despite federal expenditures and additional spending by the states, however, the increased costs of college forced an approximate doubling of tuition charges over the decade 1960–1970. The fraction of family income spent on higher education increased, and that portion of university income contributed by students or their families rose slightly.

Apportioning the Costs of College

Direct expenditures for higher education do not tell the whole story about the allocation of the costs of college. On the one hand, individuals induced into college by public subsidies pay back at least part of the subsidy through increased taxes on higher future incomes. On the other, much of the cost of education consists of the income foregone by students when they choose school instead of work.

To estimate the additional taxes paid by persons induced into college by below-cost tuition, I performed the calculations summarized in Appendix 6A. Briefly, I used estimates of the elasticity of enrollment to tuition to find the number of students in college as a result of subsidies; estimated their incremental taxes by multiplying the income attributable to college by tax rates; and calculated the present value of future taxes discounted at 6 percent. Comparisons of the present value of these taxes with the cost of public subsidies show that most if not all of the subsidization is repaid to the federal or state governments. Approximately 75 percent of the public subsidization of students in 1966, for example, is likely to be repaid in future tax receipts. With conservative assumptions, the discounted present value of taxes cumulates to $2070 per student compared to an average federal and state subsidy of $2840 per student for a four-year program. Since the federal income tax accounts for most of the tax burden, the subsidization of public education transfers funds from the state to the federal coffers.

More refined calculations than those of Appendix 6A will yield different estimates of the rate of repayment but are unlikely to change the main result. Public subsidization yields a large present value of increased tax receipts relative to the subsidy. Students do not receive a simple income transfer from the non-student public. In a sense, the tax system is a way of sharing the return to public investments in higher education by permitting added governmental services or lower taxes in the future.

The bulk of the cost of higher education is in the form of the income which students forego when they attend school. Introducing foregone income into the cost calculations raises significantly the fraction of cost financed by students or their families. In 1966 the income given up by the male college freshman was on the order of $4000 per year compared to a direct cost of $1500 for university facilities and perhaps $500 for student expenses. Thus, even ignoring potential increases in tax receipts, students and their families pay approximately 80 percent of the total cost of education.* Adjusted for foregone income and the present value of incremental taxes, the cost of higher education falls almost entirely on students and their families. The conclusion is inescapable that, despite a façade of subsidization, investment in college is financed by individuals.

Alternative Ways to Finance Higher Education

Two possible modifications of the current method of financing higher education are considered here: the use of educational loans in place of direct subsidization of students and the awarding of stipends by economic criteria.

The awarding of contingent educational loans by an Educational Opportunity Bank to finance college studies has been proposed by several groups, including the 1967 President's Panel on Educational Innovation.[14] Contingent loans are repaid as a fraction of income rather than as a lump sum and thus protect students with low future earnings from "excessive"

* The 80% estimate is derived as follows:
Total cost of college = $6000, of which $4000 is income foregone and $2000 is direct spending.
The contribution of students and their families is $4000 foregone plus $500 student expenses plus one third of university charges, or $500.
Thus, students and their families contribute $5000 of the $6000 total cost, or approximately 80%.

financial burden. The risk of investment in education is mutualized among all participants in the program. To minimize the possibility that persons with high income expectations will decide against borrowing ("adverse selection"), individuals are allowed to opt out of the program by paying an interest above that at which the bank borrows money. Thus, those opting out pay a premium that offsets the limited repayment of persons doing poorly.

In the context of the current study, the loan bank proposal raises two questions: Will students respond to bank financing in a reasonable way? If most of the cost of higher education is currently borne by the individual, what is the advantage of a loan bank?

The evidence presented here of economically rational and elastic supply behavior indicates that loan bank financing is a feasible way to pay for college and university training. In fields where stipends are currently limited, students already use loans intensively; there is no reason to believe that students in other fields will behave differently if their awards are replaced with loans. It would be difficult, however, to introduce loan financing as a supplement to current subsidies as suggested by the 1967 President's Panel. Current opportunities to obtain stipend or related support would induce most graduate students and persons of high ability or with high family incomes to reject bank financing, thereby creating problems of adverse selection.

The potential advantage of a loan bank method of financing is threefold. First, the efficiency of student decision-making is likely to be improved by the greater incentive placed on rational evaluations of the costs and benefits of college training. Second, the loan bank will eliminate the economic rent accruing to students who would attend college at higher tuition charges. The transfer of income from the community to these persons does not yield a return in the form of taxes and is probably undesirable. Third, by providing funds only for students taking loans the bank plan might alter the composition of the student body. With the elimination of economic rent, more funds may be available for persons on the margin between college and work. For these reasons the loan bank idea deserves serious attention as a feasible alternative to current methods of subsidization.

A second potentially desirable change in methods of aiding students is suggested by the analysis of this chapter. This is to grant stipends on the basis of the state of the labor market in different fields. By relating awards to economic conditions, *a labor market stipend program* would increase the responsiveness and the efficiency of the market. In addition, it would make the award system more flexible and minimize the "waste" of resources spent in economic rent. A program of this kind might operate as follows:

1) Each year a committee of manpower specialists, representing employers, professional associations, government, and academic institutions, would determine "manpower shortage or surplus" occupations on the basis of current or prospective imbalance of supply and demand, as evidenced in salaries, changes in salaries, changes in job content, vacancies, projected expenditures, and so on.

2) Shortage occupations would then receive a certain number of "manpower shortage fellowships" designed to induce additional students into the fields. Simultaneously, educational institutions would, if necessary, be granted funds to establish, enlarge, or improve programs in these areas.

3) Subsidies given to surplus occupations, on the other hand, would be reduced and, if necessary, special retraining programs established to help experienced workers shift to new fields.

4) At the same time, the Manpower Committee would offer firms assistance in making short-run adjustments to shortages or surpluses. Studies of manpower utilization might help spread "best practice" use of labor throughout the economy and thus accelerate economic growth.

Labor market stipends could be easily integrated into current support programs.

7 The Incomplete Adjustment Pattern: Doctorate Manpower

The question which arises naturally from the preceding two chapters is whether differences in lifetime income, changes in income, and scholarship opportunities explain the increase of doctorate manpower following World War II. Do these factors govern occupational choice as posited in the basic labor market model?

The present chapter uses the *incomplete adjustment* variant of the model to investigate this issue. Incomplete adjustment occurs when a market approaches but fails to attain equilibrium in the period under study. There are several reasons for expecting this adjustment path in the doctorate market in the postwar period. First, the demand for Ph.D.'s increased greatly in response to the postwar expansion of higher education and increased spending on research and development (R & D). Substantial shifts in demand are a likely precondition for lengthy disequilibria. Second, the training period for doctorate students is long, which virtually guarantees a slow, gradual adjustment of the kind described by incomplete adjustment. Third, the pattern of growth of doctorate degrees has been rapid and uneven, suggestive of a market with marked supply–demand imbalances. Finally, throughout the period public officials worried over a shortage of Ph.D.'s. According to President Kennedy, for example, "One of our most serious manpower shortages (in 1962) is the lack of Ph.D.'s in engineering, science, and mathematics."[1]

7.1 Supply of Graduates under Incomplete Adjustment

To explain the changing supply of Ph.D.'s to various specialties, a specification of the basic labor market model of Chapter 2 is employed. In the basic model the supply of labor is determined by expected wages. Changes in wage expectations depend on the deviation of previous expectations from actual wages and the rate of change of wages: *

$$(1) \qquad T_t = \alpha_0 W_t^*$$

$$(2) \qquad \Delta W_t^* = B_0(W_t - W_{t-1}^*) + B_1(W_t - W_{t-1}),$$

where (as in Chapter 2),

T_t = number of persons entering a training program;
W_t^* = expected wage,
W_t = actual wage.

Taking first differences of (1) and substituting (2) for ΔW_t^* yields

$$(3) \qquad \Delta T_t = \alpha_0[B_0(W_t - W_{t-1}^*) + B_1(W_t - W_{t-1})].$$

The expected wage term (W_{t-1}^*) in this equation is unobservable. According to the arguments in Chapter 2, however, W_{t-1}^* is a linear function of actual income W_t and equilibrium income $\overline{W}$. Substitution for W_{t-1} yields a testable relation between the number of entrants, disequilibrium income ($W_t - \overline{W}$), and changes in income:[2]

$$(4) \qquad \Delta T_t = \alpha_0 B_0[1 + (a_0/r\alpha_0)](W_t - \overline{W}) + \alpha_0 B_1(W_t - W_{t-1}).$$

With the addition of income in competitive occupations and a measure of stipend support, equation (4) is the supply equation estimated in this section.

The Model Applied to Ph.D. Manpower

The availability and quality of data determine the precise way in which the incomplete adjustment model can be applied to the doctorate market. In the absence of good data on the number of persons entering Ph.D. programs (T_t), the number of graduates five years later is used as the dependent variable. On the average, five years of continuous schooling are required to attain doctorate competence. The deviation between actual

* For ease in presentation this discussion ignores the effect of incomes in alternative specialties on the supply of Ph.D.s. Alternative income terms are added to the equation at the end.

and equilibrium income ($W_t - \overline{W}$) is measured by the difference between the discounted lifetime income in a field and the income of workers in comparable fields (for example, with similar places of employment or work activity). When lifetime incomes are unavailable, median salaries are employed. Changes in income are measured by changes in starting salaries, lifetime incomes, or median salaries, as the case may be.[3] Stipend support is measured by the mean dollar value of fellowships awarded per Ph.D. in the period of the enrollment decision. The particular variables and form of the *incomplete adjustment supply equation* used in the calculations are described below:

$$(5)\quad \ln \mathrm{DOC}_t{}^i - \ln \mathrm{DOC}_{t-5}{}^i = a_0[\mathrm{DLI} - \overline{\mathrm{DLI}}]_{t-5}{}^i - a_1[\mathrm{ALT} - \overline{\mathrm{ALT}}]_{t-5}{}^i + a_2 \ln [\mathrm{STP}]_{t-5}{}^i + a_3[\Delta \ln \mathrm{DLI}]_{t-5}{}^i - a_4[\Delta \ln \mathrm{ALT}]_{t-5}{}^i \quad (\text{all } a_i > 0)$$

where $\mathrm{DOC}_t{}^i$ = number of Ph. D's granted in the *i*th specialty in year *t*;
DLI = discounted lifetime income in the specialty;
$\overline{\mathrm{DLI}}$ = estimated equilibrium discounted lifetime income;
ALT = discounted lifetime income in competitive fields;
$\overline{\mathrm{ALT}}$ = estimated equilibrium income in competitive fields;
STP = stipend income.

With the available data, the supply equation is estimated for two short intervals, 1960–1965 and 1958–1963, and one longer span, 1953–1963. Life-cycle earnings data are obtained for the 1960–1965 period from a National Academy of Science study. Annual salaries from the National Scientific Register are used in the other intervals.[4]

The role of independent variables in explaining changes in supply can reasonably be expected to vary between the short and long period comparisons. In the short run, relatively transitory disequilibrium may be sufficiently important that the disequilibrium variables ($\mathrm{DLI} - \overline{\mathrm{DLI}}$) and ($\mathrm{ALT} - \overline{\mathrm{ALT}}$) will dominate the regression. In the longer period, changes in equilibrium should dwarf the disequilibrium and can be expected to be the principal determinant of the growth of degrees.*

Incomplete Adjustment: 1960–1965

The phenomenon to be explained in the period 1960–1965 is the remarkable variation in the growth of doctorate degrees by specialty. At one

* The hypothesis that changes in income dominate long-term supply equations is equivalent to the assumption that the market functions "properly" by eliminating disequilibrium over time. Analytically, since $\Delta\mathrm{DLI} = \Delta\overline{\mathrm{DLI}} + \Delta(\mathrm{DLI} - \overline{\mathrm{DLI}})$, the hypothesis is that $\Delta\mathrm{DLI} \approx \Delta\overline{\mathrm{DLI}}$ over long time periods, i.e., that $\Delta(\mathrm{DLI} - \overline{\mathrm{DLI}})/\Delta\mathrm{DLI}$ goes to zero.

end of the spectrum, the number of Ph.D.'s granted in mathematics increased by 131 percent and those in engineering by 161 percent. At the other, the rate of increase was 33 percent in chemistry and 22 percent in botany.

The regression calculations summarized in Panel A of Table 7.1 show that this pattern of change is well accounted for by the incomplete adjustment model. The independent variables explain much of the interfield variation in growth in an economically sensible, statistically significant way.

The chief explanatory variable is the level of disequilibrium income, represented in equation (1) by lifetime income, discounted at 6 percent, under the assumption that equilibrium incomes ($\overline{\text{DLI}}$) are similar to all specialties, and in equations (2) and (3) by lifetime income corrected for the nonpecuniary value of working in the university sector along the lines set out in Chapter 5. The corrected DLIs are theoretically and, it turns out, statistically better measures of economic incentive; by themselves they account for half of the variance in growth.

Incentive in competitive fields (ALT-$\overline{\text{ALT}}$) was estimated in a complex manner on the basis of *post*-Ph.D. mobility patterns. First, on the assumption that occupational mobility is frequent among fields with similar characteristics and ability requirements, observed mobility was used to identify likely competitors. Genetics and physiology, for example, are "close alternatives" because many experienced Ph.D.'s shift from one to the other (see Table 7.4). Second, a weighted average of disequilibrium income in alternatives was calculated using the relative number of mobile persons as weights.[5] The average is large and positive when an occupation is closely related to fields with especially high income ("shortage" areas) and large and negative in the opposite situation. It is near zero when some of the fields to which a specialty is linked are high-paying while others are low-paying or when mobility is slight.

Defined in this manner, alternative incomes have the hypothesized effect on the growth of supply in a specialty. The coefficient of the term in equations (2) and (3) is significant, opposite in sign, and roughly equal in absolute size to that on income in a field. There appears to be substantial cross-elasticity of supply among Ph.D. fields when alternative opportunities are properly identified.

Stipend support also has a significant effect on the supply of specialists. The responsiveness of supply to stipends is on the order of 0.05 (equations 2 and 3): roughly a 10 percent increase in fellowship spending increases

Table 7.1 Incomplete Adjustment Supply Equations

(The dependent variable is the log-change in the number of doctorate degrees granted)

Equation Number	Regression Coefficients and t-Statistics							R^2
	Constant	$(DLI\text{-}\overline{DLI})$[a]	$(ALT\text{-}\overline{ALT})$	ln STP	Δln DLI	Δln MA	$\ln DOC_0$	
Panel A: Changes in supply in the short-run, 1960–1965, 22 Doctorate specialties								
(1)	−1.40	0.004		0.161				0.532
	(3.18)	(2.33)		(2.83)				
(2)		0.106	−0.092	0.048				.684
		(5.36)	(2.22)	(2.92)				
(3)		0.101	−0.102	0.040	0.480			.701
		(5.09)	(2.45)	(3.46)	(0.98)			
Panel B: Changes in supply in the short-run, 1958–1963, 25 Doctorate specialties								
(4)	0.423	0.145						0.566
	(12.80)	(5.48)						
(5)	−0.152	0.056		0.113	0.949	0.096		.780
	(1.00)	(1.66)		(2.22)	(2.82)	(0.70)		
(6)	—	0.082		0.119	0.641			.769
		(3.64)		(2.70)	(4.51)			
Panel C: Changes in supply in the long-run, 1953–1963, 25 Doctorate specialties								
(7)	−0.397	0.308		0.065	0.684			0.663
	(2.11)	(0.79)		(1.03)	(3.95)			
(8)	−0.277	0.127		0.038	0.521	0.320		.729
	(1.52)	(0.34)		(0.64)	(3.80)	(2.19)		
(9)					0.191	0.445	−0.227	.754
					(13.69)	(4.01)	(2.67)	

[a] $(DLI\text{-}\overline{DLI})$ is measured by lifetime income discounted at 6% in equation (1); by the residuals from a regression of DLI on the percentage of Ph.D.'s working in the education sector in equations (2) and (3); and by the residuals from a regression of annual salary on the percentage of Ph.D.'s working in education minus the percentage working in industry in equations (4)–(9). Because civil engineering is an extreme outlier in the 1958–1963 and 1953–1963 period, the observation for civil engineering was dropped from the regression calculations. This has little effect on the results, with coefficients having similar significance and size. Of necessity, the R^2 is slightly smaller with the inclusion.

the number of Ph.D.'s by ½ percent. This estimate of the stipend effect is smaller than that reported in Chapter 6 in part because of differences in the number of fields examined. The present computation applies to 22 specialties compared with 52 in Chapter 6, and thus misses the effect of stipends in inducing persons to switch among closely related subspecialties (for instance, from one Romance language to another).

Variables measuring changes in income perform least satisfactorily in the regressions. As shown in equation (3) of Table 7.1 changes in starting salaries in the different specialties have a positive but small and relatively insignificant effect on supply. Experiments with other measures of the increase on income (log changes of discounted incomes or of starting salaries over different time intervals) and with changes in income in alternative fields yield similar results. For the 1960–1965 period the level of disequilibrium in the market appears to have determined the growth of degrees. Changes in income were of only modest importance.

From the coefficients on the disequilibrium income terms, it is possible to obtain a crude estimate of the speed of the movement to equilibrium in the doctorate market. Roughly, $10,000 in disequilibrium income (with dollars discounted at 6 percent) produces a 10 percent change in the number of Ph.D.'s entering a specialty. At the mean DLI of $170,000, the elasticity of new entrants to disequilibrium is 1.7.[6] If, following the salary calculations in Chapters 4 and 8, the flexibility of income to graduates is on the order of 0.10, approximately a decade is required to adjust to an initial $10,000 disequilibrium — five years for the training period and five and a half for the gradual adjustment of the doctorate work force.* At this rate the 1960 shortage of Ph.D. engineers would, *all else being the same,* last until 1980; that of mathematicians until 1985; while the surplus of botanists would be eliminated by 1970.[7]

Incomplete Adjustment in the Long and Short Run

Additional tests of the ability of the incomplete adjustment model to explain postwar developments are possible with salary figures from the National Scientific Register. The Register data differ in two ways from those of the National Academy of Science used in the previous calcula-

* I assume that a $10,000 disequilibrium has a 10 percent effect on supply, and that this, in turn, changes lifetime incomes by 1 percent (0.10×10 percent). As a result, an initial disequilibrium of $10,000 is reduced by $1,800 per year once graduates seek work (1% of $170,000 + $10,000). An annual charge of $1,800 cumulates to $10,000 in 5.3 years. Note that these calculations ignore possible overshooting of equilibrium or changes in responsiveness as the market approaches equilibrium.

tions: first, the sample includes many chemical and engineering specialties not distinguished in the NAS data and fewer specialties in the biological area. Second, the incomes are median salaries rather than discounted lifetime incomes. While not optimal, median salaries appear to be a good approximation to the lifetime incomes in the Register sample. They are not correlated with the average age of specialists in the fields under study (the Pearsonian coefficient is 0.016).

Despite the differences in fields and years covered and in the measures of the salary variables, the supply equation estimated for the 1958–1963 period is similar to that for 1960–1965. As Panel B of Table 7.1 shows, most of the variation in the growth of degrees is accounted for by the incomplete adjustment variable, namely disequilibrium income as measured by annual salary corrected for nonpecuniary income, change in income, and availability of scholarships. In the absence of an occupational mobility matrix for this sample, it was not possible to calculate alternative incomes by the weighted mobility procedure and so the assumption was made that alternatives were the same across specialties. Even so, the coefficient on disequilibrium income is of the same magnitude as that estimated previously, and the only noticeable difference in the regressions is the greater weight on salary changes in the 1956–1963 period.

To test the model against a more sophisticated alternative than the usual null hypothesis, the number of master's degrees, lagged two years, was added to the regression (equation 5). The hypothesis that the change in Ph.D.'s can be predicted by the change in master's degrees is decisively rejected. Incomplete adjustment is a superior explanation of developments.

The results of applying the model to a longer time interval are summarized in Panel C of Table 7.1. In this case, extension of the period of comparison alters the significance of the independent variables in the hypothesized manner. Almost all of the long-term growth of degrees is attributed to the change in salaries. Both the disequilibrium and scholarship availability variables are relatively insignificant. In addition, the number of Ph.D.'s granted in the base year and the lagged growth of master's degrees significantly affect growth (equations 8 and 9). The negative effect of base year degrees can be attributed to a reduction in elasticity as an occupation increases its share of the doctorate population and is forced to draw on persons with increasingly less interest or ability for working in the field (see Chapter 2). The positive relation between changes in M.S. and Ph.D. degrees is probably due to similar changes in conditions at the two levels of education. In the long run, adjustments in the number of workers in an occupation may be more important than intra-occupational adjustments in the relative number with master's or doctorate degrees.

Further Evidence on the Long-run Supply Curve

The way in which changes in salaries determine the supply of doctorate specialists over relatively lengthy periods of time is examined further in Tables 7.2A and 7.2B. These tables compare the rank ordering of fields by change in salaries and in degrees for the periods 1953–1963 and 1940–1965. The data in Panel A reveal a significant positive correlation between the variables in the 1953–1963 period. The Spearman coefficient is 0.71. This relation underlies the regression calculations of Table 7.1.

In Table 7.2B the analysis is extended to a 25-year interval, with a similar picture of supply responding to changes in salaries. Here we find a close correlation between the percentage change of degrees, 1940–1941 to 1965–1966, and the change in the doctorate starting salaries five years earlier. One marked exception to the pattern has been omitted from the table, however. This is chemistry, for which the recorded salaries in 1935 were inordinately low, either because of an error of measurement in the survey or because the field suffered especially greatly in the Depression. Inclusion of chemistry in the sample reduces but does not alter the significance of the observed pattern. The Spearman coefficient remains significant at 1 percent.

In sum, the statistical evidence shows that the incomplete adjustment variant of the basic labor market model adequately explains the growth of doctorate degrees, with growth depending primarily on disequilibrium in the short run and changes in equilibrium in the long run.

7.2 Additional Dimensions of Doctorate Supply

Other supply adjustments — mobility of Ph.D.'s among occupations and sectors of employment and the attainment of doctorate competence within fields — can also be studied in the incomplete adjustment framework.

Occupational Mobility

Are doctorate graduates so specialized that their entire working life is spent in a single field? Do they change specialties in response to eco-

Table 7.2A Changes in Median Annual Salaries, 1948–1957, and in Doctorate Degrees, 1953–1963

Field of Study	*Percentage Change in Salary 1948–1957 (current dollars)*	*Percentage Change in Ph.D.'s Granted 1953–1963*	*Rank of Change in Salaries*[a]	*Rank of Change in Degrees*[a]
Pathology	98.9	187.5	1	2
Mechanical Engineering	91.7	122.0	2	4
Electrical Engineering	78.7	180.2	3	3
Inorganic Chemistry	78.6	52.9	4	12
Chemical Engineering	65.8	65.4	5	8
Analytical Chemistry	65.0	67.0	6	7
Physics	61.3	47.4	7	16
Mathematics	61.1	88.1	8	5
Physical Chemistry	60.8	37.4	9	18
Aeronautical Engineering	58.3	72.2	10	6
Organic Chemistry	52.9	32.8	11	20
Civil Engineering	51.7	274.7	12	1
Metallurgical Engineering	49.8	57.8	13	11
Geology	49.6	57.4	14	10
Entomology	46.0	48.7	15	15
Pharmacology	45.0	32.4	16	21
Anatomy	44.1	40.3	17	17
Zoology	43.6	9.7	18	23
Physiology	43.1	2.2	19	24
Microbiology	41.6	50.6	20	14
Astronomy	41.4	60.6	21	9
Biochemistry	40.6	52.2	22	13
Agriculture	39.8	−7.5	23	26
Psychology	39.3	35.2	24	19
Botany	36.2	−6.3	25	25
Geography	35.3	32.2	26	24

[a] The Spearman correlation coefficient is between the rankings in columns (3) and (4) 0.71. The 1% level of significance is 0.47.

nomic incentive? Is occupational mobility a significant adjustment mechanism in the Ph.D. market?

An answer to these questions can be culled from the data contained in Tables 7.3 and 7.4. First, comparisons of the area in which doctorate specialists work with the field of their doctorate major point to considerable interspecialty mobility (Table 7.3). Approximately one in four Ph.D.'s switches the area of specialization after graduation. Only 68 per-

Table 7.2B Changes in Doctorate Starting Salaries, 1935–1960, and in Doctorate Degrees, 1940–41 to 1965–66

Field of Study[a]	*Percentage Change in Salary 1935–1960*[b]	*Percentage Change in Ph.D.'s Granted 1940–41 to 1965–66*	*Rank of Change in Salary*[c]	*Rank of Change in Degrees*[c]
Mathematics	106	555	1	3
Engineering	69	1870	2	1
Physics	66	535	3	4
Microbiology	59	351	4	13
Political Science	54	421	5	9
Genetics	48	380	6	11
Physiology	48	375	7	12
Education	47	512	8	5
Biochemistry	45	264	9	17
Psychology	45	1589	10	2
Geology	43	495	11	6
Medical Science	43	450	12	8
Pharmacology	42	385	13	10
Zoology	39	106	14	21
Economics	38	338	15	14
Agriculture	35	461	16	7
Languages & Literature	32	225	17	19
Botany	32	123	18	20
Sociology	32	266	19	16
Arts & Humanities	31	271	20	15
History	22	257	21	18

SOURCE: Degrees: National Academy of Sciences-National Research Council; Income: Appendix Table 5.5.

[a] Chemistry is omitted from the calculations as an extreme outlier due to extraordinarily low salaries in 1935. The salary reported in 1935 may be an error of measurement or the result of the temporary impact of the Depression on the field. When chemistry is included in calculations, the rank correlation drops to 0.50, which is significant at the 1% level with twenty-three observations.

[b] Salary changes are for constant 1957–58 dollars.

[c] The Spearman rank correlation coefficient is 0.66; the 1% level of significance is 0.51.

cent of the microbiology majors, for example, work in that discipline after graduation; many switch to "medical science," agriculture, and miscellaneous biological fields.

For the most part, mobility is limited to fields with related subject matter.[8] Individuals with biological or medical specialization shift to other biomedical fields; physical scientists may move from chemistry to

Table 7.3 Change in Specialization from Doctorate Major to Field of Work

		FIELD OF									
Field of Doctorate Major	*Total Degree Recipients*	*Medical Science*	*Physiology*	*Zoology*	*Pharmacology*	*Microbiology*	*Botany*	*Genetics*	*Misc. Biology*	*Biochemistry*	*Agriculture*
Medical Science	254	188 (*74.0*)[a]	11	3	7	10	—	—	4	6	1
Physiology	533	96	274 (*51.5*)	18	20	8	2	2	21	29	28
Zoology	525	22	100	245 (*46.5*)	4	17	5	8	72	9	16
Pharmacology	153	40	2	—	79 (*51.6*)	—	—	—	3	2	—
Microbiology	513	35	17	2	1	353 (*68.4*)	6	4	12	23	16
Botany	445	11	61	2	2	26	200 (*44.7*)	26	41	8	37
Genetics	155	3	9	2	—	3	7	73 (*47.1*)	9	3	39
Misc. Biology	153	8	22	14	1	6	8	2	62 (*40.5*)	9	6
Biochemistry	688	41	22	1	22	17	—	5	10	385 (*55.7*)	47
Agriculture	536	5	14	6	1	3	12	14	4	14	389 (*72.2*)
Chemistry	493	6	—	—	1	1	—	—	3	19	2
Engineering	463	—	—	—	—	—	—	—	1	—	1
Geology	433	—	1	2	—	1	—	—	2	—	2
Physics	436	—	3	9	—	—	—	—	—	—	—
Mathematics	458	1	—	—	—	—	—	—	7	—	—
Economics	436	—	—	—	—	—	—	—	1	—	3
Sociology	449	2	2	—	—	—	—	1	—	—	1
Political Science	378	1	—	—	—	—	—	—	—	—	—
History and Geography	449	—	—	—	—	—	—	—	—	—	—
Psychology	468	9	2	—	—	—	—	—	1	—	—
Language and Literature	457	1	—	—	—	—	—	—	—	—	1
Arts and Humanities	379	4	—	—	—	—	—	—	—	—	1
Education	396	3	—	—	—	—	—	—	1	—	—
Other Professionals	366	1	—	—	—	—	—	—	—	—	—
Total Working in Field	9483	477	540	304	138	445	240	135	254	507	592

Source: NAS-NRC Survey of Doctorate Recipients.

[a] Number of Ph.D.'s entering an area of work and the percentage remaining in their doctorate major (in parenthesis)

WORK

Chemistry	Engineering	Geology	Physics	Mathematics	Economics	Sociology	Political Science	History & Geography	Psychology	Language & Literature	Arts & Humanities	Education	Other Professionals
12	3	1	1	—	—	—	—	—	—	1	—	5	2
14	2	—	1	—	—	—	—	—	1	1	—	10	6
5	1	2	—	2	—	—	—	—	—	—	—	8	8
20	1	—	—	—	—	—	—	—	1	1	—	—	4
30	2	—	—	—	—	—	—	—	—	1	—	7	4
5	3	3	—	—	—	—	—	—	—	1	—	14	5
—	—	1	1	—	—	—	—	—	—	—	—	3	2
2	—	1	4	3	—	—	—	—	1	—	—	1	2
109	3	1	2	3	—	—	—	—	—	3	—	7	14
33	2	3	1	2	9	—	1	—	—	—	—	11	11
375 *(75.9)*	32	5	12	2	—	—	—	—	1	—	—	7	26
15	405 *(86.8)*	5	8	5	—	—	—	—	1	—	—	8	13
3	10	387 *(89.6)*	5	6	1	—	—	2	—	—	—	7	4
14	44	5	336 *(76.8)*	10	—	—	2	—	—	—	—	5	6
4	20	1	4	406 *(88.2)*	1	—	—	—	—	—	—	14	4
3	1	—	—	8	316 *(72.2)*	1	6	2	3	—	1	15	76
8	1	—	—	—	4	317 *(69.9)*	8	16	13	4	11	24	35
7	0	0	0	0	14	2	287 *(75.7)*	16	—	2	—	22	26
4	—	2	2	—	4	—	15	348 *(77.3)*	1	9	6	34	23
8	2	—	—	4	—	2	1	2	380 *(81.0)*	5	—	42	10
5	1	—	—	1	—	—	2	3	2	377 *(82.3)*	15	31	18
3	—	—	—	3	1	4	3	3	6	28	264 *(69.4)*	27	31
5	—	—	2	9	2	4	1	5	30	8	7	300 *(75.5)*	16
1	—	—	—	1	22	4	8	13	9	3	14	21	266 *(72.1)*
685	533	417	379	465	374	334	334	410	449	442	318	620	611

Table 7.4 Mobility of Ph.D.'s among Fields and Income of Fields of In- and Out-Migration

Specialty	*Ratio of Ph.D. Majors Remaining in the Field to All Degree Recipients in the Field*[a] (*1*)	*Ratio of Ph.D.'s Entering from Other Fields to Degree Recipients*[a] (2)	*Ratio of Specialists Working in a Field to Degree cipients [Col. (1) + Col. (2)]*[a] (*3*)	*Average Lifetime Income in Fields from Which Workers Migrate (in $ Thousands Discounted at 6%)* (*4*)	*Average Lifetime Income in Fields to Which Workers Migrate (in $ Thousands Discounted at 6%)* (*5*)
Medical Science	74.0	113.8	187.8	141	153
Physiology	51.5	49.8	101.3	129	158
Zoology	46.5	11.4	57.9	147	147
Pharmacology	51.6	48.6	90.2	147	169
Microbiology	68.4	18.3	86.7	136	157
Botany	44.7	9.2	53.9	136	143
Genetics	47.1	40.0	87.1	133	123
Biochemistry	55.7	18.0	73.7	143	158
Agriculture	72.2	38.2	110.4	131	138
Chemistry	75.9	63.0	138.9	152	166
Engineering	86.8	28.3	115.1	171	160
Geology	89.6	6.7	96.3	162	162
Physics	76.8	10.1	86.9	167	170
Mathematics	88.2	13.3	101.5	157	173
Economics	72.2	13.6	85.8	141	142
Sociology	69.9	4.5	74.4	140	141
Political Science	75.7	12.6	88.3	137	143
History & Geography	77.3	13.8	91.1	140	143
Psychology	81.0	14.9	95.9	136	145
Language & Literature	82.3	14.4	96.7	133	139
Arts & Humanities	69.4	14.5	83.9	132	137
Education	75.5	81.0	156.5	139	140

SOURCE: Number of Ph.D.'s switching fields: Table 7.3; discounted incomes: Table 5.8.
[a] All ratio figures multiplied by 100.

physics or agriculture, or from physics to engineering, and so on. The pattern of switching gives the matrix of mobility presented in Table 7.3 a nearly decomposable structure. The major blocks of fields — the biomedical sciences, the physical sciences, the social sciences, and the cultural specialties — are linked by the flow of persons from all these areas into administrative work in education and miscellaneous professions. Biological and natural sciences are linked by the mobility of chemists into biology and biochemists into chemistry.

Within the limits set by the subject matter of fields, the direction and level of mobility appear to be determined by economic incentive. Specialties with incomes above those in competitive occupations gain workers; those with relatively low incomes lose. Medical sciences, the highest paying biomedical field, for example, has the largest influx of experienced workers while low-paying botany and zoology record the greatest loss. (Table 7.4, column 3). Mobility increases the number of medical scientists by 80 percent and decreases the number of botanists by 46 percent.

To test the economic rationale of field-switching, columns 4 and 5 of Table 7.4 record for each specialty the average (weighted) lifetime income offered by fields from which in-migrants are drawn (column 4) and to which out-migrants move (column 5). For example, persons switching to medical sciences are drawn from specialties with an average DLI of $141,000, while those leaving medical science shift to fields offering $153,-000 on the average. For the pattern of occupational mobility to make economic sense, specialties ought to attract workers from fields with lower pay than those to which they lose workers. Comparison of the incomes in columns 5 and 6 shows this to be true in nearly every case. For 18 of 22 possible comparisons, the incomes in (5) exceed those in (4); in two cases, the incomes are approximately equal. In a sense, occupational mobility is similar to international trade, with occupations importing from low-paying sources and exporting to higher-paying fields.

By comparing the income in a field with the averages recorded in Table 7.4 we can make a more refined test of the economic motivation of mobility. A priori, income in a field should exceed that in the fields from which it obtains workers and be less than that in fields to which its majors move. For a majority of specialties the income figures describe this pattern. In 14 of 22 cases, incomes exceed those in the fields of in-migration; in 15 cases incomes are below those in areas of out-migration. The arithmetic of the comparison, however, understates the degree of economic motivation, for low-paying fields must by definition be exceptions from the in-migrant pattern and high-paying fields from the out-migrant pattern. If we limit the analysis to occupations in the middle of the income distribution (for instance, by eliminating the four highest and lowest paying fields) the pattern is more striking. In this comparison in 21 of 28 possible cases, the income in a given field exceeds the average in fields from which it draws Ph.D.'s.

Educational Adjustment

Changes in the educational attainment of male workers in the aggregate and within specific occupations are also influenced by economic incentive along the lines of the basic labor market model. Overall, the rate of return to doctorate training, estimated in Chapter 5 to be in the area of 10–14 percent, seems sufficiently high to motivate the postwar increase in the supply of Ph.D.'s, even allowing for the risk of investing in human capital. Similarly, estimates from other studies of the rate of return to baccalaureate training are consistent with increased undergraduate enrollment. The bachelor's degree pays off at a rate of 13–15 percent (unadjusted for ability biases), a good return by most criteria.[9] The low payoff to master's training, on the other hand, while consistent with the slower growth of M.S. than Ph.D. degrees, does not completely jibe with the increased supply of master's degrees relative to bachelor's. A more detailed analysis of the economics of master's education is needed to explain this possible inconsistency.

Within occupations there is additional evidence that changes in the education of specialists is motivated by the payoff to training. Table 7.5 shows, in particular, that the increase in the doctorate share of the labor force in engineering and science fields is significantly related to the financial advantage of the degree. Fields in which the capital value of the Ph.D. (discounted at 6 percent) greatly exceeded the value of the M.S. in 1962 experienced a relatively large shift toward doctorate manpower in succeeding years (columns 1 and 2). Similarly, the incremental value of the doctorate relative to the baccalaureate is positively correlated with changes in the ratio of Ph.D. to B.S. graduates (columns 3 and 4).

The available evidence, while meager, thus supports the hypothesis that the return to education alters the educational composition of specialized occupations. Adjustment in the labor market has an educational as well as an occupational dimension.

Sectoral Mobility

Postwar changes in the distribution of doctorate workers among sectors of employment can also be interpreted sensibly by the incomplete adjustment model. From 1948 to 1964 the fraction of Ph.D.'s in industrial employment increased, while that in educational institutions fell, often by

Table 7.5 Effect of the Capital Value of Degrees on the Educational Composition of Science and Engineering Fields

Field of Specialization	*Difference Between Capital Values of Ph.D. and M.S. (in $ Thousands, Discounted at 6%) 1962* (1)	*Percentage Change in Ph.D.'s 1961–1965 Divided by % Change in M.S. Degrees, 1959–1963* (2)	*Rank of Col. (1)*[a]	*Rank of Col. (2)*[a]	*Difference Between Capital Values of Ph.D. and B.S. (in $ Thousands Discounted at 6%) 1962* (3)	*Percentage Change in Ph.D.'s, 1961–1965 divided by the change in B.S. Degrees, 1959–1963* (4)	*Rank of Col. (3)*[a]	*Rank of Col. (4)*[a]
Mechanical Engineering	49.7	1.59	1	3	46.1	2.29	2	3
Industrial Engineering	39.6	3.06	2	1	47.5	2.97	1	1
Civil Engineering	36.7	2.06	3	2	35.3	2.73	5	2
Physical Science	27.9	1.08	4	7	37.9	1.17	4	8
Biological Science	24.9	1.11	5	5	30.7	1.39	7	6
Mathematics	23.8	0.92	6	8	27.2	.84	8	9
Agriculture	22.6	1.12	7	6	44.3	1.51	3	5
Psychology	19.8	.88	8	9	—	—	—	—
Electrical Engineering	13.6	1.31	9	4	34.4	1.62	6	4
Other Social Science	13.3	.81	10	10	−1.3	1.27	9	7

SOURCE: Income statistics, Table 5.11.

[a] The Spearman correlation coefficients are 0.70, for the Ph.D.–M.S. comparison, and 0.63 for the Ph.D.–B.S. comparison. The 5% level of significance is 0.56 and 0.60.

sizable amounts (Table 7.6A). The shift to industry was accompanied by a decline in the income differential between industry and education. In 1948 doctorate specialists in industry averaged 46 percent more than specialists in education. In 1964 the advantage was cut to 41 percent (unweighted average computed from Table 5.6). The extent of the shift to

Table 7.6A Proportion of Ph.D. Scientists Employed in Education, Industry, and Government in 1948 and 1964

	Share of Employment		
Field and Sector	*1948*	*1964*	*Ratio of Shares, 1964:1948*
All Ph.D.			
Education	54.5	53.1	.974
Industry	32.8	33.0	1.006
Government	10.9	11.8	1.083
Agriculture			
Education	64.6	64.8	1.003
Industry	10.5	11.5	1.095
Government	24.3	21.9	.901
Biology			
Education	69.8	65.5	.938
Industry	10.6	15.6	1.472
Government	17.2	18.4	1.070
Earth Sciences			
Education	58.6	53.8	.918
Industry	20.4	27.0	1.324
Government	20.0	17.7	.885
Mathematics			
Education	85.3	69.0	.809
Industry	6.2	17.6	2.839
Government	8.2	8.4	1.024
Chemistry			
Education	38.3	33.9	.885
Industry	51.3	54.3	1.058
Government	8.3	7.6	.916
Physics			
Education	61.2	52.2	.853
Industry	25.3	33.3	1.316
Government	12.5	9.0	.720
Psychology			
Education	75.9	53.7	.707
Industry	10.7	27.5	2.570
Government	12.3	17.9	1.455

Table 7.6B Rank Correlation of the Relative Change in Salaries and in Sectoral Employment, by Field[a]

Field and Sector	*Rank of Change in Nonindustrial Salaries Relative to Change in Industrial Salaries*[b]	*Ratio of Shares in*[b] *Table 7.6A*
Agriculture		
Education	1	1
Government	4	3
Biology		
Education	6	8
Government	10	7
Earth Sciences		
Education	3	4
Government	2	2
Mathematics		
Education	13	13
Government	11	9
Chemistry		
Education	5	6
Government	9	5
Physics		
Education	8	11
Government	14	14
Psychology		
Education	7	10
Government	12	12

Source: Employment by sector: *National Scientific Register*, 1948 and 1964; Income statistics: Table 5.6.

[a] In this table the change in salaries and employment are compared for all fields and sectors simultaneously, with industry as the base of comparison. Since there are seven fields and three sectors, this yields 14 observations, with two observations for each field.

[b] The Spearman correlation coefficient is 0.84; the 1% level of significance is 0.65

industry and of the decline in the industrial income differential varies markedly among fields.

In the incomplete adjustment framework, these patterns of change in employment and salaries are explicable by a supply response to an initial (in this case, 1948) disequilibrium in the level of sectoral income differentials and to the 1948–1964 change in equilibrium differentials. With respect to the effect of levels of income, the model directs attention to the relation between the 1948 differential between industry and other sectors and the ensuing shift of Ph.D.'s into industry. Presumably, industrial salaries were high in 1948 relative to education and government salaries, inducing doctorate specialists to choose industrial jobs. Assuming that the greater the industrial differential the greater is the incentive to shift to industry, we can test this hypothesis by correlating the 1948 ratios of industrial to other sectoral salaries across fields with the 1948–1964 change in industry's share of Ph.D.'s. Such a test supports the incomplete adjustment explanation. For the fields included in Table 7.6A, the Spearman rank correlation between sectoral salary differentials and mobility is 0.73, significant at 5 percent.

Changes in the equilibrium differential between sectors, as well as the initial level of disequilibrium, are likely to affect the pattern of mobility. The smaller the decline in the ratio of industrial to other salaries, the greater is the likelihood of a shift in equilibrium position favoring industry, and the more rapid will be the growth of industry's share of the doctorate work force. If this argument is correct, the change in sectoral salary differentials will be positively correlated with the change in the proportion of Ph.D.'s in industry. The correlation analysis in Table 7.6B strongly confirms this prediction. The extent to which doctorate specialists shifted their sector of employment is positively correlated with the change in salary differentials at the 1 percent level of significance. Relatively large increases in salaries in education or government reduce the rate of increase of industrial employment. To go a step further, the differential change in relative salaries may be traced to uneven growth in sectoral demands for various Ph.D. specialties. In mathematics, for example, the advent of the computer greatly increased the industrial need and actually raised the industrial salary premium. In other fields the differential effect of enrollment patterns on university demand and of R & D spending on industrial demand may account for the diversity of sectoral shifts.

7.3 Capacity of Graduate Schools

For the preceding explanation of the changed supply of Ph.D.'s to be valid, graduate schools must have the capacity to train students in the numbers and fields desired. Did universities have the requisite capacity in the 1960s?

Established Graduate Schools

Direct evidence of the ability of graduate schools to train additional doctorate students in the 1960s is presented in a 1959 Office of Education survey of the deans of over a hundred institutions. The deans were asked to evaluate the "serious barriers to expansion of present enrollment" and to estimate "the number of additional doctorate candidates whom you could accept . . . with the faculty and academic facilities . . . available at the beginning of the academic year 1960–1961, *without lowering* the quality of training.[10]

Their responses indicate that the supply of Ph.D.'s was not seriously constrained by limited academic facilities. First, there was general consensus that the chief barrier to expansion was inadequate fellowship support and student housing rather than lack of qualified faculty, laboratories, and so on.[11] Second, the deans reported substantial capacity for enrolling additional doctorate students. As Table 7.7 shows, available places in

Table 7.7 Capacity of Graduate Schools to Increase Doctorate Enrollment in 1959–60[a]

Field	*Estimated Places for Enrolling Additional Ph.D. Students in 1959–60*[a]	*No. of Ph.D.'s Granted in 1959*	*No. of Enrolled Graduate Students in 1959*	*Ratio of Additional Places to No. of Ph.D. Degrees Cols. (1)/(2)*	*Ratio of Additional Places to No. of Enrolled Graduate Students Cols. (1)/(3)*
	(1)	(2)	(3)	(4)	(5)
All	20,785	9,360	314,349	2.22	.066
Chemistry	1,443	1,009	10,676	1.43	.135
Physics	924	482	8,840	1.92	.105
History	772	324	8,895	2.38	.087
Mathematics	718	255	9,746	2.82	.074
Sociology	536	157	1,489	3.41	.360
Zoology	364	144	2,209	1.65	.065
French	307	58	1,464	5.29	.210

SOURCE: John L. Chase, *Doctoral Study* (Washington, D. C.: U. S. Government Printing Office, 1961)

[a] With no change in quality of education.

1960–1961 would have allowed a 6.6 percent increase in total graduate enrollment with no deterioration in the quality of education. Assuming that all additional places are, in fact, filled by prospective Ph.D.'s, the number of doctorate candidates could have been increased by about one third.[12] Third, and perhaps most significantly, the post-1960 growth of enrollment was completely unrelated to the availability of places in 1960. Enrollment in fields near capacity, such as mathematics, for example, increased as rapidly — or more rapidly — as in fields with substantial excess capacity. The rank correlation of capacity in 1960–1961 and the rate of increase of enrollment, 1960–1964, was insignificantly negative ($r = -0.22$), not significantly positive as required for facilities to be a serious constraint on supply.

New Ph.D. Programs

The ability of the university system to service the enormous postwar demand for doctorate training was enhanced by relatively loose entry conditions in the market for education, which permitted a substantial increase in the number of institutions and departments awarding Ph.D.'s. In 1950, 118 universities awarded doctorates; in 1966, 212. One tenth of all Ph.D.'s in 1966 and one fifth of the increase in degrees from 1950 to 1966 are accounted for by the new schools. The number of universities with doctorate programs in the fastest-growing specialty, engineering, increased especially rapidly.

While the advent of new institutions and departments probably has had some deleterious effects on the education market — for instance, a reduction in the average quality of education and the creation of excess capacity and high-cost imitative programs[13] — these effects do not appear to balance out the advantage of a high elasticity of places. For one thing, some of the new doctorate institutions, including the smaller ones offer more than scaled-down, low-quality imitations of major university programs. Some specialize in particular areas. Miami of Florida, for example, is a major school in ecology while La Jolla in California is the 21st ranking producer of earth science degrees. Others, such as Dartmouth, have been innovators in particular areas of study. The Dartmouth mathematics Ph.D. is designed more for prospective teachers than for research scholars. Competitive pressures can be expected to force the small doctorate schools to offer something different in their curricula.

Over the long run, increasing the capacity of higher education by adding new schools or expanding smaller institutions appears to enjoy a competitive advantage over the growth and concentration of degrees in a limited number of major institutions. The fraction of Ph.D.'s awarded by the top five doctorate producers (Illinois, Wisconsin, Berkeley, Harvard, Columbia) fell from 40 percent in the 1920s to 17 percent in the sixties.

7.4 Summary of the Findings: Doctorate Manpower

Chapters 5, 6, and 7 have dealt with several aspects of the labor market for doctorate workers. The principal findings of this investigation are

1) Doctorate manpower has four distinctive features: an especially large investment in human capital; considerable social subsidization of training; concentration of employment opportunities in research; and marked differences in nonpecuniary income by sector of employment.

2) The market has undergone a great boom since 1957, or thereabouts, with salaries increasing more rapidly than elsewhere in the economy. Salaries change primarily by field of study rather than by sector of work.

3) The rate of return to the Ph.D. is in the area of 10 to 14 percent, depending on the precise method of calculation. Differences in nonpecuniary income by place of work cause substantial variations in the return among fields. Risk is unlikely to deter persons from studying for the doctorate.

4) Stipends account for a sizable fraction (5–6 percent) of doctorate lifetime income, discounted at 6 percent. The availability of stipends varies among fields and over time, largely because of federal fellowship policies. Despite stipends and below-cost tuition, however, students pay for most of their education through foregone income. The taxes paid on the increased earnings of persons who choose college because of subsidies, moreover, repays most of the public subsidization.

5) Stipends influence the supply of students to specialties and the time spent earning a degree. In the long run, part of the incentive of stipends is dissipated in relatively lower salaries. It is feasible to replace the current method of financing education with loan programs.

6) The increased number of doctorate graduates in the postwar period is well explained by the incomplete adjustment variant of the basic labor market model. The degree of disequilibrium, the change in salaries, and the availability of stipends determine supply, with disequilibrium adjustment dominating short-run changes and changes in equilibrium, long-run developments.

7) Incomplete adjustment also explains the sectoral and occupational mobility of experienced Ph.D.'s and the influx of Ph.D.'s relative to less educated workers to different specialties. In each of these cases, the flow of manpower is governed by levels of disequilibrium and changes in income.

8) The availability of training facilities has not seriously hampered the

expansion of graduate education. Capacity was available to increase enrollment in the early 1960s and appears to have adjusted to the demand for training. The entry of new institutions and programs facilitates the expansion of places.

All told, the picture of the doctorate market which emerges from these findings is consistent with the basic models developed in Chapter 2, and more generally, with flexible economic behavior. The policy implications of this conclusion and of the detailed findings are developed in Chapter 12.

8 Cobweb and Incomplete Adjustment in Other College Markets

The cobweb and incomplete adjustment models provide reasonably good explanations of developments in B.S. engineering and doctorate specialties since World War II. Can they also explain the pattern of change in other high-level occupations? As the models were developed with engineering and Ph.D. manpower in mind, the answer to this question is important in determining their general validity and usefulness.

In this chapter the models are applied to the markets for four other college specialties: accounting and MBA management, which are expected to operate under cobweb adjustment; and chemistry and mathematics, expected to operate under incomplete adjustment, with a *relative* surplus of chemists and shortage of mathematicians. The rationale for these expectations are developed below.

8.1 Cobweb Adjustment in Accounting

The labor market for accounting and auditing, the third largest professional specialty in the United States, has several features indicative of cobweb adjustment. First, as in engineering, there is a very tight relation between education and work; the accountant major is chosen primarily as "the best possible training for work," and over half of recent graduates regard it as prerequisite for their current job.[1] Vocational orientation of this kind is likely to produce the supply responsiveness associated with cobweb adjustment. Second, the specialized knowledge required in the field permits only limited substitution with other professions and thus makes the number of graduates especially important in salary determination, as posited in the cobweb model. Third, the number of undergraduates choosing accounting fluctuated cyclically in postwar years relative to all male students, to nonengineering students, and to other business and commerce majors (Figure 8.1). The fluctuations are similar, though less pronounced, than those in engineering.

The educational composition of the accountant work force is also similar to that of engineering. Nonacademic training is important in the profession, and post-bachelor's education infrequent. In 1960, 56 percent of all accountants and 40 percent of those less than 35 years old did not hold a college degree, having obtained their training in correspondence schools, technical institutes, and the like.[2] Even at the level of highest competence, nonacademic work is critical, the certified public accountant award signifying the peak of technical proficiency. The number of accountants obtaining the CPA (like the number of engineers earning graduate degrees) is increasing rapidly. In 1940 there were 5,500 CPA's, in 1950, 15,000, and in 1965, 50,000, or about 10 percent of the profession.

To extend the range of applicability of the cobweb model, market conditions in accounting should differ from those in engineering. Substantial differences are found on the demand side of the market. Accountants work in a different set of industries than engineers, with nearly 50 percent employed in professional services, finance, and public administration. A large number of accountants are self-employed as proprietors or partners of small firms. Demand for accountant services increased relatively moderately in the postwar years. The growth of employment from 1950 to 1960 is wholly attributable to the expansion of the major industries of employment.* The accountant market thus appears to be less dynamic than the engineering market and closer to its long-term equilibrium.

Cobweb Model of Accounting

The cobweb model estimated for the accounting profession is specified in the following logarithmic difference equations:

(1) Supply:

$$\Delta\ln \text{ACCT}_t = a_0\,\Delta\ln \text{GRAD}_t + a_1\,\Delta\ln \text{ASAL}_{t-3}{}^{w} - a_2\,\Delta\ln \text{YSAL}_{t-3}{}^{w},$$

(2) Demand: $\Delta\ln \text{ASAL}_t = -b_0\,\Delta\ln \text{ACCT}_t + b_1\,\Delta\ln \text{PSRV}_t,$

* To be precise, had accountant employment grown at the average rate of the industries of employment of 1950, the number of accountants would have grown by 23.3 percent. The actual growth rate was 22.5 percent.

where

$ACCT_t$ = number of account graduates in year t;
$GRAD_t$ = total bachelor's degree male graduates;
$ASAL_{t-3}^w$ = weighted average of starting salaries in accounting during the freshman, sophomore, and junior years of study
SAL_{t-3}^w = similar weighted average of the earnings of young males aged 25–34;
$ASAL_t$ = starting salaries in accounting;
$PSRV_t$ = output in professional services;
t = year under study, with $_{t-3}$ referring to the sophomore year of the graduating class of year t.

This specification differs from the cobweb model of Chapter 4 in two ways. First, because accountants choose a major at the end of the sophomore year, supply is a simple one-stage process, relating graduates to weighted salaries in accounting and to the weighted earnings of young men three years earlier. The weights count salaries during the sophomore year twice as heavily as those in the junior or freshman year on the assumption that developments in the second year are especially significant in career choice. Second, output in the professional service sector, not in durable manufacturing or R & D, determines the level of demand. In the empirical analysis, alternative weighting schemes and different lag structures are applied to both the supply and demand equations.

Regression Results

Least-square estimates of the accountant model are summarized in Table 8.1A and 8.1B. The supply equations in Table 8.1A show that changes in accountant and alternative salaries explain 70 percent of the variation in graduates (equation 1), but that their role is dwarfed by changes in the number of graduates (equation 2). To focus on "nondemographic" factors, the share of graduates is chosen as the dependent variable in equations (3) and (4). Here it is evident that the cyclic variability revealed in Figure 8.1 can be explained by changes in economic incentive. Both the salary of accountants and of all young males enter the regressions with coefficients four to five times the size of the standard error.[3] Experiments with other lag patterns, including those with no a priori averaging, yield similar results, with unweighted regressions suggesting a greater role for salaries prevailing during the sophomore year.[4] Regardless of the precise

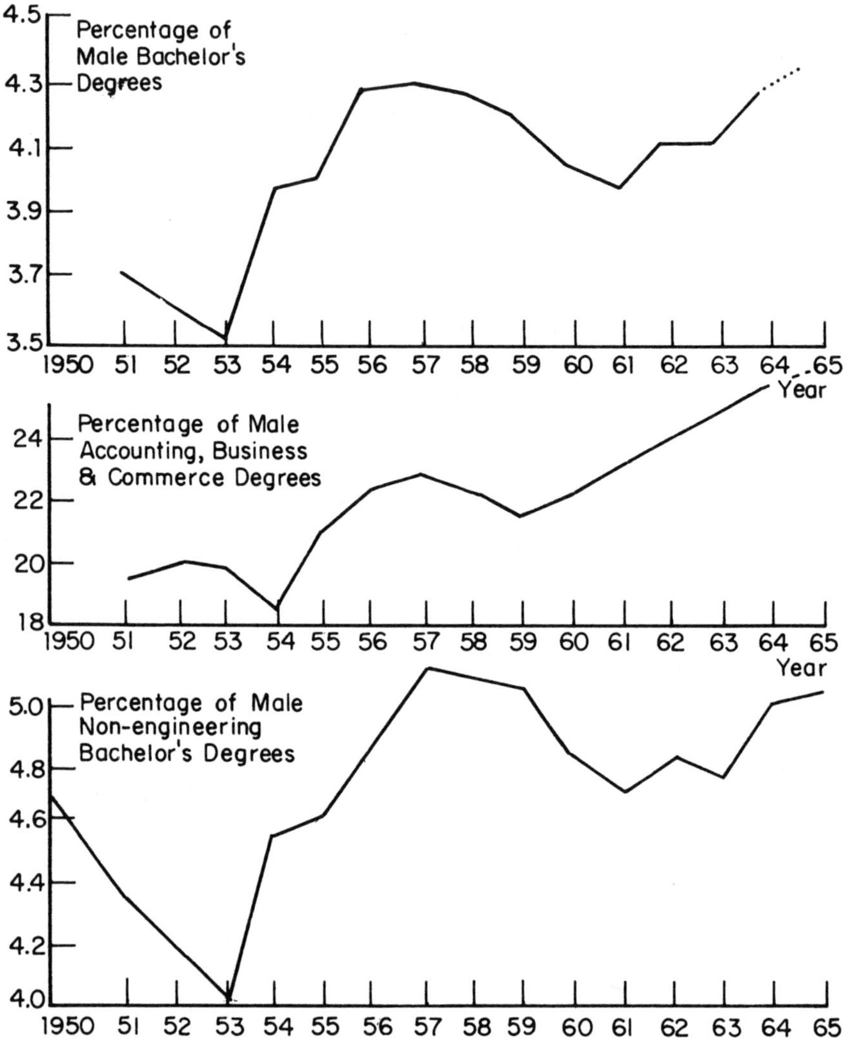

8.1 Bachelor graduates in accounting, relative to all graduates, all business and commerce graduates, and all graduates in non-engineering programs, 1951–1965

specification of the time delay, prospective accountants evidently respond to economic incentive.

Accountant starting salaries are also determined in accord with the cobweb model. In this case the regressions in Table 8.1B show that the

Table 8.1A Supply of Bachelor's Degree Accountants, 1951–1965

		Regression Coefficients and t-Statistics[a]						
Equation Number	*Dependent Variable*[b]	*Constant*	$\Delta\ln$ $ASAL_{t-3}^{wc}$	$\Delta\ln$ $YSAL_{t-3}^{wc}$	$\Delta\ln$ GRD_t	ln (ACCT/ GRAD)$_{t-1}$	R^2	*D.W. Statistic*
(1)	Δln ACCT	0.10	3.63	−5.49			0.71	1.67
		(1.59)	(3.94)	(5.75)				
(2)	Δln ACCT	—	0.78	−0.63	1.00		.86	1.77
			(0.76)	(0.57)	(4.15)			
(3)	Δln (ACCT/ GRAD)	1.45	2.02	−3.17			.70	1.36
		(4.60)	(3.78)	(5.74)				
(4)	Δln (ACCT/ GRAD)	0.73	1.69	−2.39		0.36	.77	1.56
		(2.82)	(3.46)	(3.53)		(2.03)		

[a] The levels of significance for the *t*-statistics are:

Eq. No.	1%	5%
1,2,3,	3.06	2.18
4,	3.11	2.20

[b] Δln ACCT is the log change in the number of accountant graduates and ln ACCT/GRAD, the proportion of male graduates with accountant majors.

[c] The salary variables, $\Delta\ln ASAL_{t-3}^{w}$ and $\Delta\ln YSAL_{t-3}^{w}$ are changes in weighted averages of starting salaries, with weights of 1, 2, 1, for the freshman, sophomore, and junior years respectively.

Table 8.1B Demand for Bachelor's Degree Accountants, 1951–1965

		Regression Coefficients and t-Statistics[a]					
Equation Number	*Dependent Variable*[b]	*Constant*	$\Delta\ln$ $PSRV_t$	$\Delta\ln$ $ACCT_{t-1}$	$\Delta\ln$ $ACCT_{t-2}$	R^2	*D.W. Statistic*
(1)	$\Delta\ln ASAL_t$	0.02	0.39	−0.05		0.78	2.53
		(2.29)	(6.36)	(1.81)			
(2)	$\Delta\ln ASAL_t$	0.02	0.38	−0.06	0.03	0.81	2.50
		(2.43)	(6.06)	(2.07)	(1.04)		

[a] The levels of significance for the *t*-statistics are:

Eq. No.	1%	5%
(1)	3.06	2.18
(2)	3.11	2.20

[b] The dependent variable $\Delta\ln ASAL_t$ is the log change in the salary of starting bachelor degree accountants

planned salaries reported in the Endicott survey depend on the demand for professional services (Δln PSRV) and the number of graduates at the time plans are formulated ($\Delta\ln ACCT_{t-1}$).[5] Supply lagged two periods also influences salaries, with a positive coefficient roughly half the size of that on the single lagged term, supporting the extrapolation model of expected supply formation (equation 2).*

Together, the estimated supply and demand parameters point to a highly stable market having less cyclic responsiveness than engineering. The product of the elasticity of supply and flexibility of salaries is sufficiently close to zero for a very rapid movement to equilibrium.

8.2 Cobweb Adjustment in the MBA Market

There are several reasons for expecting cobweb adjustment in the market for graduates with a master's degree in Business Administration. Like engineering and accounting, the MBA program is closely linked to the labor market. Students pursue the MBA strictly for vocational reasons, and most end up with managerial positions upon graduation. In the class of 1958, three fourths obtained jobs as business executives of some kind; 8 percent became salesmen, and the remainder teachers or engineers.[6] It seems reasonable that prospective businessmen have the awareness and responsiveness to labor market conditions required for cobweb adjustment. The pattern of supply over time depicted in Figure 8.2 provides further evidence of responsive cobweb-type behavior, with the fraction of men obtaining MBA's fluctuating cyclically, as required by the model.

The principal difference between the MBA market and the previous examples of cobweb adjustment is the relatively strong demand for MBA's in postwar years. MBA salaries were high and rapidly increasing, while the number of men choosing the field rose substantially. In 1967 a starting MBA earned $845 per month compared to $622 for equivalent bachelors's degree graduates (BBA). If this 35 percent differential continued over the life cycle, the rate of return on the degree would exceed 16 percent. From 1948 to 1968, moreover, starting MBA salaries increased more rapidly than engineering or BBA starting salaries, the wages of produc-

* According to the extrapolation equation, expected supply ($ACCT_t^p$) depends on past supply and past changes in supply:

$$\ln ACCT_t^p = \ln ACCT_{t-1} + \ln (ACCT_{t-1}/ACCT_{t-2});$$

so that

$$\ln ACCT_t^p = 2 \ln ACCT_{t-1} - \ln ACCT_{t-2}.$$

Thus, the number of graduates lagged two periods has a coefficient opposite in sign and half the size of that lagged one period. See Chapter 4 (pp. 64–65, for a more detailed discussion of this model.

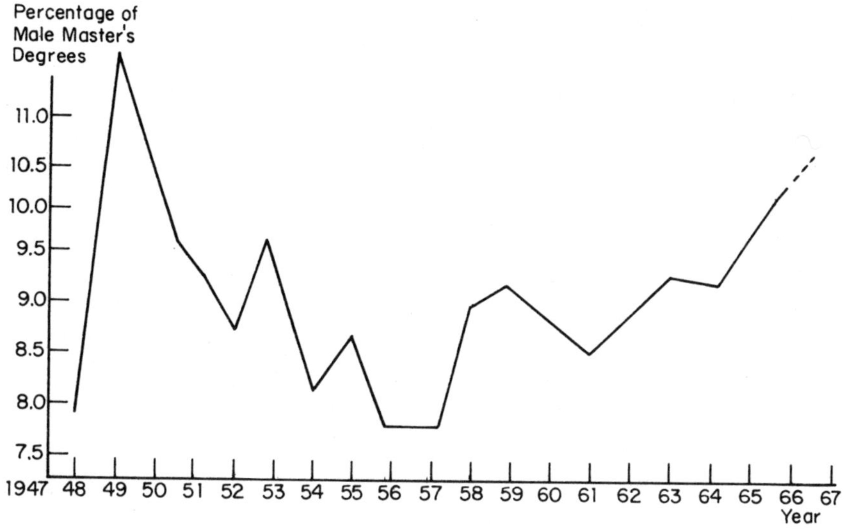

8.2 Percentage of male master's degrees awarded in business administration, 1948–1966

tion workers, or top executive compensation packages,[7] suggesting an increase in the value of MBA training.*

With incentives of this type it is not surprising that the number of men in MBA programs increased greatly. In the 1950–1965 period, the rate of increase in MBA's granted was 83 percent compared to a 31 percent decline in engineering degrees and a 7 percent increase in accountant degrees. From 1954 to 1965 the number of institutions awarding MBA's grew by 50 percent, as befits a market enjoying a substantial upward shift in demand.

Cobweb Model of MBA Management

The cobweb model to be tested in the MBA market is similar to that used for accountants:

(1) Supply:

$$\Delta \ln \mathrm{MBA}_t = a_0 \, \Delta \ln \mathrm{MA}_t + a_1 \, \Delta \ln \mathrm{MBSAL}_{t-2}{}^w - a_2 \, \Delta \ln \mathrm{BSAL}_{t-2}{}^w,$$

(2) Demand: $\Delta \ln \mathrm{MBSAL}_t = a_0 \, \Delta \ln \mathrm{GNP}_t - a_1 \, \Delta \ln \mathrm{MBA}_t,$

where MBA_t = number of MBA graduates in year t;

* Some representative rates of changes are: MBA graduates, 230 percent; engineers, 195 percent; BBA graduates, 213 percent; production workers, 132 percent.

MA_t = number of male master's graduates;
$MBSAL_t^w$ = weighted average of MBA starting salaries with weights 1, 2, 1 in years $t + 1$, t, and $t - 1$, respectively;
$BSAL_t^w$ = similar weighted average of BBA starting salaries;
GNP_t = real Gross National Product.

Equation (1) makes the decision to obtain an MBA degree dependent on the starting salaries of recent graduates* compared to the salaries of BBA graduates in business. The salaries are weighted averages, with the greatest weight given to the period two years prior to graduation. The population of prospective MBA's is taken as the number of male master's rather than bachelor's graduates because many MBA and master's candidates are older men. Statistically, changes in MBA and in master's degrees are well correlated, while those between MBA and bachelor's degrees are not.

Equation (2) makes starting salaries a function of the number of graduates and real Gross National Product. Studies of the salaries of executives find that company sales affect salaries, which suggests total output (or total sales) as an appropriate demand shift variable.[8] As salaries may also depend on profits, a measure of profits (PROF) is substituted for GNP in some calculations.

Regression Results

Tables 8.2A and 8.2B present least-squares regression estimates of the MBA model. Overall, the statistics confirm the general validity of the postulated structure: most of the variation in the change in degrees and salaries about their mean is explained in an economically sensible way.

The supply equations account for 70 to 80 percent of the change in degrees, with the starting salaries of MBA's and BBA's accorded significant opposing effects (Table 8.2A, equations 1–3). The best results are obtained in equation (2), where salaries are a weighted average of the rates in the year of enrollment and contiguous years. In this case, the salary terms have coefficients of equal absolute size and opposite signs; and the coefficient on the master's degree term is not significantly different from unity, as required for a properly specified equation. The calculations suggest an elasticity of supply on the order of 1.20. On the other hand, when all salary terms are treated equally in equation (3), the coefficients

* The beginning rates of Harvard Business School graduates are used to measure starting salaries in the statistical calculations. While the level of HBS salaries exceeds that of average MBA graduates, the *change* in HBS salaries probably provides a good indicator of changes in the state of the market.

Table 8.2A Supply of Master of Business Administration Graduates, 1949–1966

(The dependent variable is Δln MBA, the log change in the number of MBA graduates)

		Regression Coefficients and t-Statistics[a]				
Equation Number	*Constant*	Δln MA_t	Δln $MBSAL_t^w$	Δln $BSAL_t^w$	R^2	*D.W. Statistic*
(1)	−0.02	1.28	0.031	—	0.74	2.38
	(.70)	(3.99)	(2.86)			
(2)	−0.09	1.46	1.19	−1.32	.79	2.81
	(1.96)	(4.65)	(1.88)	(1.84)		
(3)[b]	—	1.53	0.80	−1.31		
		(6.08)	(2.06)	(2.84)	.73	2.65

SOURCE: The MBA salary series is taken from the salaries of Harvard Business School graduates, the BBA series from the Endicott Placement Survey.

[a] The levels of significance for the *t*-statistics are:

Eq. No.	1%	5%	10%
(1)	2.92	2.12	1.76
(2),(3)	2.95	2.13	1.77

[b] In equation (3) unweighted salary figures are used.

on the MBA and BBA salaries diverge noticeably, the coefficient of master's degree is two standard deviations away from unity, and the R^2 drops somewhat. While the simple 1, 2, 1 weighting scheme may not be optimal, it is superior to the unweighted alternative.

Regression equations (1)–(3) of Table 8.2B represent the demand side of the market. They show that salaries are determined by the number of graduates and shifts in demand, as measured by profits or real GNP, in accord with the cobweb model.* In the MBA, as in the engineering and accountant markets, moreover, salaries appear to respond to shifts in supply with a lag. The number of graduates one and two periods earlier are better explanatory variables than current supply. In equations (2) and (3) the coefficients on these terms have the appropriate size and sign for the extrapolation model of expected supply. The impact of supply lagged two periods (Δln MBA_{t-2}) is positive and half the absolute value of supply lagged one period (Δln MBA_{t-1}).

By substituting the salary equation (2) of Table 8.1A into equation (1), the overall operation of the model can be summarized with a "cobweb

* Intercorrelation of profits with GNP made it difficult to determine the independent effect of each when both terms entered the regression equation.

Table 8.2B Demand for Master of Business Administration Graduates, 1949–1966

(The dependent variable is $\Delta\ln \text{MBSAL}_t$, the log change in MBA starting salaries)

		Regression Coefficients and t-Statistics						
Equation Number	*Con-stant*	$\Delta\ln$ MBA_t	$\Delta\ln$ MBA_{t-1}	$\Delta\ln$ MBA_{t-2}	$\Delta\ln$ GNP_t	$\Delta\ln$ PROF_t	R^2	*D.W. Statistic*
(1)	0.04	−0.04	−0.16		0.81		0.707	2.70
	(4.53)	(.60)	(3.80)		(4.43)			
(2)	0.05	−0.03	−0.18	0.10	0.60		.788	2.69
	(5.24)	(.57)	(3.36)	(2.29)	(3.13)			
(3)	0.06	−0.02	−0.20	0.12		0.14	.792	2.47
	(8.95)	(.35)	(3.78)	(3.21)		(3.19)		

Source: The MBA salary series are taken from the salaries of Harvard Business School graduates, the BBA series from the Endicott Placement Survey.

[a] The levels of significance for the *t*-statistics are:

Eq. No.	1%	5%	10%
(1)	2.95	2.13	1.77
(2),(3)	2.98	2.15	1.78

equation" relating the number of graduates to the number of MBA's seeking work and the level of demand two years earlier. An estimate of this equation is given below, with reasonably good statistical results. The coefficient on the number of graduates two years earlier is negative, as required for cobweb behavior, and considerably below unity, as required for a stable market. The level of demand ($\Delta\ln$ GNP) has the expected positive effect on the number of graduates.

$$\Delta\ln \text{MBA} = \underset{(1.77)}{-0.06} + \underset{(4.22)}{1.78}\,\Delta\ln \text{MA}_t \underset{(1.39)}{-0.20}\,\Delta\ln \text{MBA}_{t-2} + \underset{(1.78)}{0.94}\,\Delta\ln \text{GNP}$$

$$R^2 = .662$$
$$\text{D.W.} = 2.95$$

Cobweb adjustment in the MBA case is stable and dampened, with greater cyclic responsiveness than in accounting and less than in engineering.

8.3 Incomplete Adjustment in Chemical Professions

Throughout the postwar period chemistry and chemical engineering lost ground relative to other specialized occupations. The rate of increase in employment was far below that for most college careers; the fraction of males selecting chemical work declined drastically; and salaries were low in comparison to alternatives. In this section I use the incomplete adjustment model to examine the functioning of the market for chemical specialists under these conditions. First, the evidence pointing to a *relative* surplus of chemists and chemical engineers is reviewed. Then I estimate an incomplete adjustment supply equation using the rule of acceleration developed in Chapter 2, and consider the effect of changes in supply on salaries.

Surplus Manpower in the Chemical Market

The evidence of a relative surplus of chemical specialists in the 1950s and 1960s is threefold:

First, the proportion of male college students choosing chemistry and chemical engineering majors fell markedly throughout the period. At all levels of education the chemical professions experienced a substantial decline in degrees compared to other fields. The decline is concentrated at the postgraduate level, with a near-halving in the fraction of master's and Ph.D.'s granted in the field (see Table 8.3).

Table 8.3 Degrees in Chemical Professions, 1950–1965

	All Male	*Chemistry*	*Chemical Engineering*
Bachelor, 1950	286,652	9,134	4,474
1965	279,777	8,111	3,050
Percent Change	−2.4	−11.2	−31.2
Master's, 1950	41,237	1,368	698
1965	76,211	1,362	803
Percent Change	84.8	−0.4	15.0
Doctorate, 1950	2,925	914	172
1965	7,741	1,277	362
Percent Change	145.3	39.7	110.5

SOURCE: Tables 3.6 to 3.8.

Second, employment of chemists relative to other workers in the main industries of work tell a similar story. Many chemists and over half of the chemical engineers are employed by chemical and petroleum firms. Since the chemical industry is a leading growth sector, with substantial increases in output, R & D, and employment, the demand for chemical specialists would *ceteris paribus* have increased greatly. The fact that demand did not increase points to a sizable intra-industrial shift in skill coefficients against chemists and chemical engineers. Indeed, from 1950 to 1960 the number of chemists per worker declined from 48 per thousand to 37 per thousand in the chemical industry and from 18 per thousand to 11 per thousand in petroleum and coal. The average rate of growth of jobs in chemist-employing industries was 27.4 percent compared to an increase in chemist employment of just 17 percent.

Finally the level and rate of change of chemists' salaries are consistent with this picture of a weak market. As shown in Table 8.4, scientists and

Table 8.4 Incomes in the Chemical Industry

		Chemical Industry		*All Manufacturing*	
Scientists and Engineers	*Year*	*Dollars*	*Percent*	*Dollars*	*Percent*
Starting B.S. salary	1966	660/ month		693/ month	
Starting Ph.D. salary	1966	1032		1120	
Change in B.S. salary	1949–66		134.0		143.2
Change in Ph.D. salary	1949–66		133.5		147.2
Production Workers					
Average hourly earning	1966	2.98		2.71	
Change in hourly earnings	1949–66		109.9		96.4

SOURCES: Los Alamos Scientific Laboratory, Bureau of Labor Statistics.

engineers in the chemical industry earned less in 1966 than those in other industries. In addition, they had smaller increases in salaries from 1949 to 1966. By contrast, production workers in chemical plants had exceptionally high pay and large increases in wages.

From the employment, education, and salary figures, it is clear that the *relative* position of chemistry and chemical engineering worsened in the postwar period.[9] Does the incomplete adjustment model help explain the response of the market to this development?

Incomplete Adjustment Supply Behavior

The incomplete adjustment model of Chapter 2 suggested that markets with substantial disequilibrium would obey a rule of acceleration of supply. According to the rule, the rate at which supply moves toward equilibrium is determined by the level of wages. Changes in the rate (for example, the acceleration of supply) are governed by changes in wages.* Does the rule apply to the postwar chemist market?

To test the applicability of incomplete adjustment to the chemical case, changes in the number of chemist and chemical engineering degrees were examined in relation to salaries several years earlier. This analysis supports the validity of the model and of the acceleration rule. First, as Table 8.5 shows, the annual acceleration (change in the rate of change) of Ph.D. degrees in chemistry compared to all Ph.D.'s is closely linked to changes in relative salaries five years earlier. The Spearman coefficient is 0.89, significant at 1 percent. In this test a five-year lag was chosen because approximately five years are spent studying for the Ph.D. in chemistry. The salaries of doctorate engineers are used as the measure of the alternative possibilities facing prospective chemists.

The regression calculations presented in Table 8.6 specialize the relation and extend it to master's graduates.

In equation (1) the acceleration of the ratio of chemist to all male degrees (in logarithmic form) is regressed on the change in relative salaries lagged five years. The coefficient on the salary term is positive and highly significant as predicted by the acceleration rule. In equation (2) the change in degrees lagged one period is added to the equation and obtains a significant negative coefficient. Equation (3) applies the model with similar success to M.S. chemists. The response of the change in supply to changes in salaries is on the order of 0.70 to 0.90. A 1 percent increase in salaries increases by 0.70 to 0.90 percent the speed with which supply moves toward equilibrium.

For a more discriminating test of the incomplete adjustment model, the acceleration equations can be compared with supply equations in which changes in salary determine changes in supply, as opposed to the acceleration of supply. Equations of this type are presented in Panel B of Table

* The acceleration rule is derived as follows. Let W_t = actual relative wage of chemists to alternative specialists, and $\overline{W}$ = the equilibrium relative wage. Then the incomplete adjustment supply equation is

$$\Delta T_t = a(W_t - \overline{W}), \text{ where } \Delta T_t = \text{change in supply.}$$

The second difference of supply is

$$\Delta(\Delta T_t) = a\Delta(W_t - \overline{W}).$$

With a fixed equilibrium wage, this reduces to a relation between the acceleration of supply and the change in wages:

$$\Delta^2 T_t = a\Delta W_t.$$

Table 8.5 Acceleration of Change in Number of Doctorate Degrees in Chemistry Compared to Changes in Ratio of Ph.D. Chemist to Ph.D. Engineer-Scientist Salaries, Lagged Five Years, 1952–1966

Year	*Share of Ph.D. Degrees Awarded in Chemistry* (1)	*Change in Share of Degrees* (2)	*Accelera-tion of Change* (3)	*Ratio of Ph.D. Chemist to Ph.D. Engineer-Scientist Salaries, Lagged 5 Years* (4)	*Change in Ratio of Salaries* (5)	*Rank of Ac-celera-tion*[a,b] (6)	*Rank of Changed Ratio of Sal-aries*[b] (7)
1952	0.141			—			
1953	.126	−0.015		—			
1954	.118	− .008	0.007	0.841			
1955	.121	.003	.011	.893	0.052	3	2
1956	.116	− .005	− .008	.881	− .008	10	8
1957	.122	.006	.011	.985	.096	2	1
1958	.112	− .010	− .016	.887	− .098	12	12
1959	.115	.003	.013	.928	.041	1	3
1960	.114	− .001	− .004	.898	− .030	9	10
1961	.109	− .005	− .004	.909	.011	8	6
1962	.101	− .008	− .003	.926	.027	7	4
1963	.100	− .001	.007	.917	− .009	4	9
1964	.091	− .009	− .008	.873	− .004	11	11
1965	.087	− .004	.005	.898	.025	5	5
1966	.089	.002	.006	.907	.009	6	7

SOURCES: Degree data: Office of Education. Salary data: Engineer-scientist salaries from Los Angeles Scientific Laboratory; Chemist salaries: the American Chemical Society, with the 1950 and 1951 figures estimated on the basis of salaries and scientists and engineers in the chemical industry. Experiments with other salary series yield similar results.

[a] Ties resolved by taking figures to additional places.

[b] The Spearman correlation coefficient is 0.89; the 1% level of significance is 0.71.

8.6 for M.S. and Ph.D. chemists. In both cases the acceleration rule provides a better explanation of developments than the alternative supply equation.* Analogous, though less strong, results are obtained for bachelor's chemistry and chemical engineering graduates.[10]

A different type of evidence of incomplete adjustment supply behavior is presented in the flow diagrams of Figure 8.3. The diagrams show the kind of jobs and postgraduate education obtained by chemistry majors in the classes of 1951 and 1958. The fraction of majors working in the chemical profession fell from 56 percent in 1951 to 45 percent in 1958. Behavior

* As the coefficient on the lagged change in supply term in equations (2) and (3) is close to unity, however, the hypothesis that changes in supply are determined by changes in salaries by the level of salaries cannot be entirely rejected. The regression results favor the acceleration rule, but not decisively.

of this kind can be viewed as a sensible response to a disequilibrium surplus of specialists in the chemist market.

The findings of Chapters 5 and 7 offer further support for the incomplete adjustment hypothesis. In Chapter 5 the discounted lifetime income of chemists was seen to be below those of comparable specialties, as

Table 8.6 Supply of Doctorate and Master's Chemists, 1955–1966

Equation Number	*Level of Degree*	*Regression Coefficients and t-Statistics*[a] *Constant*	*Change in Relative Salaries*[b]	*Lagged Change in Degrees*	R^2	*D.W.*
PANEL A: Supply regressions with the *acceleration* of the log change in chemist degrees relative to all male degrees as the dependent variable, 1955–1966						
(1)	Ph.D.	0.00	1.22		0.68	2.00
		(.02)	(4.61)			
(2)	Ph.D.	−0.03	0.70	−0.94	.84	2.02
		(1.90)	(2.54)	(3.00)		
(3)	M.S.	−0.03	0.86	−0.81	.54	2.39
		(1.61)	(1.84)	(2.31)		
PANEL B: Supply regressions with the log change in chemist degrees relative to all male degrees as the dependent variable, 1955–1966						
(4)	Ph.D.	− .03	.64		.54	1.97
		(2.75)	(3.42)			
(5)	M.S.	− .03	.42		.09	1.06
		(2.47)	(.98)			

[a] The levels of significance for the *t*-statistics are:

Eq. No.	1%	5%
(1),(4),(5)	3.17	2.23
(2),(3)	3.25	2.26

[b] Relative salaries for Ph.D.'s are measured by the ratio of Ph.D. chemist to engineering salaries lagged five years. Relative salaries for M.S. graduates are measured by the ratio of M.S. chemist to M.S. engineering salaries lagged three years.

would be expected under surplus conditions. In the moving cross-sectional regressions of Chapter 7 the relatively slow growth of Ph.D.'s in chemistry and other "low-paying fields" was attributed to this disequilibrium situation.

In sum, time series supply regressions, the occupational decisions of chemistry majors, and cross-sectional comparisons of lifetime incomes and supply support the application of the incomplete adjustment model to the chemists' market.

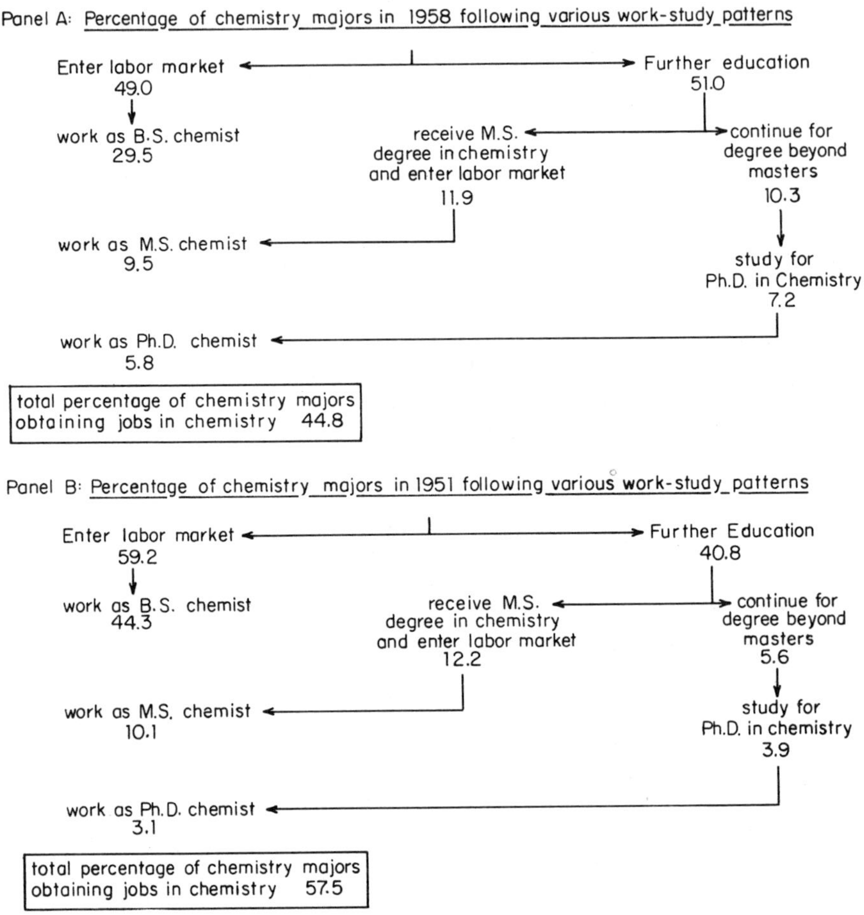

8.3 Post-bachelor's degree work and study patterns of chemistry majors in the class of 1958 compared to the class of 1951

Demand for Chemists

For equilibrium to be restored in a market with a surplus of workers, the salary of specialists must increase as supply declines. To check this requirement of incomplete adjustment, salary determination equations were calculated for B.S., M.S., and Ph.D. chemists and chemical engineers. The explanatory variables in these regressions are the number of graduates in the field (DEG), investment in the chemical industry (INV), research and development spending (RDC), and industrial output (PROD) in the industry.

The regression results are contained in Table 8.7. In almost all cases

Table 8.7 Demand for Chemical Specialists: Salary Determination Regressions, 1951–1966

(The dependent variable is the log change in starting salaries)

Equation Number	*Level and Degree*	*Regression Coefficients and t-Statistics*[a]							
		Constant	$\Delta \ln DEG_{t-1}$	$\Delta \ln DEG_{t-2}$	$\Delta \ln INV$	$\Delta \ln RDC_{t-1}$	$\Delta \ln PROD$	R^2	*D.W.*
1	B.S.	−1.95	−0.40	0.20	0.05	0.21	0.28	0.918	2.94
		(4.39)	(5.29)	(3.23)	(2.99)	(4.53)	(4.46)		
2	B.S.C.E.[b]	−0.94	−0.11	0.06	0.04	0.15	0.14	.609	1.67
		(1.46)	(.97)	(0.66)	(1.45)	(2.13)	(1.52)		
3	M.S.	0.03	−0.07	0.12	0.05	0.13	—	.552	2.81
		(2.70)	(.70)	(1.78)	(1.29)	(1.58)			
4	M.S.C.E.	0.05	−0.24	0.11	0.09	0.01	—	.488	1.96
		(3.95)	(2.19)	(1.51)	(2.16)	(.16)			
5	Ph.D.	0.04	−0.06	0.03	0.05	0.10	—	.397	2.50
		(3.08	(1.86)	(1.36)	(1.47)	(1.19)			

SOURCES: Salary figures: American Chemical Society, Los Alamos Scientific Laboratory. Industry figures: Federal Reserve Board, Commerce Department, National Science Foundation. Degree figures: Office of Education.

[a] Definition of abbreviations:

DEG = number of degrees awarded in the level and specialty under study.
INV = dollars of investment in the chemical industry.
RDC = dollars of research and development spending in the chemical industry.
PROD = current industrial output in the chemical industry, as indexed by the Federal Reserve Industrial Output Series.

[b] C.E. = Chemical Engineering.

the number of graduates has the required negative effect on salaries, usually with a one- or two-year lag. Graduates in the previous period significantly reduce the starting salaries of B.S. chemists (equation 1) and the salaries of M.S. chemical engineers (equation 4) and Ph.D. chemists (equation 5). For B.S. chemical engineers and for M.S. chemists the number of graduates has a negative effect on salaries but with a standard error of estimate of roughly similar size (equations 2 and 3). Graduates lagged two periods also enter the salary equations with a generally significant coefficient. In each of starting salary regressions this variable obtains a positive coefficient approximately half the absolute value of that on graduates lagged one period. This is in accord with the extrapolation of expected supply model that fit the engineering, accountant, and MBA markets. The flexibility of B.S. salaries is on the order of 0.20 percent; that of M.S. and Ph.D. salaries ranges from 0.05 to 0.10 percent.[11]

Changes in demand also help determine salaries. For B.S. chemists and chemical engineers investment, R & D, and current output in the chemical industry have substantial effects on salaries (equations 1 and 2). For M.S. and Ph.D. specialists, who are unlikely to work on problems directly related to current production, investment and R & D are important (equations 3–6). The absence of demand shift variables for the university sector, which employs many postgraduate chemists, explains the relatively low R^2 in the demand equations in these cases.

8.4 Incomplete Adjustment in Mathematics

Although mathematics is "queen of the sciences," not until the mid-1950s, when employment and degrees in the field began expanding at phenomenal rates, did her reign extend to the labor market. From 1950 to 1966 the number of employed mathematicians increased by upward of 300 percent, the share of degrees awarded in mathematics more than doubled, and salaries rose at rates far above the economy-wide average. In the 1957–1966 period the median beginning rate for a Ph.D. increased by 48 percent in industry and 60 percent in education, compared to an increase in manufacturing wages of just 32 percent.[12] By 1968 a starting B.S. mathematician commanded a salary of $742 per month in industry, an M.S. $885, and a Ph.D. $1325.[13] The simultaneous growth of employment, degrees, and salaries points to a shortage of workers in mathematics and a movement toward equilibrium along an incomplete adjustment path.

A rigorous test of the applicability of the incomplete adjustment model to the mathematics market is difficult to perform. Professional mathematics societies have not been as diligent in surveying salaries as chemical and engineering societies. The evidence that does exist, however, tends to support the validity of the model.

On the supply side, there are three indications of incomplete adjustment behavior. First, the flow diagrams contained in Figure 8.4 show a sizable increase in the fraction of mathematics majors employed in the field during the decade of the fifties. Over one fourth of the class of 1950 obtained jobs as mathematicians compared to one eighth of the class of

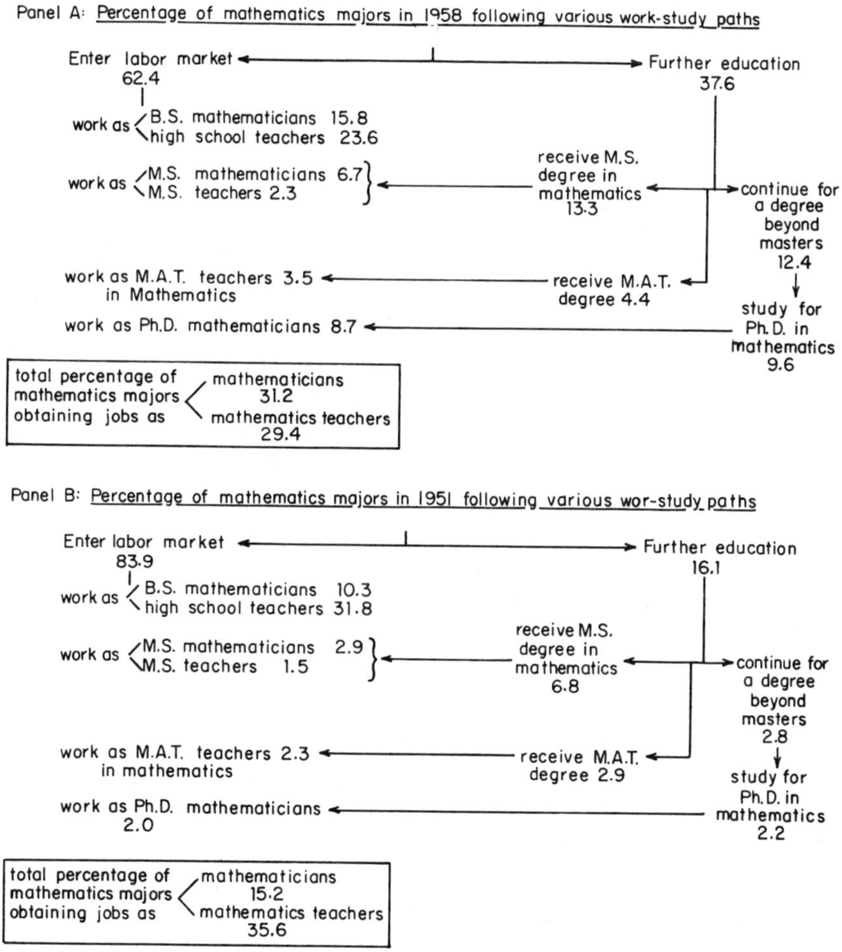

8.4 Post-bachelor's degree work and study patterns of mathematics majors in the class of 1958 compared to the class of 1951

1958. While this is indirect evidence of incomplete adjustment, it points to a sizable supply response to disequilibrium shortage.

Second, the long-term growth of doctorate degrees in mathematics is closely correlated with relative salaries in the field. Figure 8.5 shows, in

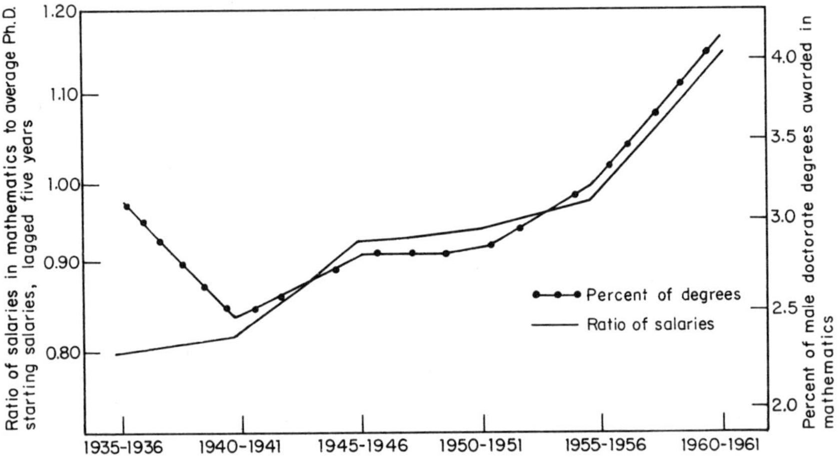

8.5 Proportion of Ph.D. degrees awarded to males in mathematics compared to the ratio of starting salaries in mathematics to the average doctorate starting salary five years earlier, by quinquennium, 1940–1965

particular, that the fraction of Ph.D.'s in the field varies over time in accordance with the ratio of mathematics to average doctorate starting salaries. Only during the World War II period do the changes in degrees and salaries diverge. Again the evidence is fragile, but indicative of the supply responsiveness required by the model.

Third, in the computations of Chapter 5, mathematics obtained a discounted lifetime income far above its equilibrium level, which is to be expected in a market with a shortage of workers. The relatively high income of mathematicians "explains" the rate of increase in degrees in the 1960–1965 period, indicating a supply response of the incomplete adjustment type.

Demand for Mathematicians

An underlying cause of the apparent shortage of mathematicians in postwar years is not hard to discover. The advent of computer technology in industry shifted demand upward by a considerable amount. At the B.S. level, employment increased greatly in such computer-using industries as aircraft, insurance, and electrical equipment, and in computing centers. Not surprisingly, a large fraction of mathematicians report considerable use of computer techniques and numerical analysis on the job.[14] The timing of the spurt in mathematics degrees also directs attention to the role of computer technology, for bachelor's and master's degrees began increasing rapidly in about 1956–1957, two to three years after the onset of substantial usage of computers in government and industry.

The growth of industrial job opportunities induced many students to select mathematics as their career and thus raised the demand for mathematical training. As a result the demand for faculty in the field increased greatly. The number of new personnel in mathematics rose from 4.5 percent of all new faculty in 1953 to 6.3 percent in 1965. Difficulty in attracting mathematicians from industry also added to the number of vacant teaching positions. These postwar shifts in industrial and academic demand seem sufficient to create disequilibrium shortages of the kind needed for incomplete adjustment.

Finally, the increased supply of mathematics graduates has reduced the rate of change of salaries as required by the model. In the 1957–1967 decade the annual change of doctorate starting salaries reported to the American Mathematical Association is negatively correlated with changes in the number of doctorate graduates relative to the level of demand. In industry, the rank correlation of the percentage change in salaries with new Ph.D.'s per dollar of real GNP is −0.70 and with new Ph.D.'s per computer, −0.79. In academia, changes in starting rates are correlated at −0.70 with the changing ratio of Ph.D.'s per enrolled student (the 5 percent level of significance is 0.64 in these comparisons).

Thus, the mathematics case confirms the ability of the incomplete adjustment model to explain developments in a market with a shortage of workers.

9 Demand for Education and the Market for Faculty

In preceding chapters the supply of specialized workers was assumed to depend on the occupational decisions of students rather than on the availability of training facilities. This assumption can be tested by examining the responsiveness of universities to changes in the demand for training. Since faculty members are the principal determinants of the supply of facilities, an analysis of the faculty market has special importance. In this chapter three aspects of the operation of this labor market are considered: the effect of changes in the demand for education on the interfield composition of the faculty; the determination of the scale of employment and salaries in the context of the simultaneous allocation model of Chapter 2; and the influence of economic incentive on the choice of an academic career by new and experienced Ph.D.'s.

9.1 The Interfield Composition of Faculties

In an educational system that responds to the needs of the labor market, changes in the demand for training will generate changes in the composition of faculty and in the supply of training facilities. Increased demand for mathematical training, for example, will lead to increased employment of mathematics faculty. Has the U.S. system operated in this way in the years since World War II?

Enrollment and New Faculty

Table 9.1 and Figure 9.1 present evidence regarding this question. The table compares changes in enrollment and in the number of new faculty

Table 9.1 Percentage Changes in Enrollment and in New Faculty, by Major Field, 1960–1964, 1954–1964

	1960–64 Percentage Change of–				*1954–64 Percentage Change of–*			
	Enrollment[b]	*New Faculty*	*Rank of*[a]		*Enrollment*[b]	*New Faculty*	*Rank of*[a]	
Field	*(1)*	*(2)*	*(1)*	*(2)*	*(3)*	*(4)*	*(3)*	*(4)*
Languages	82.6	61.2	1	4	267.6	408.4	3	1
Political Science	64.8	88.3	2	2	137.7	211.5	8	9
Library Science	60.5	36.9	3	13	72.9	28.8	15	19
English	59.7	58.1	4	5	625.6	173.4	1	10
Sociology	59.6	108.1	5	1	111.5	306.7	10	2
Biology	54.8	38.8	6	16	146.2	138.8	7	15
Psychology	44.2	51.9	7	6	149.8	273.8	5	3
Mathematics	42.6	48.2	8	9	366.6	227.0	2	8
History	38.8	71.1	9	3	162.1	237.2	4	5
Philosophy	36.7	34.5	10	14	123.4	240.1	9	4
Fine Arts	35.0	49.0	11	8	105.8	234.3	11	6
Education	33.7	57.2	12	10	97.5	167.2	12	11
Economics	30.2	17.4	13	17	82.2	128.7	13	16
Home Economics	29.3	0.5	14	21	−12.4	27.0	21	20
Chemistry	27.6	31.6	15	15	72.3	134.7	16	14
Physics	21.7	51.7	16	7	48.9	233.3	6	7
Health Fields	19.7	40.3	17	11	47.4	72.8	18	18
Business & Commerce	18.7	37.3	18	12	68.9	106.5	17	17
Religion	11.3	15.4	19	19	33.4	165.6	19	12
Engineering	6.6	14.1	20	20	80.1	158.5	14	13
Agriculture	5.6	17.0	21	18	−2.1	−6.6	20	21

SOURCES: National Education Association, *Teacher Supply and Demand* (1954–1964); Office of Education, *Earned Degrees Conferred* (1954–1966; and 1960–1964); *Enrollment for Advanced Degree* National Science Foundation, *Graduate Student Enrollment and Support in American Universities and Colleges, 1954.*

[a] Summary of rank correlation analysis:

Spearman coefficient for 1960–64 = 0.56
Spearman coefficient for 1954–64 = 0.75
1% level of significance is 0.52

[b] Enrollment is estimated as the sum of graduate enrollment and the number of bachelors graduates in the following two years. Because of changes in the sample of universities reporting new faculty, the 1954–64 comparisons are valid only with regard to magnitude.

by field in a relatively short period of time (1960–1964) and over the 1954–1964 decade. The figure shows the fraction of new faculty and of enrollment in four fields biannually from 1953 to 1965. Both sets of data reveal a close connection between the pattern of enrollment and that of newly

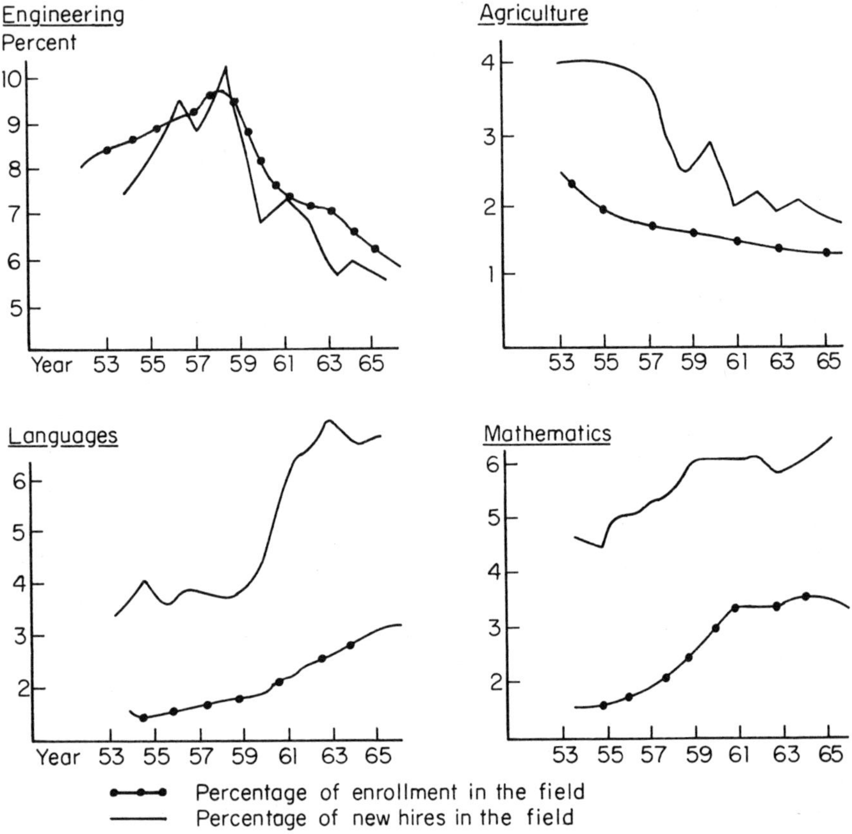

9.1 Proportion of new faculty and of enrollment in four major fields of study, 1953–1965. Enrollment is estimated as the sum of graduate enrollment and undergraduate degrees two years later. In the interval 1955–1958 graduate enrollment is an interpolation of 1954 and 1959 figures.

SOURCE: National Education Association, *Teacher Supply and Demand*; Office of Education: *Earned Degrees Conferred* and *Enrollment for Advanced Degrees*; National Science Foundation: *Graduate Student Enrollment and Support in American Universities and Colleges, 1954.*

hired faculty. First, the rank correlations in the table show that relative changes in enrollment are accompanied by similar changes in new appointments in the short and long run. The Spearman coefficient increases from 0.56 to 0.75 as the time interval is lengthened, possibly because budgetary and labor market constraints ease in the long run. Second, when the number of *unfilled* budgeted positions is added to the number of newly hired faculty to measure *desired* appointments, the correlation is even higher. In this instance changes in enrollment are nearly perfectly rank-correlated with changes in the desired number of new faculty. For the 1960–1964 interval the Spearman coefficient is 0.93. This suggests that universities attempt to alter the composition of faculties in the direction of the changed demand for education to a greater extent than is actually feasible. Third, the figure shows that biannual changes in the proportion of newly hired faculty in a field are well correlated with changes in the fraction of students enrolled. When engineering enrollment peaked in 1958, for example, so too did new faculty personnel in the field.

From these computations it is clear that the composition of new appointments and enrollment are closely related. The direction of causation is not self-evident, however. The empirical regularities might be due to the response of universities to educational needs. They might also result from the response of enrollment to changes in the number of openings resulting from new appointments. There are several reasons for attributing the results to the "responsiveness" of universities rather than to a limitation on openings for students. First, the potential constraint on enrollment cannot account for the near-perfect correlation between desired new faculty and enrollment. Second, the constraint hypothesis fails to explain the increased correlation between the actual number of newly hired faculty and enrollment as time proceeds (a constraint on available places ought to be stronger in the short run). Third, although the number of new appointments is an appropriate measure of investment in teachers, it is a poor measure of the total number of places that might constrain enrollment.

The evidence on the changing *quality* of newly appointed faculty, as reflected in the proportion of new teachers with a Ph.D., also supports the "responsive university" hypothesis. In this case, quality deteriorates in rapidly expanding fields and improves in those with limited gains in enrollment, apparently because universities accept less qualified faculty when demand pressures are great. Similarly, there is a strong negative correlation between the change in the quality of new faculty depicted in Figure 9.2 and changes in enrollment relative to the supply of Ph.D.'s.*

These considerations lead to the conclusion that universities adjust the mix of new faculty to the demand for education, as required of a respon-

* In both the interfield and time series comparisons, the changed proportion of faculty with Ph.D.'s is rank-correlated with changes in demand at the 2 percent level. However, in the case of the annual changes it is necessary also to take account of the number of available Ph.D.'s.

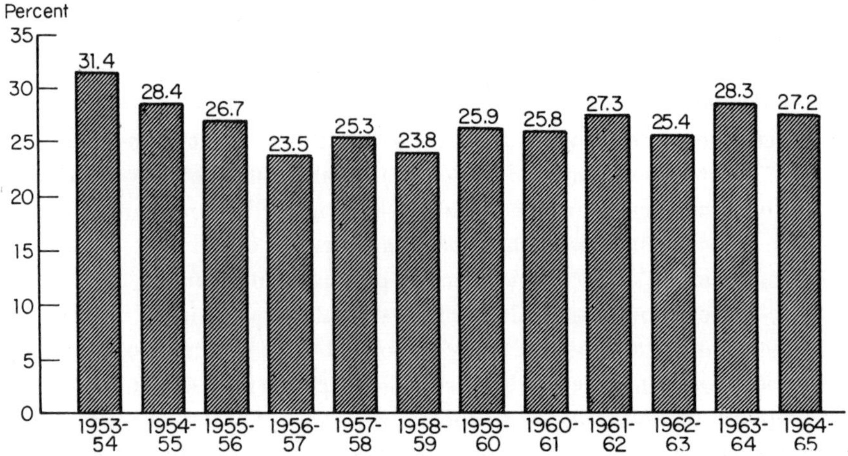

9.2 Percent of newly appointed college teachers with doctor's degree, 1953–1965.)
SOURCE: National Education Association, *Teacher Supply and Demand.*

sive educational system. In this sense the supply of places is elastic with respect to demand.[1]

A Hiring Standards Approach

The pattern of quality variation just described suggests the applicability of a hiring standards — or queue — model of demand to the faculty market. A model consistent with the observed variation in the quality of newly appointed faculty can be constructed from the following postulates:

1) that, within a range of relative salaries, universities prefer doctorate to nondoctorate faculty (either for reasons of prestige or productivity);

2) that, outside the range of preference, the elasticity of substitution of non-Ph.D.'s for Ph.D.'s is very high;

3) that the supply of doctorate teachers is less elastic than that of the other potential faculty.[2]

Under these conditions universities hire Ph.D.'s until the area of substitution is reached, whereupon they turn to faculty with fewer academic qualifications. As a result the quality of new appointments will depend on the demand for faculty relative to the supply of Ph.D.'s.

Readily available evidence about the supply and demand of doctorate and other faculty are consistent with the proposed model. Regression calculations presented in section 9.3 show that the number of new doctorate faculty depends critically on the number of recent graduates and thus has only limited elasticity. The supply of less-qualified persons, on the other hand, consists of master's graduates, high school teachers, and business or government officials who are drawn from a large, diverse and presumably elastic population.* On the demand side, crude calculations indicate that the elasticity of substitution of non-Ph.D. for Ph.D. faculty is high (8.0).[3] As a first approximation, the hiring standards-queue approach offers a reasonable description of the faculty market.

Constraints on Responsiveness

Universities are limited in their ability to adjust faculty employment to desired levels by several factors: the external labor market, which determines the availability of faculty, the internal market, which restricts salary variation, and the budget constraint that limits total spending. Because of these constraints, the salaries offered by universities in some fields are too low to attract the desired number of teachers. As a result, job vacancies in the form of unfilled budgeted positions are found in the university system. In 1964 vacancies were concentrated in mathematics, economics, and physics, where from 14 to 18 percent of new budgeted positions went unfilled in 1964.

The relation between vacancies and salaries is examined in Table 9.2.[4] Column 1 presents incremental vacancy rates — the ratio of vacant positions to the number of new budgeted positions in eight scientific fields. Column 2 shows the ratio of industrial to academic salaries. There is a substantial positive correlation between salaries and vacancies, which suggests that relatively high nonacademic earnings lie behind the pattern of vacancies. The supply of faculty at the usual academic rates is limited in such fields as economics and mathematics, where nonacademic salaries are high.

The obvious response to vacancies is to increase salaries in fields with many unfilled positions. This response is barred to universities by the internal labor market and budgetary constraints. According to a National Education Association survey, 90 percent of universities adhere to the internal constraint that requires rough equality of salaries in all specialties and thus prevents the needed increases in shortage areas.[5] Evidence on the range of salaries and changes in salaries among fields shows the constraint

* In the 1960s, from 30 to 40 percent of new faculty were former high school teachers or workers in the government or industrial sector (*Teacher Supply and Demand,* National Education Association, Washington, D.C., 1967).

to be generally effective. There is an extraordinarily narrow interfield salary structure in higher education. The highest paying specialty (economics), for example, has a bare 14 percent advantage over the lowest (agriculture), compared to a 45 percent differential in industry. Similarly, the coefficient of variation in the rate of change in salaries among fields was just 0.109 for education compared to 0.201 for industry in the 1948–1964 period.

Table 9.2 Incremental Vacancy Rates in Academic Institutions Compared to the Ratio of Industrial to Academic Salaries, 1964

Field	*Incremental Vacancy Rate*[a] (1)	*Ratio of Industrial to Academic Salaries 1964* (2)	*Rank of*[b] (1)	(2)
Physics	.177	1.47	1	3
Economics	.162	1.72	2	1
Mathematics	.143	1.65	3	2
Psychology	.123	1.45	4	4
Chemistry	.095	1.40	5	5
Biology	.069	1.33	6	7
Agriculture	.028	1.08	7	8
Geology	.017	1.37	8	6

SOURCES: National Education Association, *Teacher Supply and Demand* (1964); National Science Foundation, *National Scientific Register* (1964).

[a] The incremental vacancy rate is the fraction of new budgeted positions unfilled in a given year.

[b] The Spearman coefficient is 0.88; 1% level of significance is 0.83.

The budget constraint prevents universities from raising salaries in all fields by the amount needed to eliminate vacancies. With financial limitations, the marginal cost of an across-the-board increase exceeds the benefit of filling shortage positions.

Circumventing Constraints

Several factors counteract the constraints on university responsiveness and facilitate the adjustment of faculty to educational needs. First, the production of faculty within universities, which transforms current demand for training into future supply of potential teachers, limits the possible extent of teacher shortages. Second, with over 2200 separate institutions of higher education in the United States, the education market is relatively decentralized and competitive and can be expected to enjoy the allocative advantages of a flexible competitive system. Third, the resources available to universities grew greatly in the postwar years: the fraction of GNP spent on higher education doubled from 1950 to 1966; the increased number of master's and doctorate graduates enlarged the supply of potential faculty and places.[6]

University administrators also consciously use nonsalary incentives to circumvent constraints on behavior. Variation of the rate at which faculty members are promoted is a frequently used tool for differentiating real income by field without violating the internal salary constraint. Increases in pay associated with higher rank have, after all, a similar effect on lifetime income as "pure" increases at a given level of responsibility. In the major universities for which detailed figures exist, rapid promotion of natural and social scientists in the 1960s produced a 7–8 percent advantage in discounted lifetime income over humanities faculty. By comparison, the scientists enjoyed a bare 5 percent differential in salaries when age, rank, and experience are held fixed.[7]

Other nonsalary tools — office facilities, secretarial and research assistance, hours of teaching, computer facilities, special research centers or libraries — are also widely used to sweeten offers in particular fields. While eye-catching examples of these incentives can easily be found (the Berkeley Radiation Laboratory, for example, designed to keep E.O. Lawrence and high-particle physics at Berkeley, and the Cowles Foundation at Yale to attract scholars in mathematical economics), it is not possible at present to evaluate their monetary worth.

Finally, irrespective of university action, the labor market thwarts the internal salary constraint by offering men in shortage fields advantageous nonacademic income opportunities. For the average academician, consulting, lecture fees, royalties, and such, account for 10 percent of total earnings; for the teachers actually receiving such moneys, they account for 25 percent. The concentration of opportunities in high-paying fields widens the interspecialty income differential among faculty. In 1961–1962 the interfield coefficient of variation in income jumped from 0.146 to 0.180 by the inclusion of nonteaching income.[8]

Thus, despite limited use of pure salary incentives, universities have several ways of attracting specialists in fields in great market demand. These mechanisms are an adequate though by no means perfect substitute for a flexible salary policy.

9.2 The Faculty Labor Market Model

In a properly functioning educational system the scale of faculty employment, as well as the composition of newly appointed faculty by field, will adjust to changes in education and labor market conditions. Adjustments in total employment are examined next in the context of the simultaneous allocation model of Chapter 2. For statistical convenience and in the absence of adequate data, nonacademic salaries are treated as exogenous rather than endogenous in the calculations. Elimination of the nonacademic sector reduces the model to a two-equation simultaneous system:

Simplified Faculty Model

(1) Demand for faculty:

$$\Delta\ln \text{FAC}_t^D = a_0\,\Delta\ln \text{ENR}_t + a_1\,\Delta\ln \text{INC}_t - a_2\ln(\text{FAC/STD})_{t-1} - a_3\,\Delta\ln \text{SAL}_t.$$

(2) Supply of faculty:

$$\Delta\ln \text{FAC}_t^D = \alpha_0\,\Delta\ln \text{SAL}_t - \alpha_1\,\Delta\ln \text{ISAL}_t + \Delta\ln \text{QUL}_t.$$

(3) Market Clearing:

$$\Delta\ln \text{FAC}_t^D = \Delta\ln \text{FAC}_t^S.$$

FAC = number of faculty (endogenous);
SAL = salary of faculty (endogenous);
ENR = number of enrolled students;
INC = income of universities;
(FAC/STD) = ratio of faculty to students;
ISAL = nonacademic salaries;
QUL = number of specialists qualified to teach.

The solution of these equations for the endogenous variables FAC and SAL yields the reduced form of the system. Because the model is overidentified, with two variables omitted from equation (1) and three from equation (2), the reduced form coefficients do not provide a unique estimate of the structural parameters.* They do, however, show the way in which the market is affected by exogenous changes. For this reason both reduced form and the structural equations are estimated in the regression

* The equations are overidentified because the number of variables omitted from each exceeds the number of exogenous variables minus one. See M. Nerlove *Estimation and Identification of Cobb-Douglas Production Functions* (Chicago, Ill.: Rand-McNally, 1965).

calculations. The model is applied to the entire university system and to individual institutions and departments.

Aggregate Employment and Salary

Table 9.3 summarizes least-squares estimates of the reduced form employment and salary equations for the entire university system. In the even-numbered years from 1920 to 1964 for which data exists, changes in the number of faculty are well explained by the employment equations (1)–(4), with both shifts in demand due to enrollment, the income of univer-

Table 9.3 Reduced Form Employment and Salary Equations of the Faculty Labor Market Model, 1920–1964[a]

Equation Number	*Even-numbered Years Covered*	*Regression Coefficients and t-Statistics*[b]						
		Constant	Δln ENR	Δln INC	Δln ISAL	Δln QUL	ln (FAC/STD)$_{-1}$	R^2
PANEL A: Employment Equations—the Dependent Variable is Δln FAC								
(1)	1920–1964	−0.06 (1.93)	0.33 (4.45)	—	—	0.22 (2.33)	−0.40 (3.56)	0.847
(2)	1920–1924, 1952–1964	—	0.50 (5.96)	—	−0.10 (1.63)	0.01 (.10)	−0.18 (5.26)	.761
(3)	1932–1964	—	0.21 (4.26)	0.24 (3.10)	−0.14 (1.10)	0.31 (4.47)	−0.11 (2.23)	.924
(4)	1932–1942, 1952–1964	—	0.37 (3.13)	0.16 (1.19)	−0.14 (1.09)	—	−0.16 (4.33)	.883
PANEL B: Salary Equations—the Dependent Variable is Δln SAL								
(5)	1920–1942, 1952–1964	0.02 (0.73)	0.29 (1.82)	—	0.14 (1.31)	−0.02 (.20)	—	0.340
(6)	1932–1942, 1952–1964	—	−0.09 (0.39)	0.43 (1.78)	0.11 (0.45)	—	0.05 (0.63)	0.640

SOURCES: For enrollment, employment, and income figures: Office of Education; for salary figures: B. Ruml and S. Tickton, *Teaching Salaries, Then and Now* and National Education Association.

[a] The years chosen in the samples are dictated by the availability of data and problems of war periods. The income of universities (INC) is available only for the period 1932–1964.

[b] The levels of significance of the *t*-statistics are:

Eq. No.	*1%*	*5%*
(1),(3)	2.90	2.11
(2),(5)	2.95	2.13
(4),(6)	3.01	2.16

sities, and attempts to attain the desired faculty-student ratio; and shifts in supply due to the number of specialists and nonacademic salaries contributing to the explanation. Each regression has a substantial coefficient of determination and significant estimates of the critical parameters.

The demand-shift variables account for roughly two thirds of the R^2, with enrollment having an especially sizable effect on employment: ignoring university income, the enrollment-elasticity is about one half (equation 2); the inclusion of income reduces the coefficient, indicating that part of the enrollment effect is related to its possibly complex link to income.[9] Since demand has a substantial effect on employment only when supply is elastic, the estimates point to an elastic supply of faculty.

Rearrangement of terms in the employment equation produces a relation for the faculty : student ratio, a variable of central importance in models of education. As shown in Figure 9.3, the ratio varies considerably

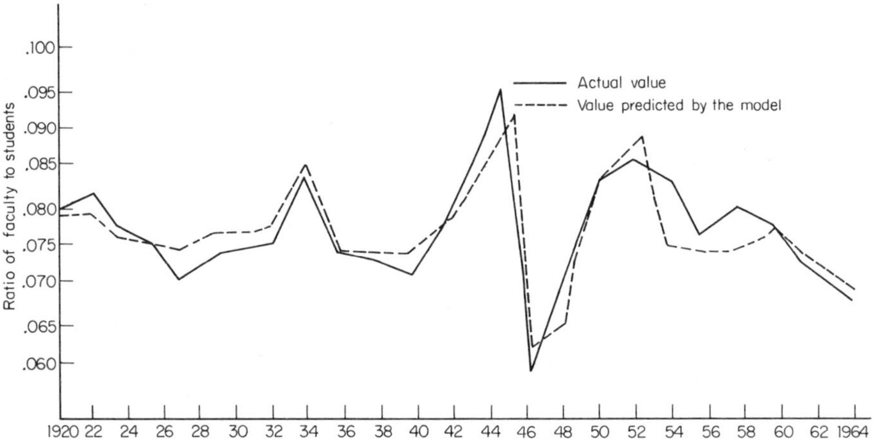

9.3 Faculty-student ratios 1920–1964

from year to year in accord with changes in the explanatory variables of the model. Except for normative purposes, the oft-assumed constancy of the faculty : student ratio is invalid and can be replaced by an economic explanation of its variation over time.

In contrast to the "good" employment regressions, the reduced-form salary equations give poor statistical fits to the historical experience (Table 9.3, equations 5–6). No current period variable, with the exception of the budget of universities, has a well-defined effect on salaries. For various reasons — the existence of the internal salary constraint, nonprofit motivation, and so on — salary determination is a more complex phenomenon than initially envisioned. The model must be modified to explain the pattern of changes in salary.

Aggregate Supply and Demand

Tables 9.4A–9.4C summarize two-stage (and, for comparative purposes, single-stage) least-squares estimates of the structural supply and demand equations for the entire university system. To take account of complexities in salary determination, lagged variables are introduced into the demand equation, with considerable success. The overall results of the calculations provide general support of the model, with estimated coefficients

Table 9.4A Structural Supply Equations of the Faculty Labor Market Model, 1920–1964

(The dependent variable is Δln FAC, 1920–1942 and 1954–1964)[a]

		Explanatory Variables and t-Statistics[b]				
Equation Number	*Estimating Technique*	*Constant*	Δln SAL	Δln ESAL	Δln QUL	R^2
(1)	Ordinary least squares (OLSQ)	0.058 (6.85)	0.47 (4.68)	−0.05 (.92)	0.15 (1.67)	0.74
(2)	Two-stage least squares (TSLQ)	0.059 (5.28)	0.83 (2.96)	−0.11 (1.31)	0.11 (0.56)	0.63

[a] In Tables 9.4A, 9.4B, and 9.4C 1952 is omitted from the supply equation as an extreme outlier, due to the Korean War. Regressions with 1950–52 yield similar results to those in the table; the choice of years in the demand equations is dictated by the limited observations on the university income series.

[b] The levels of significance for the *t*-statistics are: 1%, 2.98; 5%, 2.15.

Table 9.4B Demand Equation with Dependent Variable Δln FAC, 1934–1942 and 1952–1964

		Explanatory Variables and t-Statistics[a]					
Equation Number	*Estimating Technique*	*Constant*	Δln SAL	Δln ENR	Δln INC	ln (FAC/STD)$_{-1}$	R^2
(1)	TSLS	—	−0.14 (.48)	0.40 (3.06)	0.12 (.65)	−0.14 (3.24)	0.79

[a] The levels of significance for the *t*-statistics are: 1%, 2.98; 5%, 2.15.

Table 9.4C Demand Equations with Dependent Variable Δln SAL, 1934–1942 and 1952–1964

		Explanatory Variables and t-Statistics[a]						
Equation Number	*Estimating Technique*	*Constant*	Δ ln FAC	Δln FAC_{-1}	Δln INC	Δln INC_{-1}	ln $(FAC/STD)_{-1}$	R^2
(1)	TSLQ	—	−0.04		0.45		0.05	0.62
			(.10)		(2.69)		(.55)	
(2)	OLSQ	—	−0.37	−0.61	0.44	.44		0.87
			(1.62)	(3.09)	(4.17)	(3.98)		
(3)	TSLQ	—	−0.46	−0.62	0.47	.45		0.86
			(1.94)	(3.09)	(4.37)	(4.05)		

[a] The levels of significance for the *t*-statistics are

Eq. No.	*1%*	*5%*
(1)	2.98	2.15
(2),(3)	2.95	2.13

indicative of supply and demand elasticities on the order of 1.0.[10] Even with the modified salary equation, however, there is an indication that the model misses some of the complexities of the market and could be improved further.

In the case of supply, the equations cover only the even-numbered years from 1920 to 1942 and from 1954 to 1964, with odd years and the World War II period omitted because of the absence of salary data, and the Korean interval (1950–1952) omitted, as an extreme outlier, with little effect on the results. The measures of independent variables are crude: academic salary is the mean professorial salary, not discounted lifetime incomes; the alternative is the average earnings in industry; the number of qualified specialists is approximated by estimates of living Ph.D. and master's graduates. Despite the approximate nature of the data, however, equations (1) and (2) accord the independent variables correct signs and explain from 60 to 75 percent of the variance of employment. Academic salaries are highly significant;* alternative incomes and the stock of specialists are insignificant, probably because industrial earnings are a poor measure of alternatives facing faculty, and the stock a crude measure of qualified specialists.† Because of the incorrect measures of these variables,

* The highly significant constant in the regression may reflect the gradual improvement over time in academic working conditions. In first difference equations the constant picks up the influence of omitted variables that change smoothly.

† Note that because industrial salaries measure the nonacademic income opportunities of faculty as well as the incentive to leave academia, the coefficient on this term should, in any case, be smaller than that on the academic salary variable.

the other regression coefficients are biased. The impact of academic salaries, in particular, is likely to be understated: at the minimum, the elasticity of supply is about 0.80; taking account of the bias, it is probably in the area of 1.00.[11]

A more diverse set of results is obtained with the estimated demand equations (Tables 9.4B and 9.4C). Regressions with current period variables yield contradictory pictures of the market. When employment is the dependent variable, demand is affected by enrollment and the lagged faculty:student ratio (Table 9.4B, equation 1). When salary is dependent, income is the key explanatory variable (Table 9.4C, equation 1). In the salary case the best results are obtained with the addition of lagged income and employment (equations 2 and 3); the R^2 increases substantially and explanatory variables are accorded significant, sensible coefficients. Under this specification the flexibility of salaries to employment ($\Delta \ln$ SAL $\div$ $\Delta \ln$ FAC) is 0.50 in the short run and roughly unity in the long run. University income also has a lagged impact on employment. Budgetary rigidity and nonprofit motivation may be reducing the speed of adjustment to additional funding.

While the addition of lagged employment and income variables improves the ability of the model to explain changes in salary, it does not present a consistent picture of the demand for faculty. The factors affecting salaries are not identical to those affecting employment in the demand regressions. The indication of differential determination of salaries and employment is perhaps not surprising in view of changes in the quality of new faculty and in the number of vacancies that are not reflected in the salary or employment figures. A more complex model that allows for these factors is probably needed to explain observed developments. For the purpose of this chapter, however, the simultaneous allocation model suffices. As it stands, the model gives a tolerably good explanation of past changes in employment and salaries and provides strong evidence that universities adjust faculty employment (and thereby openings for students) to the demand for training. The working assumption that occupational decisions determine the supply of graduates is thus justified by these calculations.

Institution and Department Employment

A valid economic model should be able to explain disaggregate cross-sectional as well as aggregate time series phenomena. To test the ability of the faculty model in this regard, data on employment, university income, and enrollment in 40 major universities and departments in 1952 and

1962 were gathered and used to estimate the reduced form employment equation of the model. By the usual statistical criteria, the model does a good job of accounting for the 1962 pattern of faculty employment and the 1952–1962 changes in employment (Table 9.5), and thus passes this

Table 9.5 Determinants of Faculty Employment for 42 Institutions and Departments

Total Academic Employment, 1962[a]

(1) $\ln(\text{FAC}) = -2.23 + .55 \ln(\text{INC}) + .34 \ln(\text{STD})$ $\quad R^2 = 0.84$

$\qquad\qquad (6.10) \quad (9.12) \qquad\quad (4.14)$

(2) $\ln(\text{FAC/STD}) = 1.03 + .85 \ln(\text{INC/STD})$

$\qquad\qquad (12.1) \quad (14.62)$ $\quad R^2 = 0.94$

Change in Employment, 1952–1962[a]

(3) $\Delta\ln(\text{FAC/STD}) = 0.83 + 0.87\, \Delta\ln(\text{INC/STD})$ $\quad R^2 = 0.78$

$\qquad\qquad (1.2) \quad (11.30)$

Employment in Engineering Departments, 1962[a,b]

(4) $\ln(\text{EFAC})$

$= -1.6 = .25 \ln(\text{INC}) + .52 \ln(\text{ESTD}) + .11 \ln(\text{EGRAD})$ $\quad R^2 = .75$

$\qquad (0.6) \quad (3.00) \qquad\quad (5.24) \qquad\quad (2.85)$

SOURCE: *American Colleges and Universities for basic data.*

[a] The levels of significance for the *t*-statistics are: 1%, 2.58; 5%, 1.96.

[b] Previously undefined variables are: EFAC = engineering faculty; ESTD = engineering enrollment; and EGRAD = fraction of enrolled engineers in graduate programs.

test. As can be seen in the table, the coefficients on the income and enrollment terms explain most of the variation in employment in a consistent manner. The coefficients on parameters in the cross section (equations 1 and 2) and moving cross section (equation 3) regressions are roughly equal, suggesting a stable behavioral relation over time, and compare plausibly with those from the time series calculations.

Generally, the cross section elasticities exceed the time series elasticities presented earlier, probably because the former pick up long-term, permanent adjustments while the time series estimates reflect short-run behavior: the employment-income elasticity, for example, is 0.55 in the former case and 0.20 in the latter, while the enrollment elasticities are 0.34 and 0.21–0.37 respectively. These differences are sufficiently small, however, as to paint a similar picture of responsiveness.

The coefficients in the engineering and total faculty regressions also differ, it should be noted, in a sensible way, with income having a less significant effect on the number of engineering teachers than on the total faculty, and enrollment having a larger effect (compare equations 1 and 4 in Table 9.5). The smaller income effect for engineering is readily explicable by relatively high engineering salaries. The greater impact of enrollment is probably due to the possibility of transferring funds across departments to meet changes in departmental needs. Finally, the positive impact of graduate students on engineering but not on total faculty employment[12] can be traced to the dual role of graduate students in the education process. As students requiring faculty time, graduates make heavy demands on employment: as substitute teachers, laboratory instructors, and section men they reduce demand. In engineering, where relatively few obtain research or teaching assistantships, the former effect dominates, while overall the two effects balance out.

9.3 Doctorate Faculty

We turn next to the choice of an academic career by both new and experienced Ph.D.'s.

New Doctorate Faculty

The number of *inexperienced* Ph.D. graduates hired as faculty changed greatly in postwar years.* In 1955 fewer than 3000 graduates received first academic appointments; in 1965, over 6000. Part of the variation in the number of new appointments results from changes in the willingness of graduates to accept academic jobs. In 1955, 52 percent decided to work for universities, in 1965, 58 percent. Can the change in the supply of new Ph.D.'s to the academic sector be explained by the allocation model?

Two-stage least-squares estimates of the supply equation of the model (with both academic and nonacademic salaries treated as endogenous for the period 1950–1966) provide an affirmative answer.† Annual changes in the number of new Ph.D.'s choosing academic work are explicable by changes in the number of graduates and in relative salaries:

$$\Delta \ln \text{DFAC} = \underset{(6.35)^a}{0.70\,\Delta \ln \text{DOC}} + \underset{(2.70)^a}{0.95\,\Delta \ln \text{SAL}} - \underset{(2.00)^b}{0.70\,\Delta \ln \text{ISAL}} \qquad R^2 = 0.94, \quad \text{D.W.} = 2.39,$$

* The statistics cited relate to *inexperienced* graduates only. I omit about 45 percent of doctorate graduates because they hold full-time jobs at the time of receipt of the degree. See *Teacher Supply and Demand in Universities, Colleges, and Junior Colleges,* National Education Association, for detailed figures on the number of inexperienced and experienced Ph.D. graduates.

† The other variables in this system are enrollment, real Gross National Product, and industrial research and development expenditures. Enrollment shifts the demand for faculty; real GNP and R & D raise the nonacademic demand for specialists.

where

DFAC = number of inexperienced doctorate faculty;
DOC = number of inexperienced graduates;
SAL = salary of faculty;
ISAL = salary of experienced scientists and engineers in industry;
^{a} = significant at 1%; ^{b} = significant at 5%.

From this regression it is apparent that the selection of academic or nonacademic work is governed by economic incentive. The faculty and non-faculty salary terms have significant roughly equal opposite effects on supply, with an elasticity slightly below unity.

The *differential* increase of new Ph.D. faculty by specialty can also be explained within the model. In this case, however, the absence of salaries by specialty limits analysis to the reduced-form employment equation. For the 15 specialties for which data exist, changes in employment for short and long periods of time are accounted for by differential changes in three variables — enrollment, doctorate graduates, and the fraction of graduates employed as faculty in the base years:

Short-run (1960–1964)

$$\Delta \ln \text{DFAC} = \underset{(1.47)}{0.31} + \underset{(1.84)^b}{0.22}\,\Delta \ln \text{ENR} + \underset{(10.30)^a}{1.04}\,\Delta \ln \text{DOC} - \underset{(1.68)}{0.09}\,\ln \text{SHR},$$
$$R^2 = 0.87$$

Long-run (1954–1964)

$$\Delta \ln \text{DFAC} = \underset{(1.83)}{0.56} + \underset{(2.26)^b}{0.26}\,\Delta \ln \text{ENR} + \underset{(5.49)^a}{0.88}\,\Delta \ln \text{DOC} - \underset{(1.95)^b}{0.16}\,\ln \text{SHR} \quad ;$$
$$R^2 = 0.76$$

where

DFAC = the number of inexperienced doctorate faculty;
ENR = the number of enrolled students;
DOC = the number of inexperienced doctorate graduates;
SHR = the fraction of inexperienced graduated employed as faculty in the base year;
^{a} = significant at 1%; ^{b} = significant at 5%.

The chief explanatory variable here is the supply of graduates, which clearly limits possible increases in new Ph.D. faculty. The negative fit on the share term shows that the limitation becomes increasingly stringent as the proportion of graduates electing to teach increases. Although less significant, the positive impact of enrollment on new faculty points to an adjustment in the composition of doctorate teachers to changed educational needs.

Mobility of Experienced Ph.D.'s

Do experienced Ph.D. workers also select their area of employment on the basis of economic incentive? What is the role of the sectoral mobility of experienced men in the allocation of Ph.D.'s among employers?

There are two sets of evidence pertaining to these issues: a recent study by the National Academy of Sciences–National Research Council on "the factors involved in switching from academic to nonacademic employment and vice versa" [13] and the sectoral employment data examined in Chapter 7.

Gross mobility among sectors of employment is quite high according to the NAS-NRC study, with many Ph.D.'s moving into or out of academic jobs. By 1963, when the study was conducted, over one in four living Ph.D. graduates had made such a shift at least once. With more time for mobility, older specialists reported even greater numbers of shifts; half of the 1935 cohort, for example, had shifted into or out of academic work during their lives. Perhaps because of postwar prosperity, recent cohorts report more frequent changes at similar stages in the life cycle.

Despite sizable gross flows, however, *net* sectoral mobility was slight in the 1935–1963 period, with the number of Ph.D.'s entering academia roughly equal to the number leaving (Table 9.6). Within particular subperiods, an economically sensible pattern of net flows is discernible. During World War II for example, and in the early 1950s, when enrollment fell, the flow favored nonacademic work. In the post-1955 period, when enrollment and salaries in academia increased, experienced workers shifted to higher education.

Although net flows averaged just 0.18 percent of the doctorate work force per annum and had a peacetime peak of only 0.26 percent, they are an important element in the gradual reallocation of doctorate workers among sectors of employment. With approximately 250,000 Ph.D. specialists in 1968, for example, a flow of 0.18 percent of the stock produces a shift of about 500 persons. For comparison, the usual change in the sectoral allocation of *new* Ph.D.'s is on the order of 2–3 percent of graduates, or roughly 500 persons also. Thus, although experienced workers are less responsive than new Ph.D.'s, they are equally important in the allocative process.

Table 9.6 Distribution of Doctorate Workers between Academic and Nonacademic Employment and Percentage Changing Place of Employment, 1935–1963

Time Period for Change in Place of Employment	*% of Ph.D.'s in Academic Work at Start of Period*	*Relative No. Leaving Academic Employment*	*Net Change*[a,b]	*Relative No. of Ph.D.'s Leaving Nonacademic Employment*	*% of Ph.D.'s in Nonacademic Work at Start of Period*
1935–1940	0.602	0.035	−0.009	0.044	0.398
1940–1945	.591	.079	−0.047	.032	.409
1945–1950	.586	.071	0.014	.057	.414
1950–1955	.613	.050	−0.026	.024	.387
1955–1960	.595	.035	0.007	.042	.405
1960–1963	.611	.034	0.007	.041	.389
1963 resulting distribution and total flows	0.622	0.138	−0.012	0.126	0.378

SOURCE: National Academy of Sciences — National Research Council, *Careers of Ph.D.'s.*

[a] Because of the entrance of new Ph.D. graduates into the market, the percentage of Ph.D.'s in a sector does not equal the sum of last period's percentage and the net flow.

[b] Minus sign signifies movement from academic to nonacademic work.

As a means of *increasing* sectoral employment, however, the flow of experienced personnel is of minor significance. Here, a shift of 500 persons amounts to just 10 percent of the number of inexperienced Ph.D.'s hired as faculty and perhaps 15 percent of the number hired as nonacademic specialists in a given year.

Concluding Comments

From the detailed analysis of this chapter two principal findings emerge. First, and most significantly, the investigation provides strong evidence of a responsive educational system in which facilities constraints are of only minor importance. Second, the econometric computations substantiate the usefulness of the simultaneous allocation model as a tool of analysis. They show (i) that employment in the entire system and in individual institutions or departments adjusts to educational needs, (ii) that the supply of faculty responds to monetary incentive, and (iii) that (as in other markets) salaries are determined with a lag. In sum, given the constraints under which it operates, the *education market* functions in a flexible, economically rational way.

10 Career Plans and Occupational Choice

Our empirical investigation of career choice has thus far considered only the surface connections between market conditions and labor supply. The individual perceptions of job opportunities, expectations of income, and marginal aspects of decision-making that underlie the theory of choice have been ignored. Chapters 10 and 11 fill this analytic gap with an examination of *survey* data regarding career plans, labor market information, and the economic factors that affect students decisions. Survey evidence provides a perspective on supply different from that of econometric calculations and, in the absence of controlled experimentation, is necessary for understanding the operation of the market.[1]

10.1 The Survey Questionnaire

In the 1966–1967 academic year, a questionnaire consisting of three pages of questions and an instruction sheet was mailed to approximately 10,000 randomly selected male students in the Boston area and 1,000 additional men in the University of Massachusetts at Amherst. The Boston area colleges covered by the survey were Harvard University, Massachusetts Institute of Technology, Boston University, and the University of Massachusetts at Boston. Twenty-eight hundred usable questionnaires were returned, giving a response rate of about 25 percent.[2] Women students were excluded from the survey because their career decisions are likely to involve different considerations from those of men. A copy of the completed questionnaire is contained in Appendix B.

Questionnaire responses were examined for the entire group of students taken together. Preliminary analysis revealed only slight variation in replies according to school affiliation, the principal cause of variation being the interfield composition of student bodies (engineers at M.I.T., for example). Thus, aggregation into a single sample is legitimate in the present instance.

The chief problem with the survey is the possibility of "response bias" due to differences between respondents and nonrespondents. Although the absence of a direct check on nonrespondents prevents a definitive analysis of the bias, the available evidence points to a small impact. First, many results depend on comparisons of subgroups of respondents and will be valid unless the behavior of nonrespondents is perversely related to the groupings. Second, few differences in answers are found between respondents from schools or classes with differing rates of response. The questionnaires from small classes where personal distribution guaranteed a very high rate of return are similar to those for the entire sample. Third, virtually identical questions in more carefully controlled studies elicit similar responses. (See the discussion in Appendix C.) Failure to adjust for response bias may limit the scope of the survey but is unlikely to seriously distort its substantive finding.

10.2 The Career Decision

When do students choose a career? Are decisions final or subject to change? How much consideration is accorded alternative possibilities? How do college studies relate to career plans?

Timing and Flexibility

Figure 10.1 summarizes the survey evidence regarding the timing and flexibility of career plans. Two aspects of the decision process stand out in the responses:

1) In most cases final career plans are made during the college period. Three fourths of the undergraduates responding to the questionnaire and seven eighths of the graduate students regard the school years as the time of decision. A sizable minority of graduate students, in fact, claim to be still in the process of final selection (Panel A). Consistent with these responses is the fact that most students report having seriously considered alternative occupational possibilities since graduation from high school (see Panel B).

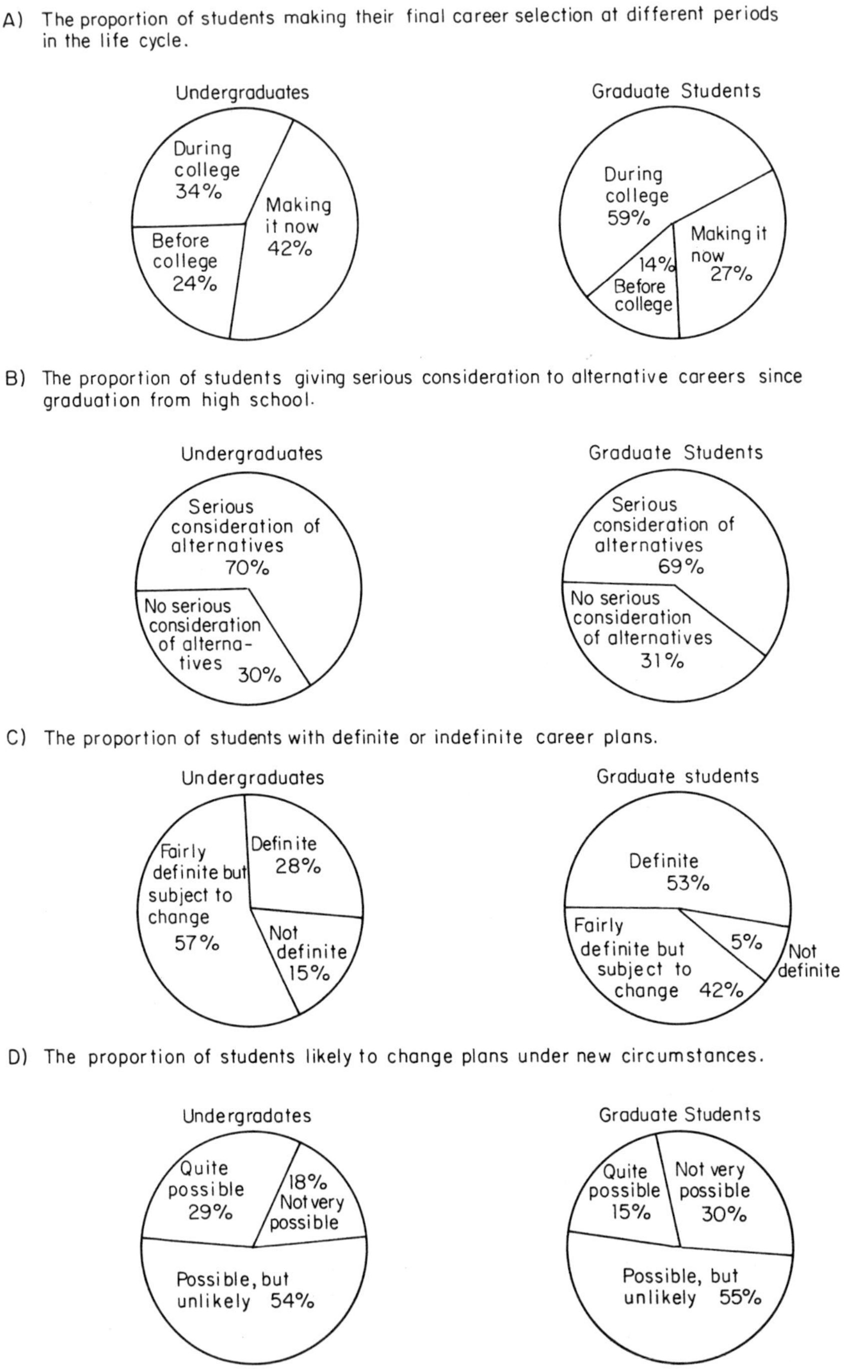
A) The proportion of students making their final career selection at different periods in the life cycle.
Undergraduates
During college 34%
Making it now 42%
Before college 24%
Graduate Students
During college 59%
Making it now 27%
14% Before college
B) The proportion of students giving serious consideration to alternative careers since graduation from high school.
Undergraduates
Serious consideration of alternatives 70%
No serious consideration of alterna-tives 30%
Graduate Students
Serious consideration of alternatives 69%
No serious consideration of alternatives 31%
C) The proportion of students with definite or indefinite career plans.
Undergraduates
Fairly definite but subject to change 57%
Definite 28%
Not definite 15%
Graduate students
Definite 53%
Fairly definite but subject to change 42%
5%
Not definite
D) The proportion of students likely to change plans under new circumstances.
Undergradates
Quite possible 29%
18% Not very possible
Possible, but unlikely 54%
Graduate Students
Quite possible 15%
Not very possible 30%
Possible, but unlikely 55%

10.1 Selected aspects of the career decision process, undergraduate and graduate males, 1967

2) For many students, career plans are amenable to change during college in response to new information or conditions. According to Panel C of the figure, the plans of nearly 60 percent of the undergraduates and 42 percent of graduate students are subject to change, though fairly definite. Fifteen percent of the undergraduates report that they have not yet made a definite choice. Similarly, a sizable minority of undergraduate and graduate students believe that additional information about job opportunities would alter their plans. The majority regard a change as "possible but unlikely" (Panel D).

What is important about this picture of decision-making is its consistency with the regression analysis of preceding chapters. According to the regression calculations, the supply of graduates responds to market stimuli during college and is only slightly affected by a lagged response to new conditions. The survey confirms this pattern of responsiveness and time delay.

The time at which a student makes his career decision and his amenability to change varies according to intended area of specialization (Table 10.1). In fields with lengthy cumulative training, early decisive commitments are frequent. Students in medical and scientific specialties, for example, tend to choose their careers before college (column 1) to give only limited attention to alternatives thereafter (column 2) and to remain in their chosen major (column 3).

Undergraduates in the sciences are more likely to have definite plans than other students (column 4). Nearly all biology majors report definite or fairly definite career plans compared to 75 percent of sociology majors. As a consequence, the scientific and medical markets can be expected to operate differently from those for nonscientists. Adjustments in supply will be slower, and more time will be required to attain equilibrium. The statistical findings of substantial cobweb fluctuations in engineering and disequilibrium in chemistry, mathematics, and doctorate fields are consistent with this evidence.

College Studies and Career Choice

For most students the selection of a college major and of an occupation are closely related decisions. According to the survey responses presented in Figure 10.2, the majority of undergraduates and over 80 percent of graduate students expect to work permanently in the area of their college major (Panel A). Even those students expecting to work outside the major are generally vocationally motivated, the majority choosing the field for the

Table 10.1 Career Plans of College Students, by Major Field of Study

	(1) Percentage of Students Choosing Career Before College	(2) Percentage Giving Serious Consideration to Alternatives	(3) Percentage Switching Majors in College	(4) Percentage with Career Plans Which Are —			(5) Percentage Intending to Seek Employment in Major Field		
				Definite	*Fairly Definite*	*Indefinite*	*Permanently*	*For Some Time*	*Not at All*
				UNDERGRADUATES					
Biology	37	62	10	38	54	8	75	12	13
Chemistry & Geology	36	61	10	29	57	14	83	7	10
Engineering	25	66	8	31	60	9	67	13	20
Physics	32	69	10	23	59	18	74	7	19
Mathematics	28	68	14	21	63	17	65	4	31
Economics	14	79	20	25	55	20	42	23	35
Sociology	11	83	23	22	53	25	38	15	47
Psychology	24	70	22	37	45	18	58	18	24
Government	17	77	18	28	53	18	46	19	35
English	18	75	14	22	56	22	40	10	50
History	17	76	13	28	53	20	31	20	49
Languages	31	64	15	25	64	11	53	19	28
Arts and Philosophy	32	65	8	42	45	12	73	3	24
Business	20	73	8	18	69	12	63	11	26

Table 10.1 (*Continued*)

			GRADUATE STUDENTS						
Biology	12	70	41	59	41	0	84	2	14
Chemistry and Geology	10	60	30	37	58	5	89	1	10
Engineering	20	61	23	47	46	8	82	5	13
Physics	23	63	29	56	40	4	96	1	3
Mathematics	18	60	35	63	28	10	83	3	14
Economics	11	81	55	55	39	5	82	9	9
Government	14	74	24	39	53	8	70	14	16
Other Social Sciences	7	76	60	74	26	0	93	0	7
English, History, and Languages	11	73	52	66	34	0	84	7	9
Arts and Philosophy	15	83	49	56	39	4	79	8	13
Business	5	84	65	46	51	4	78	7	15
Education	9	91	68	64	36	0	95	0	5
Law	12	78	49	51	39	10	67	6	27
Medicine	28	55	26	85	15	0	94	2	4

career preparation it offers. Prospective lawyers, for example, study political science to obtain potentially useful vocational training. Less than 10 percent of the survey respondents gave enjoyment of the subject as the principal reason for choosing a major. The dominance of vocational considerations suggests that the consumption component of college may be relatively small after all.

The educational and occupational plans of undergraduates differ by area of specialization.* Almost all students in the scientific fields plan on graduate or medical school, while many in business expect to work upon graduation. Column (5) of Table 10.1 shows that majors in engineering, business, science, philosophy and the arts (including architecture and music) usually foresee a permanent career in the field of their major. By contrast, students in social science, English, and languages often expect to work in other areas.

Interfield differences in the likelihood of working in the college major disappear at the graduate level, where nearly everyone is in a field related to his future occupation. Table 10.1 (column 5) shows, for example, that 82 percent of graduate economics students, 82 percent of engineering students, 84 percent of the biologists, and a like number of others expect permanent jobs in their fields of study.

As students move up the educational ladder a relatively large number change their major. Panel B of Figure 10.2 and column 3 of Table 10.1 present the survey data regarding this form of mobility. The figure shows that over 40 percent of graduate students switched majors, generally upon entry to graduate school. Switching is common in fields where undergraduate curricula are often unavailable, such as law, business, or education (Table 10.1, column 3). The value of mathematical training induces students with a variety of career intentions to major in mathematics as undergraduates. Nearly half of the baccalaureate mathematics majors earning Ph.D.'s in the 1957–1961 period received their doctorates in other fields.[3]

The relationship between occupational choice and college studies is not unidirectional. Success or failure in academic work affects the career

* The vast majority of undergraduate respondents plan some postgraduate training. This is the culmination of a long-term increase in graduate or professional training, particularly at high-quality institutions, and is not attributable to the 1967 draft law, which deferred graduate students. In the country as a whole the ratio of first-year graduate students (including older persons) to bachelor's graduates rose steadily from 0.32 in 1954 to 0.72 in 1965.

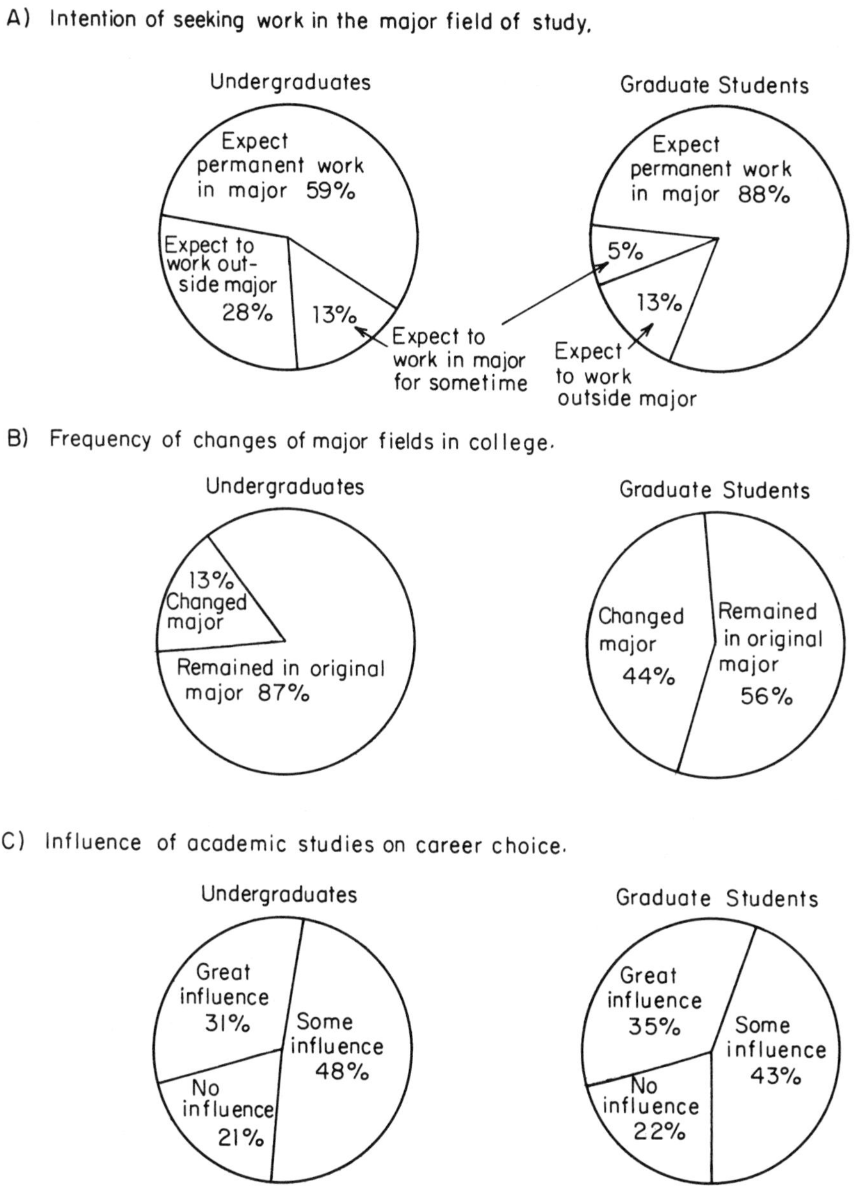

10.2 The relation of college studies to career choice

plans of many students. One third feel that academic success or failure greatly influences their career decision while another third see a more moderate influence (Figure 10.2, Panel C). Classwork is especially important to individuals considering academic careers, with 50 percent of prospective teachers citing academic studies as an important guide in career choice compared to 17 percent of prospective businessmen.

10.3 Interrelation of Specialties

In this section the relation of field of study to occupation and the alternative careers considered by students are examined in greater detail. The tools of analysis are an education–occupation matrix like that of Chapter 3, which shows the career intentions of students by fields of study, and an alternative career matrix, whose elements are the number of students with different alternative career possibilities.

Education-Occupation Coefficients

Table 10.2 presents separately the row coefficients from the 1967 education–occupation matrix for undergraduate and graduate students. The coefficients are the *fraction* of students in each major planning work in the relevant careers. For example, the figure in row 1, column 1, indicates that 21 percent of undergraduate biology majors intend to become biological or agricultural scientists.

The relation of fields to careers described by the coefficients fits a sensible pattern. Among undergraduates there is a wide dispersion of row coefficients in fields like the social sciences and limited dispersion in the sciences. Psychology is the only undergraduate social science major closely tied to work in the field. In engineering, on the other hand, the major is definitely preparation for the career. Sixty-five percent of engineering students foresee permanent jobs as engineers. In other fields, schooling is closely related to area of work when teaching is included with the principal occupation. Sixty-one percent of the English students, for example, plan on literary or teaching careers. Two thirds of the language majors anticipate teaching. Four fifths of "arts and humanities" majors expect jobs in areas related to their majors. All fields send some persons into business and teaching. At the graduate level, the matrix approaches a one-to-one correspondence between training and work. Here, most students in every field, including the social sciences, intend to work in the area of their major as scientists or as teachers.

The relationship of schooling to work can also be examined from the perspective of occupations. Rearrangement of the education–occupation matrix by dividing elements by column totals shows the fraction of specialists in different occupations trained in various majors. Not surprisingly, these "column coefficients" show a substantial dependence of careers on particular college fields. Both scientific and nonscientific occupations draw on students from a limited set of related majors. Fifty percent of the prospective public officials, for example, major in political science. A majority of those interested in business study business (47 percent), economics (11 percent), or engineering (20 percent).

In sum, there is a close relation between college majors and careers. Evidently students select majors for the vocational preparation they offer and plan to work in careers for which the major provides training. This means that the demand for education depends on the demand for specialized labor and that the number of graduates determines the supply of specialists, as postulated in the models of Chapter 2.

Alternative Careers

Some evidence on the potential cross-elasticity of supply among occupations — the likelihood of their competing for the same workers — is presented in the alternative occupation matrix of Table 10.3. The matrix records the fraction of students who consider a career to be the closest alternative to their present choice. The element in column 2, row 2, for example, shows that 31 percent of prospective lawyers view business as their principal alternative career.

The matrix has a well-defined pattern, with students in the sciences considering science, medicine, or engineering as the main competitors for their talent while those outside the sciences regard nonscientific work as their closest alternative. Nearly two thirds of the prospective physicists, for example, give serious consideration to scientific, engineering, or medical jobs compared to just one fourth of the nonscientists.[4] Some occupations — business and, to a lesser extent, medicine and teaching — are seriously considered by students in all specialties. Many prospective scientists and businessmen have thought of a career in engineering.

The tendency of men in particular occupations to consider fields with similar subject matter does not restrict the matrix coefficients completely. There is substantial *diversity* in the alternatives of students in most fields. One third of the potential engineering work force, for example, expressed

Table 10.2 Education–Occupation Matrix 1967: Percentage of Students Intending to Work in Specified Occupations

Major / *Intended Occupation*	*Biological and Agricultural Scientists*	*Medicine*	*Chemist and Geologist*	*Engineer*	*Physicist*	*Mathematician & Statistician*	*Other Sciences*	*Social Scientist*	*Social Worker*	*Government*	*Law*	*Literary Careers*[a]	*Architect*	*Entertainment*[b]	*Clergy*	*Business & Accounting*	*Teaching*	*Miscellaneous Others*	*Total*
								UNDERGRADUATES											
Biology	21	54	3	0	1	0	0	1	0	1	1	1	1	1	2	2	11	0	100
Chemistry and Geology	5	11	54	0	4	0	2	0	0	0	1	0	0	0	0	1	20	2	100
Engineering	0	1	2	65	0	0	1	0	0	1	0	0	1	1	0	21	5	2	100
Physics	0	4	1	10	54	1	4	1	0	0	2	0	2	0	0	2	19	0	100
Mathematics	2	2	1	12	2	30	2	0	3	0	2	0	0	1	0	13	27	3	100
Economics	0	6	0	2	0	0	0	9	0	6	21	1	1	1	0	45	7	1	100
Sociology	1	11	1	0	0	0	2	14	2	0	14	9	3	1	0	17	21	4	100
Psychology	0	7	0	0	0	0	0	32	7	2	2	5	2	3	0	2	29	9	100
Government	1	2	0	0	0	1	0	3	0	20	41	2	1	0	1	11	17	0	100
English	0	7	0	0	0	1	0	3	3	0	4	26	0	7	1	12	35	1	100
History	0	10	1	0	0	0	0	2	0	12	24	3	0	0	1	17	29	1	100
Languages	0	3	0	3	0	0	6	0	0	8	8	0	0	0	0	6	64	2	100
Arts and Philosophy	2	0	0	0	2	3	0	0	0	2	2	5	23	29	2	3	26	1	100
Business	0	0	0	1	0	1	0	1	1	1	8	11	0	1	0	72	2	1	100
Education	0	0	0	0	0	0	0	0	5	0	0	0	0	10	0	0	77	8	100

Table 10.2 (*Continued*)

								GRADUATE STUDENTS											
Biology	23	5	0	0	0	0	0	0	0	0	0	0	0	0	0	3	68	1	100
Medicine	0	96	0	0	0	0	0	0	0	0	0	0	0	0	0	0	4	0	100
Chemistry and Geology	1	3	27	7	0	0	5	1	0	0	3	0	0	0	0	3	50	0	100
Engineering	1	0	1	60	0	0	2	0	0	0	0	0	1	0	0	9	22	4	100
Physics	0	0	0	2	49	0	2	0	0	0	0	0	0	0	0	3	44	0	100
Mathematics	0	0	0	15	0	18	0	0	0	0	0	0	0	3	0	3	60	1	100
Economics	0	3	0	3	0	0	0	30	0	0	0	0	0	0	0	14	50	0	100
Government	0	0	3	3	0	0	0	0	0	26	0	3	5	3	0	5	52	0	100
Other Social Sciences	0	0	0	0	0	0	0	29	17	2	0	0	2	0	2	0	45	3	100
Law	0	0	0	0	0	0	0	0	0	3	88	2	0	0	0	5	2	0	100
English, History, Languages	3	3	0	0	0	0	0	0	0	0	3	3	0	0	0	0	88	0	100
Art, Music, Religion	0	0	0	4	0	0	2	0	0	2	0	6	18	14	17	32	18	5	100
Business	0	0	0	1	0	1	0	0	0	3	1	2	1	1	0	83	7	0	100
Education	0	0	0	0	0	0	0	5	0	0	0	5	0	0	0	5	82	3	100

[a] Literary careers include authors, journalists, public relations personnel, and advertising specialists.
[b] Entertainment careers include actors, TV and radio personnel, and musicians.

Table 10.3 Percentage of Students Considering Various Careers as the Closest

Intended Career / CLOSEST ALTERNATIVE CAREER	ALL NON-SCIENCE	*Business*	*Law*	*Accounting*	*Government*	*Social Science*	*Social Work*	*Clergy*	*Literary Careers*	*Entertainment*	*Architecture*	MEDICINE	TEACHING
Business	39	8	14	1	5	4	1	1	2	1	2	5	17
Law	56	31	0	2	10	3	2	1	4	1	2	8	27
Accounting	27	13	0	0	0	7	7	0	0	0	0	13	13
Government	59	16	14	0	7	1	1	1	7	1	11	3	19
Social Science	46	6	9	1	8	4	4	6	8	0	0	5	12
Social Work	65	0	5	5	0	25	0	15	10	0	5	0	25
Clergy	20	0	10	0	0	0	5	0	0	5	0	10	42
Literary Career	54	9	9	1	8	5	5	1	9	7	0	7	29
Entertainment	58	11	9	0	2	9	2	0	17	4	4	2	24
Architecture	36	8	0	0	5	0	0	3	10	10	0	3	13
Medicine	39	10	10	0	5	5	2	2	2	2	1	6	22
Teaching	49	12	8	1	7	5	1	4	6	4	1	9	4
Chemist	22	11	2	0	0	5	0	0	0	2	2	11	22
Geologist	28	8	4	0	4	0	0	4	4	0	4	8	20
Mathematician	28	8	0	4	2	4	0	0	6	4	0	2	21
Biologist	27	5	2	4	0	2	0	4	4	4	2	19	16
Physicist	23	6	5	1	2	7	0	1	0	1	0	6	14
Aeronautical Engineer	35	27	2	0	0	0	0	2	0	2	2	2	5
Chemical Engineer	37	0	18	0	0	5	0	0	0	0	14	5	18
Civil Engineer	22	11	0	0	0	0	0	0	0	0	11	0	22
Electrical Engineer	30	16	3	0	1	3	0	2	1	2	2	7	13
Metallurgical Engineer	23	19	0	0	0	4	0	0	0	0	0	8	15
Mechanical Engineer	39	18	3	0	0	3	0	6	0	3	6	3	21
Other Engineers	24	7	4	1	1	3	0	3	1	3	1	5	23

[a] Medicine and teaching are not included in the total nonscience category.

a serious interest in nonscientific fields. Twenty percent of the medical and premedical students considered law or business as their closest alternative compared to just 13 percent considering biological science. A similar scattering of coefficients is found for other occupations.

In short, the characteristics and ability requirements of occupations do

Alternative to Their Intended Career

ALL SCIENCE INCLUDING FIELDS NOT LISTED HERE	*Chemist*	*Geologist*	*Mathematician*	*Biologist*	*Physicist*	ALL ENGINEERS	*Aeronautical Engineer*	*Chemical Engineer*	*Civil Engineer*	*Electrical Engineer*	*Metallurgical Engineer*	*Mechanical Engineer*	*Other Engineers*	MISCELLANEOUS OTHERS	*Total*
8	1	1	2	1	2	27	2	3	1	12	1	4	4	4	100
4	1	0	0	1	1	3	0	0	0	1	0	0	2	2	100
21	7	0	7	7	0	14	0	0	0	7	0	0	7	12	100
6	0	0	1	1	3	4	0	0	0	3	0	0	1	9	100
24	0	3	8	4	8	7	1	0	1	4	0	1	0	6	100
0	0	0	0	0	0	5	0	0	5	0	0	0	0	5	100
15	0	0	5	5	0	0	0	0	0	0	0	0	0	13	100
6	0	0	0	0	5	3	0	0	0	0	0	0	3	1	100
8	0	4	2	2	0	6	0	0	0	2	2	0	2	2	100
21	0	0	5	8	5	24	0	0	5	8	8	3	0	3	100
24	5	1	1	13	1	8	2	1	0	3	0	1	1	1	100
20	3	1	4	3	6	15	1	1	1	5	1	2	4	3	100
28	4	0	9	4	11	17	0	11	0	4	2	0	0	0	100
24	8	4	4	4	4	20	0	0	4	88	4	0	4	0	100
31	0	0	2	2	27	14	6	2	0	2	0	2	2	4	100
19	3	0	2	2	7	14	0	2	0	4	0	4	4	5	100
23	5	1	11	0	5	33	2	1	0	18	1	2	9	1	100
32	5	2	9	0	16	26	0	2	0	7	5	7	5	0	100
10	5	0	0	5	0	29	9	0	0	5	5	5	5	1	100
23	6	0	11	6	0	29	0	6	6	6	0	11	0	4	100
27	0	2	8	0	16	23	5	3	0	0	2	6	7	0	100
26	4	8	7	4	0	28	0	12	4	8	0	0	4	0	100
12	3	0	6	0	3	18	0	6	0	6	3	0	3	7	100
16	1	0	3	1	10	26	3	1	1	14	0	4	3	6	100

not constrain the possibilities of students to a narrow group of related fields. As a result, changes in the attractiveness of a particular occupation are likely to have widely dispersed effects on the market, and the cross-elasticities of supply may be more uniformly sized than might otherwise be expected.

10.4 Information in the College Market

One requirement for a properly functioning labor market is that suppliers be well informed about alternative opportunities. The evidence examined next shows that the college market fulfills this requirement.

Subjective Adequacy of Information

As a first step in determining the adequacy of ocupational information students were asked whether they consider the information available *at the time of their decision* as adequate for a wise choice. Most students expressed a reasonable degree of satisfaction with the available information. On the average, information was rated as adequate by 60 percent of the undergraduates and 65 percent of the graduate students, and as barely adequate by an additional 25 percent. A relatively small minority, comprising 16 percent of the undergraduates and 12 percent of the graduate students, consider the available information inadequate.

Students who regard their information as inadequate are found in every field, though with a concentration in nonscientific occupations (where approximately twice as many believe themselves poorly informed as in the sciences). At the *minimum,* however, in every occupation one in ten students views himself as inadequately informed about job opportunities, and one in seven anticipates changing his career plans given additional information. All occupations thus contain some potentially mobile persons and are likely to be affected by changes in economic incentive or in information about job opportunities.

Sources of Information

Students were asked to rate the importance of six sources of career information: family, local community, teachers, guidance counselors, public media, and employment. The first two sources involve personal contacts likely to be sharply circumscribed by the student's background; the others should be available to nearly everyone.[5]

Employment, contact with college professors, and the public media are rated as the most important sources of information (Figure 10.3). Half of the graduate students cite employment and teachers as very important, which reflects the opportunity for career-related summer or part-time jobs and contact with faculty at the graduate level. While of lesser overall importance, personal contacts are highly valuable to some students, particularly those intending to work in "traditional professions." Forty-two percent of medical students, for example, rate the family as a major source

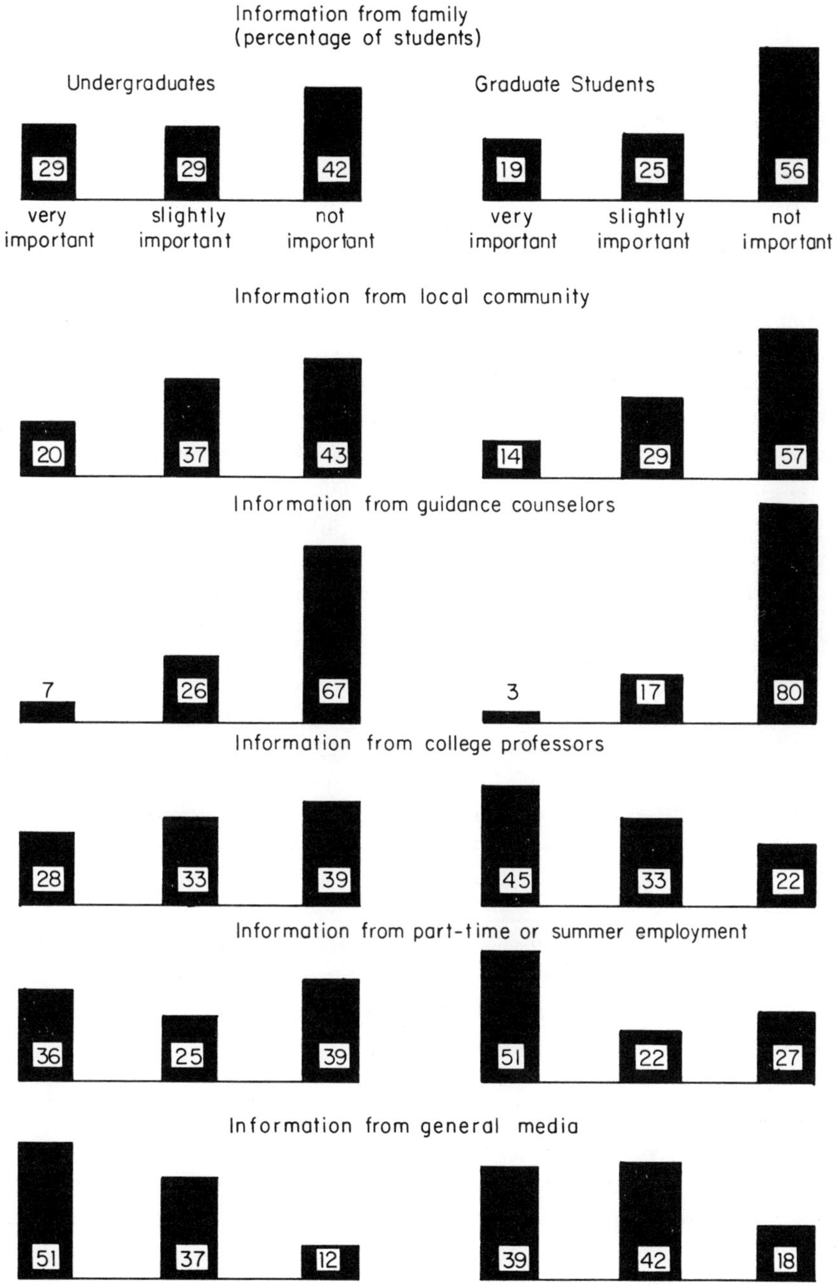

10.3 The importance of channels of job information to undergraduate and graduate students in 1967

of information compared to 29 percent of students in other fields. Occupational inheritance is clearly important in medicine. Guidance counselors are useful to virtually no one.

The significance of employment and teachers in the information network is confirmed by a comparison of the channels used by students who regard information as adequate and those regarding it as inadequate. Forty-seven percent of undergraduates with adequate information view employment as an important source compared to just 25 percent of those who consider information inadequate. Analogous figures for the proportion relying on college teachers for information are 30 and 22 percent respectively.

Reliance on part-time or summer work for information about prospective careers may be a relatively new phenomenon associated with the postwar increase in the fraction of college students obtaining work. From 1947 to 1967 the labor participation of male students roughly doubled.[6] If job-related work has in fact increased and if work experience is, as seems reasonable, an exceptionally good source of information, the information network probably improved in the postwar period.

Accuracy of Information

That students consider themselves well informed does not prove the adequacy or accuracy of their information. This can be done only by comparing student perceptions with actual market conditions. Tables 10.4A,

Table 10.4A Student Perceptions of the Earnings in Five Well-Known Careers[a]

	Mean Ratings of Earnings (1 = highest, 5 = lowest)			*Rank of*	
	At Start of Career (1)	*With 15 Years' Experience (2)*	*Actual Earnings after 15 Years' Experience[b] (3)*	*(2)*	*(3)*
Engineer with Master's degree	2.20	3.49	9,560	4	4
Lawyer	3.17	2.50	14,920	2	2
Doctor	2.72	1.63	19,567	1	1
Professor with Ph.D. degree	3.97	4.51	8,916	5	5
Businessman with MBA degree	2.68	2.54	13,186	3	3

[a] The student ratings presented in Tables 10.4A, B, and C relate to undergraduates only. The ratings of graduate students are virtually identical.
[b] *U.S. Census of Population*, 1960.

Table 10.4B Student Perceptions of Changes in Earnings over the Life Cycle in Five Well-Known Careers

	Change in Mean Rating, from Start of Career to 15 Years (1)	*Actual Ratio of Income after 15 Years to Starting Salary*[a] (2)	*Rank of* (1)	(2)
Engineer with Master's degree	−1.29	1.34	5	5
Lawyer	.60	2.21	2	2
Doctor	1.10	2.68	1	1
Professor with Ph.D. degree	−.54	1.65	4	4
Businessman with MBA degree	−.14	1.74	3	3

[a] *U.S. Census of Population*, 1960. The change in the income of businessmen with the MBA is estimated by the change for all salaried managers.

Table 10.4C Student Perceptions of Changes in Job Opportunities and Need for Workers in Five Well-Known Careers

	Mean of Student Ratings of Improvements in Job Opportunities in Recent Years (1 = highest; 5 = lowest) (1)	*Percentage Changes in Income 1950–1960*[a] (2)	*Rank of* (1)	(2)	*Mean of Student Ratings of Society's Need for Workers (1 = lowest; 5 = highest)* (5)
Engineer with Master's degree	1.76	89	1	1	2.90
Lawyer	4.07	72	5	5	3.94
Doctor	3.13	81	4	2	1.60
Professor with Ph.D. degree	2.80	79	2	3	2.09
Businessman with MBA degree	3.00	75	3	4	4.23

[a] American Association of University Professors, *Bulletin* (Summer 1965).

10.4B, and 10.4C present such a comparison for the mean student ranking of the chief economic characteristics of five "well-known" careers. If students have accurate information they will surely know about the market for these occupations.

The comparisons show remarkable agreement between the perceived and actual position of professions. First, Table 10.4A shows that the

Table 10.5 Student Information on the Doctorate Labor Market Compared to Actual Conditions

	PANEL A: Perceived versus actual earnings in ten Ph.D. specialties					PANEL B: Perceived improvement in job opportunities versus changes in earnings				
	Percentage of Students Rating Earnings High (1) or Low (2) Relative to Average Ph.D. Earnings		*% With High Ratings Minus % With Low Ratings*	*Rank of Col. (3)*	*Rank of Discounted Lifetime Income in 1960*	*Percentage of Students Rating Improvements in Opportunities as Relatively*		*% With High Ratings Minus % With Low Ratings*	*Rank of Col. (3)*	*Rank of Changes in Discounted Lifetime Income, 1950–60*
						High	*Low*			
Field	*(1)*	*(2)*	*(3)*	*(4)*	*(5)*	*(1)*	*(2)*	*(3)*	*(4)*	*(5)*
Chemistry	60	3	57	3	3	3	53	−50	2	4
Engineering	90	1	89	1	1	3	80	−77	1	5
History	20	80	−60	9	9	82	6	76	9	12
Mathematics	25	14	11	5	5	12	32	−20	4	1
English	2	84	−82	10	10	82	3	79	10	7
Genetics	5	18	−13	6	7	14	26	−12	6	6
Botany	1	49	−48	8	8	51	3	48	8	8
Economics	41	10	31	4	4	11	30	−19	5	3
Physics	62	4	58	2	2	3	61	−58	3	2
Political Science	19	34	−15	7	6	32	19	13	7	9

Table 10.5 (*Continued*)

	PANEL C: Perceived versus actual stipend support					PANEL D: Perceived need for additional workers				
	Percentage of Students Rating Stipend Support as		*% With High Ratings Minus % With Low Ratings*	*Rank of Col. (3)*	*Rank of Proportion With Stipends in 1963*	*Percentage of Students Rating Social Need as*		*% With High Ratings Minus % With Low Ratings*	*Rank of Col. (3)*	*Rank of Discounted Life Income in 1960*
Field	*High* (1)	*Low* (2)	(3)	(4)	(5)	*High* (1)	*Low* (2)	(3)	(4)	(5)
Chemistry	69	4	65	2	4	47	7	40	3	3
Engineering	50	10	40	3	5	68	8	60	1	1
History	11	66	−55	10	10	8	73	−65	10	9
Mathematics	31	10	21	4	7	25	16	9	6	5
English	12	65	−53	9	9	12	69	−57	9	10
Genetics	16	22	−6	5	1	34	16	18	5	7
Botany	3	48	−45	8	2	6	54	−48	8	8
Economics	16	23	−7	6	6	34	15	19	4	4
Physics	72	4	68	1	3	50	7	43	2	2
Political Science	15	42	−27	7	8	33	35	−2	7	6

SOURCES: Discounted Incomes: Table 5.8. Changes in lifetime income: National Academy of Sciences-National Research Council, *Profiles of Ph.D.* Fellowship availability: Table 6.2.

student ordering of professions by the income of experienced workers (column 2) is perfectly correlated with the actual ordering (column 3).[7] Second, the information presented in Table 10.4B indicates that students are aware of the shape of age–earnings curves. Fields with steep curves (law, medicine) rise in the rankings between the onset of work and fifteen years' experience, while those like engineering, with flat curves, fall (columns 1 and 2). Third, although improvements in job opportunities or society's need for workers are imprecise phenomena, perceptions of their relative position also seem to be in accord with actual conditions (Table 10.4C).* The ranking of professions by changed opportunities is well correlated with changes in earnings, one potential measure of improved opportunities. The rating of need presented in column 5 places doctors at the top of the list, and thus agrees with the evaluation of most public and private manpower agencies.

It may be concluded that students have accurate information about the characteristics of the five well-known professions.[8]

Information about Doctorate Specialties

Are students well informed only about these well known professions or do they also have accurate information of more specialized careers?

The survey findings contained in Table 10.5 reveal an accurate assessment of the market for specialized doctorate careers. In this case students were asked to identify the three doctorate fields out of a group of ten ranking highest in a specific characteristic and the three ranking lowest. There was a general consensus in the ratings. As columns 1 and 2 of Panel A show, nearly everyone, for example, placed engineering in the top triad by earnings, and history in the bottom triad. To test the accuracy of the student evaluations the rankings are summarized by subtracting the fraction with low ratings from that with high ratings (column 3); this summary statistic is then ranked in column 4 and correlated with the ranking of fields by the actual characteristic presented in column 5.

In the case of the main economic variable, earnings (Panel A), student perceptions of the position of the various fields are nearly perfectly correlated with the actual positions. Moreover, the correlation is not due to simple recognition that pay is higher in technical jobs. As columns 4 and

* In theory, changed opportunities would be measured as a shift in the equilibrium or long-run demand for specialists. Depending on the adjustment mechanism, this might be reflected in changed salaries, employment, or vacancies. In a field like medicine, changes in the number of schools or in admission policies might be interpreted as improved opportunities.

5 show, within the sciences, social sciences, and humanities, perceived and actual income levels are perfectly aligned. Students know that Ph.D. engineers earn more than physicists and physicists more than chemists.

Further evidence that students are accurately informed about the doctorate market is shown in Panel B where improvements in job opportunities are compared to changes in lifetime income. Despite the imprecise meaning of "improvements" in opportunities and the dated estimate of changes (1950–1960), the student ratings are well correlated with the actual ranking. The Spearman coefficient is 0.71, significant at 1 percent.

Panel C of the Table 10.5 shows, surprisingly, that the availability of fellowships is the characteristic about which students are worst informed. Neither undergraduate nor graduate students seem to be aware of the extensive support given biological sciences, rating the most strongly supported fields — genetics and botany — fifth and eighth in availability (column 5). Perhaps they falsely infer that high-paying fields necessarily receive many fellowships.

Finally, the ranking of occupations by social need summarized in Panel D mirrors the ranking by level of income (cf. columns 4 and 5). For these occupations, either perceived need is a function of income or the market is paying the highest salaries in fields with the greatest perceived social value.

11 Expectations and Marginal Decision-Making

The preceding chapter has gone part of the way toward establishing the "micro-foundations" of the economic theory of occupational choice. It has shown that the timing and flexibility of decisions are compatible with the theory, that the selection of a field of study is a good indicator of the career decision, and that students have, for the most part, the kind of occupational information needed for rational supply behavior.

This chapter takes the next logical step in analyzing student decision-making. It compares student income expectations and perceptions of career characteristics to actual incomes and measures of the characteristics. Then it examines the career decisions of two groups of students whose behavior is especially relevant to the theory, those identified as marginal suppliers or as money-oriented.

These investigations offer a good micro-test of the economic theory of choice, for they are based on actual expectations, not rankings of position, and cover a larger sample of careers than the tests presented earlier.

11.1 Expectations of College Students

Do students have reasonable income expectations? Do they consider foregone income in their educational plans? What weight do they *explicitly* place on monetary incentive?

Expectations of Income Opportunities

Survey evidence regarding the realism of student anticipations of future incomes, of the possibility of wealth, and of the variability of earnings are presented in Figure 11.1 and Table 11.1. The figure compares the average

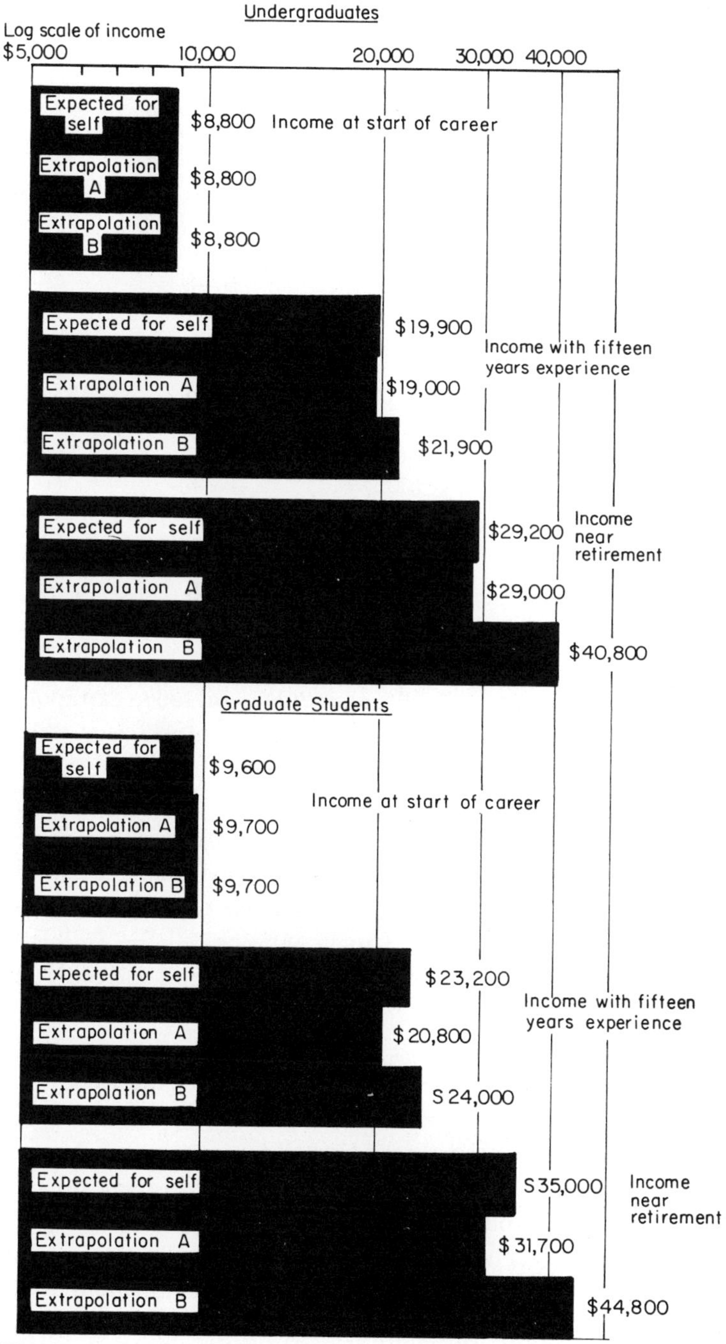

11.1 The incomes students expect in their career compared to extrapolations of 1966 incomes, by level of education and life-cycle status

Table 11.1 Student Expectations of Income, 1967

	At Start of Career	*Fifteen Years Later*	*Near Retirement*
Expected for average worker in career:			
1. Undergraduates	$8,350 (.376)[a]	$17,440 (.539)	$23,700 (.565)
2. Graduates	$9,030 (.288)	$18,140 (.523)	$25,000 (1.826)
Expected for self, students with above-average expectations:			
3. Undergraduates	$9,100 (.419)	$22,700 (.718)	$35,400 (.886)
4. Graduates	$10,000 (.273)	$27,800 (.738)	$43,800 (1.756)

[a] Figures in parentheses are the coefficients of variation in expectations.

income that students expect for themselves in their chosen careers with income projections for three periods in the life cycle: at the start of work, after 15 years' experience, and near retirement. The projections are extrapolations of the income of college graduates in 1966: extrapolation A assumes a 2 percent increase in real income in the future, extrapolation B, a 3 percent increase.

A close relation between expected and projected incomes is shown in the figure. For the beginning of their careers, the earnings that students expect for themselves are virtually identical to the extrapolated incomes. For periods further in the future, the personal income expectations lie between the A and B projections. Undergraduate expectations are especially close to the A projection, which assumed a 2 percent rate of increase. Graduate students have more sanguine expectations. In both cases, the anticipations of future income appear reasonable.

Students were asked to estimate the income that the average college-trained worker in their field could expect as well as what they expected for themselves. The mean income foreseen for average workers and the coefficient of variation (standard deviation divided by the mean) are shown in Table 11.1, lines 1 and 2. These estimates diverge noticeably from the personal income expectations recorded in Figure 11.1. On the average, students expect other workers to earn less than they themselves. The difference in expectations ranges from a 5 percent advantage foreseen by undergraduates at the start of work ($8,800 expected for one's self compared to $8,350 expected for average workers) to a 25 percent advantage expected by graduate students when they approach retirement.

This pattern of anticipations is examined further in lines 3 and 4 of the table, which focus on students with above-average expectations. Approximately half of the respondents fit into this category. The greatest deviation in income expectations is for graduate students looking at the period near retirement. In this case optimistic students expect an 85 percent personal premium.[1]

Two factors appear to underlie the higher personal income expectations of these students. First, many of those in the high-quality institutions covered in the sample probably possess the abilities, background, and knowledge needed for above-average income. The especially high incomes expected by optimistic graduate students, for example, are primarily due to several Harvard Business School students who plan to earn incomes associated with millionaire status. As very high earnings are not unheard of for graduates of the Harvard Business School, these intentions may reflect a realistic evaluation of market opportunities. A second reason for the anticipated personal premium may be what Adam Smith has termed "the over-weaning conceit which the greater part of men have of their own abilities . . . (and) good fortune." [2]

Relative Income Comparisons

As a second step in examining expectations, students were asked whether their careers offered higher earnings, greater variation in earnings, greater opportunity for wealth, and the prospect of greater increases in income than the *average college career*. Assuming that respondents are evenly distributed among fields, the distribution of careers must fall evenly about the median,* with the result that half view their careers as above average and half as below average.[3]

For the average level of earnings in a career, this pattern of evaluations prevailed: 52 percent of students labeled as true the statement, "Earnings in my career are higher than those in most college-level careers"; 48 percent labeled it false. A similar distribution fits evaluations of the chance for

* The assumption that students are comparing their respective fields to the median may not be entirely valid, but is necessary for evaluating the reasonableness of responses. Obviously if 100 percent of students thought their fields were above or below average, they would be unrealistic. Using the uniform distribution as a measuring rod is the best that can be done, given the wording of the questionnaire and available information.

great wealth. Approximately half of the respondents rated their careers as above average in the chance to earn great wealth while half did not. From these data it appears that students have reasonable perceptions of the relative income status of careers and of the relative opportunity to achieve wealth. For possible increases in income and the variation of income in careers, on the other hand, the survey responses suggest that students have a somewhat unrealistic perception of the market. Forty-six percent anticipated more rapid increases of income in their intended careers than in other college level careers; 39 percent anticipated the same rate of change; while just 15 percent expected less rapid increases. Similarly, over two thirds of the survey respondents regarded variation of earnings in their chosen careers as being above average — which, under the assumptions of the analysis, cannot occur in reality.[4]

In contrast to these data, however, responses to other survey questions dealing directly or indirectly with increases in income and variation point to a realistic view of the market.

With respect to changes, the expected increase implicit in anticipated levels of income conforms, according to Figure 11.1, to past rates of change. More significant, perhaps, despite the general tendency to overestimate relative changes, rankings of fields by expected and actual change are closely correlated (see section 11.3). Similarly, the variation of expected incomes corresponds to the variation of actual incomes over the life cycle (see Table 11.2), and the ranking of fields by perceived and actual variation are in accord (section 11.3).

The picture of how students perceive changes in income and variation of income is thus mixed. They appear to exaggerate the position of their careers in relation to other college level careers but not the actual level of income or variation. It may be that the observed deviations from a symmetric distribution of responses simply reflect special concern about the potential variation of personal income in the risky future.

Table 11.2 Variations in Expected and Actual Income
(Coefficients of variation over the life cycle)

Life Cycle Position	*Expected Income*		*Census Income (1960)*
	Undergraduate	*Graduate*	
Start of career	0.38	0.29	0.40
15 years' experience	0.54	0.52	0.85
Near retirement	0.57	0.74	0.90

Foregone Income

In addition to the income earned from work, the income lost by attending school should enter occupational and educational decisions. Accordingly, students were asked: "What do you estimate your yearly (before-tax) earnings would presently be if you were not in school? Assume you were working today in a full-time permanent job." Their responses are summarized in Table 11.3.

Table 11.3 Estimated Foregone Income, 1966–67
(Frequency distribution in thousands of dollars)

Academic Status	*<$4*	*$4–5*	*$5–6*	*$6–7*	*$7–8*	*$8–9*	*$9–10*	*$10+*	*Average*
Undergraduate	9.0	22.9	33.7	16.5	11.4	3.3	3.2	0.0	$5700
Graduate	1.0	3.2	9.6	15.3	27.5	23.1	20.4	0.0	7600

The student estimates compare favorably with the actual earnings of young workers. In 1966, 20-year-old high school graduates and college dropouts earned approximately $5,600–5,800 while college graduates aged 25 made about $7,800 per year.[5] Students thus appear to be well informed about the income opportunities lost through school attendance. Do they take account of these foregone earnings in career and educational decisions?

The survey question requesting students to list "the cost or sacrifice" of school shows that many, though by no means all, are explicitly aware of foregone income. Roughly half of the graduate students and two fifths of the undergraduates volunteered "money," "time," or "employment" as the cost of education. Each of these factors is an element in foregone income. An additional 40 percent of the students listed "living experience" as a cost. This is also related to foregone income. Finally, one third mentioned tuition and one twentieth the postponement of marriage.*

Economic Rationale of College

By comparing estimates of foregone income with expected future incomes it is possible to assess the economic rationale of attending college. If at reasonable rates of interest future earnings compensate for foregone income, the choice of college can be viewed as an economically rational

* The percentages sum to more than 100 because students often listed more than one cost.

decision; otherwise it is a noneconomic decision to be explained by non-pecuniary factors.

At both undergraduate and graduate levels, student perceptions of the differential of future over foregone income are substantial and far in excess of the differentials required for an investment in education to payoff at 6 or 10 percent. Undergraduates, for example, expect earnings after completing school to exceed current income foregone by 55 percent; graduate students foresee a 26 percent advantage to continued schooling. Assuming that undergraduates plan on four additional years of education and graduates students on two,* these figures can be compared with the 46 and 21 percent required for education to pay off with a 10 percent discount rate.[6] If students expect similar differentials for the entire working life, the implicit rate of return to education is 12–13 percent in both cases. When the earnings of graduate students during school are added in, the return to graduate training rises to 16 percent. These "subjective" rates of return correspond to the actual rates described earlier in Chapter 5. It may be concluded that the decision to attend college is economically rational and based on a realistic view of the market.

Subjective Importance of Income

Table 11.4 presents some evidence on the subjective role of income and other characteristics in the choice of a career. The dominant factor in decisions is evidently *interest* in work. More than 80 percent of the students rate interest as very important in career choice, compared to less than 25 percent rating other characteristics as very important (column 1). Although interest in work dominates the career decision, income is still given a significant subjective role. First, to a sizable minority of students, income is a very important factor also. Second, income appears to have special significance in marginal comparisons. Column (4) of the table shows that income and interest are the principal factors that distinguish a chosen career from its closest alternative. At the same time, the majority of students report that when income differs between the chosen and alternative careers, it is *higher* in the former. While not conclusive, this suggests a marginal role for income in the career decision along the lines of the economic theory developed in Chapters 1 and 2.

* The average undergraduate in the sample was midway between his sophomore and junior years. Since most plan to enroll for graduate training, a reasonable estimate of the length of additional schooling is four years. The average graduate student in the sample was in his second year of study and would anticipate approximately two additional years of school.

Table 11.4 Perceived Importance of Job Characteristics in Choosing Career

	Percentage of Students who regard the Characteristic as:			*Percentage of Students Who Perceive Differences in the Characteristic Between Chosen and Alternative Careers*
	Very Important	*Somewhat Important*	*Not Important*	
Characteristic		UNDERGRADUATES		
Earnings	16	49	35	84
Interest	82	12	6	83
Variety of Places of Employment	25	41	33	76
National Need	14	39	47	75
Stability of Earnings and Employment	21	47	32	70
Years of Education Required	10	33	57	68
Sacrifice of Entry	17	44	39	66
		GRADUATE STUDENTS		
Earnings	13	46	41	84
Interest	84	10	5	87
Variety of Places of Employment	26	37	37	75
National Need	13	48	49	67
Stability of Earnings and Employment	12	43	45	67
Years of Education Required	11	27	62	70
Sacrifice of Entry	13	45	42	68

11.2 Expectation of Income by Specialty

To test the realism of income expectations and the reliability of labor market information, this section turns to an examination of the interfield concordance of expected and actual income. The first step is to determine whether or not students with different majors or occupations have significantly different income expectations. Then the accuracy of expectations is tested by rank-correlating them with market salaries.

Levels of Income

Tables 11.5 and 11.6 present the incomes expected by students according to their major field and intended occupation, respectively. The figures

Table 11.5 Incomes Expected by Students, According to Field of Study in 1967, and Analysis of Variance of Expectations[a]

PANEL A: UNDERGRADUATES

Major Field	*Income at Start*	*Income after 15 Yrs.*	*Income upon Retirement*
All Fields	8,350	17,440	23,690
Biology	9,510	20,940	26,850
Chemistry and Geology	8,830	16,780	19,900
Engineering	8,840	16,840	23,900
Physics	9,520	17,760	23,360
Mathematics	8,920	17,990	24,880
Economics	8,270	18,130	25,320
Sociology	8,530	17,540	23,690
Psychology	7,710	16,330	20,590
Government	7,710	16,300	22,250
English	7,260	17,200	21,290
History	7,430	17,200	23,450
Languages	7,180	14,580	17,710
Arts and Philosophy	6,920	14,780	21,610

ANALYSIS OF VARIANCE TABLES[b]

1. For starting salaries.

Source of variance	*Degrees of freedom*	*Sum of squares*	*Mean square*
Major	12	793	66.08
Error	1655	15686	9.47
Total	1667	16479	

F = 6.97

2. For salaries after 15 years.

Source of variance	*Degrees of freedom*	*Sum of squares*	*Mean square*
Major	12	6213	517.75
Error	1635	139385	85.25
Total	1647	145598	

F = 6.07

3. For salaries near retirement.

Source of variance	*Degrees of freedom*	*Sum of squares*	*Mean square*
Major	12	13426	1118.83
Error	1581	271971	172.024
Total	1593	285397	

F = 6.50

Table 11.5 (*Continued*)

PANEL B: GRADUATE STUDENTS

Major Field	*Income at Start*	*Income after 15 Yrs.*	*Income Upon Retirement*
All Fields	9,020	18,140	24,980
Biology	8,932	17,020	21,460
Chemistry and Geology	9,620	16,490	20,610
Engineering	10,710	18,370	23,490
Physics	10,400	16,660	20,240
Mathematics	9,000	16,260	21,110
Economics	8,910	16,460	22,880
Other Social Sciences	8,620	15,500	19,580
Government	7,720	14,670	19,910
Arts and Philosophy	6,860	11,980	15,870
English-History	7,950	13,780	17,600
Languages			
Business	9,360	23,280	35,960
Education	7,410	13,360	16,640
Law	7,450	19,720	31,410
Medicine	9,600	26,500	34,290

ANALYSIS OF VARIANCE TABLES[b]

1. For Starting Salaries:

Source of variance	*Degrees of freedom*	*Sum of squares*	*Mean square*
Major	14	1519	108.50
Error	959	5327	5.55
Total	973	6846	

F = 19.38

2. For Salaries After 15 Years:

Source of variance	*Degrees of freedom*	*Sum of squares*	*Mean square*
Major	14	12,693	906.64
Error	940	18,666	19.86
Total	954	31,359	

F = 45.65

3. For Salaries Near Retirement:

Source of variance	*Degrees of freedom*	*Sum of squares*	*Mean square*
Major	14	45,582	3255.86
Error	914	272,389	298.02
Total	928	314,971	

F = 10.93

[a] All income figures pertain to the average expected for the average worker in a career, not the income expected by the student for himself. Analysis of the personal expectations of students yields results similar to those in the table.

[b] The 1% levels of significance for the *F*-statistic are 2.20 (Panel A) and 2.09 (Panel B).

Table 11.6 Incomes Expected by Students, According to Intended Career in 1967, and Analysis of Variance of Expectations[a]

Prospective Career	*Income at Start*	*Income after 15 Years*	*Income Near Retirement*
All Careers	8,690	17,800	24,350
Biological and Agricultural Science	8,440	15,600	20,270
Medical Specialty	10,370	26,200	33,660
Chemistry	9,830	16,000	20,110
Government	7,610	17,590	24,260
Chemical Engineering	9,000	15,910	22,520
Aeronautical Engineering	9,500	16,000	22,000
Civil Engineering	8,500	15,220	19,940
Electrical Engineering	9,530	16,560	21,300
Metallurgical Engineering	9,690	16,480	21,440
Mechanical Engineering	9,630	17,390	25,290
Other Engineering	9,520	17,630	29,540
Architecture	7,670	17,020	24,400
Physics	10,690	17,920	22,620
Mathematics and Statistics	8,790	17,420	22,200
Social Science	8,780	16,320	21,280
Social Work	6,350	11,790	15,370
Geology and Oceanography	8,320	13,130	15,180
Literary Careers	7,130	17,320	24,440
Clergy	5,670	8,440	12,560
Business	8,810	20,520	31,550
Accounting	7,750	17,200	25,060
Law	7,760	19,530	28,700
Entertainment	7,040	20,380	24,810
Teaching	7,920	13,650	17,150
Scattered Sciences	10,210	16,700	21,770

ANALYSIS OF VARIANCE TABLES[b]

1. For Starting Salaries:

Source of variance	*Degrees of freedom*	*Sum of squares*	*Mean square*
Occupation	25	2,124	84.96
Error	2,574	18,859	7.33
Total	2,599	20,983	

$F = 11.60$

Table 11.6 (*Continued*)

Prospective Career	*Income at Start*	*Income after 15 Years*	*Income Near Retirement*
2. For Salaries After 15 Years:			
Source of variance	*Degrees of freedom*	*Sum of squares*	*Mean square*
Occupation	25	25,895	1,035.80
Error	2,537	202,773	79.93
Total	2,562	228,668	
	F = 12.96		
3. For Salaries Near Retirement:			
Source of variance	*Degrees of freedom*	*Sum of squares*	*Mean square*
Major	25	42,436	1,697.44
Error	2,457	601,388	244.77
Total	2,482	643,824	
	F = 6.93		

[a] As in Table 11.3, all income figures pertain to the average income foreseen for the average worker in a career, not to personal income expectations.
[b] The 1% level of significance for the F-statistic is 1.79.

reveal significant differences in expectations for the start of work, after fifteen years' experience and near retirement by area of specialization. Mathematics majors, for example, have much higher income expectations than language majors — $8920 versus $7180 at the start of their working life; $17,990 versus $14,580 after 15 years' experience; $24,480 versus $17,720 near retirement (Table 11.5, Panel A). Similarly, prospective doctors, businessmen, and lawyers generally expect higher earnings in their careers than do future teachers, social workers, and clergy (see Table 11.6). Statistically, the analyses of variance computations summarized in each table attribute a significant fraction of income variation to occupation or field of study, as the case may be. The array of mean expected incomes can thus be taken as a picture of how students perceive the structure of salaries.

Rank correlation comparisons of the expected incomes with incomes observed in the market point to a realistic formation of expectations and a well-informed body of decision makers. Despite difficulties in obtaining up-to-date measures of actual income for fields comparable to those in the survey,[7] all of the comparisons yield Spearman coefficients significant at 1 percent or better.

First, the comparisons in Table 11.7A and 11.7B show a very close

Table 11.7A Rank Order Comparison of Expected and Actual Starting Salaries, by Undergraduate Major

Major	*Rank of Expected Starting Salary 1967*[a]	*Rank of Actual Salary of Majors*[a,b] *1960*
Physics	1	2
Mathematics	2	6
Engineering	3	1
Chemistry and Geology	4	5
Sociology	5	12
Economics	6	4
Business	7	3
Psychology	8	9
Government	9	7
History	10	11
English	11	13
Languages	12	14
Arts and Philosophy	13	8
Education	14	10

SOURCE: Actual salary figures from *Two Years After the College Degree*, National Science Foundation (Washington, D.C.).

[a] The rank correlation coefficient is 0.67. The 1% significance level is 0.64.

[b] The 1960 salaries of the class of 1958 are likely to be good indicators of starting salaries.

correlation between the rank order of expected *starting salaries* and actual earnings of young graduates several years earlier. In Table 11.7A the expected salaries of students in 14 undergraduate majors is correlated with the actual salaries of graduates in these fields in 1960 at 0.67. In Table 11.7B the ranking of intended occupation by expected salary is correlated with the ranking of occupations by the 1960 earnings of young college graduates at 0.67.

Second, for the limited number of fields in which more recent data exist, both the level and rank order of expected salaries are closely aligned with actual earnings in the market. The correlation between student expectations and the 1967 rates given for nine sharply defined scientific-engineering fields by the College Placement Council is 0.85. With respect to levels of earnings, graduate students intending to work as engineers anticipate starting at $10,700, on the average, while surveys report that beginning M.S. engineers earned from $9,500 (Endicott placement data) to $10,000 (College Placement data) in industry in 1966–1967. Since students are in contact with recruiters, with recent graduates, and through summer

Table 11.7B Rank Order Comparison of Expected and Actual Starting Salaries, by Intended Occupation

Occupation	*Rank of Starting Salaries Expected by 1967 Undergraduates*[a]	*Rank of 1960 Earnings of Young College Graduates*[a,b]
Physics	1	6
Medical Specialty	2	1
Chemistry	3	12
Mechanical Engineering	4	9
Electrical Engineering	5	2
Other Engineering	6	7
Aeronautical Engineering	7	3
Business	8	4
Social Science	9	11
Mathematics and Statistics	10	8
Civil Engineering	11	10
Biological and Agricultural Science	12	17
Teaching	13	16
Law	14	5
Accounting	15	14
Architecture	16	15
Government	17	13
Clergy	18	18

SOURCE: Actual salary figures are from U.S. Census of Population (1960), *Occupation by Earnings and Education.*

[a] The rank correlation coefficient is 0.67. The 1% level of significance is 0.56.

[b] The earnings figures are for men aged 25–34 as reported in the U.S. Census of Population.

or part-time work, with prospective employers, accurate notions of the going rate for beginners is perhaps not surprising.

Further analysis of the connection between expected and actual salaries indicates that realistic expectations and accurate knowledge are not limited to starting rates. The incomes expected for fifteen years' experience and near retirement are well correlated with the actual income of middle-aged and older workers. In particular, the rank order of salaries by intended occupation and by 1960 Census income in 18 comparable specialties produces the following Spearman coefficients:

At the start of career	$r = 0.67$
With 15 years' experience	$r = 0.60$
Near retirement	$r = 0.86$

The 1 percent significance level is 0.56.

From these correlations it appears that students have good information about earnings over the entire life cycle and realistic expectations about the distant future.

For a more refined test of student perceptions of earnings over the life cycle, the ratio of income expected near retirement to expected starting salaries was compared with the actual gradient of cross-sectional age–earnings curves. If students have correct knowledge of the life-cycle pattern of earnings in their chosen career, the ratios of expected incomes will mirror the actual ratios. The data in Table 11.8 indicate that this is the

Table 11.8 Perceived and Actual Life-Cycle Earnings Curves

Intended Occupation	*Ratio of Salary Expected Near Retirement to Expected Starting Salary* (*1*)	*Ratio of the Salary of Specialists Aged 55–64 to the Salary of Specialists Aged 25–34*[a] (2)	*Rank of*[b] (*1*)	(2)
Law	4.21	3.07	1	1
Business	3.58	2.06	2	3
Medical Specialty	3.25	2.42	3	2
Accounting	3.23	1.41	4	7
Government	3.19	1.51	5	4
Architecture	3.18	1.43	6	6
Mechanical Engineering	2.63	1.30	7	11
Social Science	2.43	1.50	8	5
Civil Engineering	2.34	1.39	9	8
Aeronautical Engineering	2.32	1.25	10	12
Electrical Engineering	2.24	1.19	11	14
Clergy	2.24	1.23	12	13
Teaching	2.16	1.37	13	10
Chemistry	2.05	1.38	14	9

Source: Actual salaries: U.S. Census of Population 1960, *Occupation by Earnings and Education.*

[a] The number of occupations for which comparisons of earnings by age, education, and occupation was limited to fourteen by the available census data.

[b] The Spearman rank correlation coefficient is 0.84. The 1% level of significance is 0.65.

case. Students expect large gains in income over the life cycle (column 1) in occupations with steep age–earnings curves (column 2). The rank correlation coefficient is 0.84, significant at 1 percent.

It can be concluded that students have the knowledge of life-cycle earnings posited in the human capital analysis of behavior.

Relative Incomes

For a proper allocation of the work force, individuals must correctly perceive income in alternative occupations as well as in their chosen specialty. At the least they should be aware of where their careers fit in the income array of high-level occupations. Table 11.9 summarizes the

Table 11.9 Student Perceptions of Relative Income Position of Intended Occupations

Intended Occupation	*Percentage of Students Who View Income as Above the College Average* (1)	*Income of Men with Five or More Years of College, 1960* (2)	*Rank of*[a] (1)	*Rank of*[a] (2)
Medical Specialty	91	$19,794	1	1
Law	79	16,082	2	2
Electrical Engineering	79	10,243	2	6
Aeronautical Engineering	78	10,418	4	4
"Other" Engineering	76	9,806	5	8
Mechanical Engineering	75	9,844	6	7
Physics	72	10,409	7	5
Business	71	13,842	8	3
Chemical Engineering	67	9,457	9	11
Mathematics & Statistics	60	9,437	10	13
Accounting	56	9,669	11	9
Metal & Mining Engineering	50	8,968	12	14
Chemistry	47	8,931	13	15
Architecture	38	8,868	14	16
Entertainment	31	6,995	16	20
Social Science	34	9,447	15	12
Literature	28	8,324	17	18
Government	27	9,661	18	10
Biology	25	7,387	19	19
Teaching	16	8,391	20	17
Clergy	6	4,611	21	21

SOURCE: Income figures, *U.S. Census of Population, 1960.*
[a] The rank correlation coefficient is 0.88. The 1% level of significance is 0.52.

survey evidence regarding this assessment. Column 1 records the fraction of students who place their chosen occupations high in the income array; column 2 records actual 1960 incomes in those occupations. The rankings in columns 3 and 4 show a near perfect correlation between these measures of perceived and actual position. It appears that students are well aware of interfield differentials and have the facts needed for rational comparisons of alternatives.

11.3 Perceptions of Other Characteristics

Students have realistic perceptions of the economic characteristics of occupations other than income. The analysis described next shows that their evaluation of the variation in earnings, the chance for great wealth, likely increases in income, and opportunity for personal success correspond to the actual state of these characteristics as indicated in income distributions.

Variability of Income and the Chance for Wealth

In Table 11.10 perceptions of income variability and the chance for great wealth in high-level occupations are compared with measures of these characteristics from the 1960 Census. Column 1 records the proportion of students rating a field high in variability; column 2, a measure of the variation among students in expected income; column 3, the interquartile deviation of incomes reported in the census. By inspection it is clear that these measures are in broad agreement about the extent of variability or risk in particular occupations. In each case, law and business are, for example, rated high in risk while scientific and academic specialties are viewed as safe, stable alternatives. Statistically, the rankings are significantly correlated at 1 percent.

Columns 4, 5, and 6 of Table 11.10 show respectively the fraction of students rating a field high in opportunity for wealth, the proportion actually earning over $15,000 in the career in 1959, and the skew of the income distribution. Again, perceptions are in close accord with the observed phenomena. Nearly every student, for example, foresees a substantial opportunity for wealth in business and law, where earnings above $15,000 are frequent and where income is skewed to the right, while no one anticipates such opportunities in religious and social work. The rank correlation of the percentage of students viewing a career as wealth-producing (column 4) with the percentage of specialists earning over $15,000 (column 5) or with the skewness of income (column 6) are significant at 1 percent.

From the calculations it seems safe to conclude that students have a realistic view of the variation of income among careers and of the relative opportunities for earning large incomes.

Changes in Income

Do students anticipate a continuance or a reversal of past changes in income? Is the extrapolation coefficient in an expectations equation positive (as assumed in Chapter 2) or negative?

Analysis of the number of students expecting average, above average, and below average gains of income points to a positive linkage. Students planning to work in occupations with substantial past increases — for example, mathematics — foresee sizable increases. Those intending to enter occupations with moderate increases, on the other hand, expect small future gains. Overall, the rank correlation between past and expected changes in salary among fields is significant at 5 percent, regardless of the precise sample or measures of income used.

Abilities and Economic Rent

An important characteristic of occupations is the opportunity afforded persons with special abilities to rise to the top. Table 11.11 presents the survey evidence regarding student perceptions of the opportunity for personal economic success and the potential return to special abilities in their chosen career. There is a wide variation in the perceived payoff to abilities among the occupations. The majority of students in the fields of law and business, for example, regard their careers as offering considerable opportunity for personal success or failure; approximately two thirds expect to achieve above-average earnings, while less than two fifths of the prospective doctors, teachers, and social workers (column 1) have such expectations.

There are also substantial occupational differentials in anticipated ability rents — the expected percentage differential between personal and average income in a career. In the fields of medicine and social work students who expect to do better than average foresee a maximum ability rent of 15–20 percent (with 15 years' experience), while, on the other hand, persons entering entertainment occupations expect abilities to be very handsomely rewarded. In this case the percentage differentials between the income expected for the individual and that expected for the average worker in the field ("ability rents") are on the order of 300 to 500 percent, which is probably a realistic evaluation of the return to talent in entertainment.

Table 11.10 Measures of Expected and Actual Variation in Income and Opportunities for Wealth Compared to Variation and Skew of Income Distributions, by Occupation

	Perceived and Actual Variation of Income			*Perceived and Actual Chance for Great Wealth*		
Occupation	*Per Cent of Students Who Believe Their Career Has Greater Than Average Variation in Income* (1)	*Coefficient of Variation of Income Expected by Students After 15 Years' Experience* (2)	*Interquartile Range of Actual Income Divided by the Median*[a] (3)	*Percentage of Students Who Believe There Is Opportunity to Become Wealthy in Their Career* (4)	*Fraction of Workers With Incomes of $15,000 or More*[a] (5)	*Quartile Measure of Skew (minus Sign Means Skewed Left)*[b] (6)
Biological and Agricultural Science	67	0.377	0.48	25	2	−0.03
Medical Specialty	72	.381	1.14	79	52	[c]
Chemistry	54	.265	0.47	37	5	0.13
Geology	69	.303	.74	44	11	.36
Chemical and Petroleum Engineering	47	.220	.44	32	9	.00
Aeronautical Engineering	59	.248	.46	38	8	.06
Civil Engineering	61	.238	.61	28	7	−0.02
Electrical Engineering	58	.271	.43	35	7	−.05
Metallurgical Engineering	56	.263	.44	40	13	−.10
Mechanical Engineering	68	.297	.48	43	7	0.10
Other Engineering	59	.332	.59	46	—	.21

Table 11.10 *(Continued)*

Architecture	86	.355	.73	67	19	.29
Physics	55	.267	.51	20	11	.08
Mathematics and Statistics	76	.348	.74	26	6	−0.10
Social Science	78	.366	.62	43	11	0.14
Social Work	57	.225	.54	0	2	.02
Government	66	.266	.58	20	6	.12
Literary Skills	85	.422	.78	58	12	.11
Clergy	56	.241	.62	6	1	−0.14
Law	91	.402	1.12	91	34	0.35
Business	89	.608	0.86	87	41	.27
Accounting	63	.347	.57	69	8	.14
Entertainment	96	.696	1.40	78	11	.36
Teaching	55	.372	0.45	14	7	−0.31

[a] Actual income figures from the *U.S. Census of Population, 1960.*

[b] The quartile measure of skew is Bowley's statistic $(Q_3 - Q_2) - (Q_1 - Q_2)$ divided by Q_2 where Q_1 = first quartile income: Q_2 = median income and Q_3 = third quartile income.

[c] The large number of physicians and surgeons with incomes above $15.000 does not permit computation of the skew coefficient.

Table 11.11 Expectations of Personal Economic Success

Intended Occupation	*Percentage of Students Expecting Above-Average Earnings*	*Anticipated Ability Rents*[a] *Start of Career*	*With 15 Years' Experience*	*Near Retirement*
Biological and Agricultural Science	44	4	26	44
Medical Specialty	37	1	17	20
Chemistry	44	8	26	26
Geology and Oceanography	42	14	22	45
Chemical and Petroleum Engineering	73	12	22	22
Aeronautical Engineering	57	18	25	32
Civil Engineering	72	10	21	36
Electrical Engineering	62	14	28	37
Metallurgical Engineering	52	25	30	49
Mechanical Engineering	46	17	35	35
Other Engineering	53	11	24	33
Architecture	44	10	55	72
Physics	38	6	10	16
Mathematics and Statistics	40	10	31	52
Social Science	50	8	32	28
Social Work	26	5	14	14
Government	49	13	33	60
Literary Careers	46	8	29	45
Clergy	44	8	29	45
Law	60	20	76	118
Business	69	17	76	107
Accounting	50	9	9	28
Entertainment	33	12	306	531
Teaching	39	11	24	31
Scattered Sciences	30	5	26	34

[a] As defined in the text, ability rent refers to the percentage differential in the income a person expects for himself as opposed to the average worker in his career.

Overall, the perceptions of the potential payoff to ability shown in Table 11.11 correspond to the actual payoff indicated in the income distributions for the occupations. First the fields that rank highest in the fraction of students expecting above-average earnings or in "anticipated ability rent" also rank highest in the dispersion, or skewness, of income. Rank correlations of the data in Table 11.11 with those in 11.10 yield Spearman coefficients significant at 1 percent in all cases. Individuals thus expect ability to be richly rewarded in fields with "loose" income distributions. Second, in every field the percentage by which personal income expectation exceeds the average increases over the life cycle. This is in accord with the greater dispersion of income about its central tendency as a cohort ages.

11.4 Marginal Decision-Making

The theory of labor supply is based on the response of persons initially indifferent among careers to economic stimuli. These marginal suppliers alter career plans when salaries change. Here we consider the survey responses of two groups of students with some of the characteristics of the marginal suppliers — those with very flexible career plans and those with special interest in income. Do these individuals respond to economic incentives in accordance with the economic theory of occupational choice?

Marginal Suppliers and Career Plans

There are several (overlapping) groups of survey respondents whose career plans have the characteristics expected of marginal suppliers — students unsure of their career choice, those lacking strong interest in particular occupations, those dissatisfied with available information, those paying close attention to alternatives, and so on. From those categories I identify marginal suppliers as students expressing great likelihood of changing career plans upon receipt of new information. Students in this category appear willing to alter their plans when market conditions change. In addition, they exhibit other characteristics of marginality as well:

— a tendency to give serious consideration to alternative careers while in college (82 percent report such considerations, compared to 50 percent of students unlikely to change careers with more information);

— great dissatisfaction with the adequacy of information;

— a tendency to select a career at a relatively late date compared to other students. (Virtually all of the marginal persons make their career decisions during their college years and none in high school.)

— a substantial likelihood of majoring in a field unrelated to their anticipated vocation (25 percent do not expect to work in their major, compared to 10 percent of other students).

There is thus a reasonable correspondence between these students and the marginal suppliers of economic theory.

Table 11.12 Income in the Career Choice of Marginal and Other Suppliers[a]

Student Response to New Career Information	Importance of Earnings in the Career Decision			Importance of Interest in Work in the Career Decision		
	Very	*Somewhat*	*Not*	*Very*	*Somewhat*	*Not*
Strong possibility of change in career plans	17	52	31	74	17	9
Career change possible but unlikely	16	50	34	84	11	5
Career change not very possible	15	41	44	89	7	4

[a] Marginal suppliers are identified as those who report a strong possibility of changing career plans given new job information.

The survey findings in Table 11.12 indicate that economic factors play an especially large role in the career decisions of students identified in this way. First, many of these students weigh income heavily in their career decisions. Seventy percent who are likely to change careers given new conditions view income as very or somewhat important compared to 56 percent of those unlikely to respond to new information. Contrarily, interest in work is relatively less important to the marginal suppliers, with 74 percent rating interest as very important compared to 90 percent of their peers. For the population under study these differences are statistically significant.

Table 11.13 Expected Levels of Income of Marginal and Other Suppliers[a]

Student Response to New Career Information	Expected Income		
	At Start	*With 15 Years' Experience*	*Near Retirement*
Strong possibility of change	$8,060	16,530	22,630
Career change possible, but unlikely	$8,360	17,370	23,500
Career change not very possible	$8,840	19,320	26,240

[a] For identification of marginal suppliers see Table 11.12, note a.

The data in Table 11.13 provide further evidence on the role of income in the career choice of marginal suppliers. According to the table, these persons have relatively pessimistic income expectations, with lower anticipated incomes than other students for all periods of their working life. Not surprisingly, in view of this pattern, the marginal suppliers are also pessimistic about the possibility of receiving above-average incomes in their fields and of earning more than they could get in its closest alternative. Fifty-four percent expect income below the college average compared to 46 percent of other students. Nearly a third believe that income is higher in the closest alternative to their present career choice. By contrast, just a quarter of students with a small likelihood of changing careers given new information foresee higher earnings in the alternative.

In short, it looks as though the marginal suppliers are dissatisfied with current income prospects and are searching for more lucrative careers. Income appears especially important in their career decisions, as predicted by the theory of choice.

Economic Man

The one respondent in seven who rates income as very important in career decisions is akin to the proverbial "economic man." His decision should be particularly responsive to economic stimuli.

Comparisons of career decisions by the importance of income confirm this expectation. Money-oriented students choose occupations which offer especially high pay and in which income is expected to increase rapidly in the future. They are especially aware of the economic significance of education. Fewer than 10 percent see no cost or sacrifice to college compared to 20 percent of those uninterested in income. Moreover the economically oriented students report more flexible career plans than other students. Seventy-five percent express a willingness to change careers upon the receipt of new information compared to 65 percent of those with no interest in income. These differences suggest that the monetarily oriented are especially aware of and likely to respond to economic stimuli and thus provide part of the "margin of adjustment" by which the market responds to changes in economic conditions.

Marginal Incentive and Career Choice

The survey question asking students to compare incomes in their chosen career with the income in its closest alternative provides a final test of the marginal aspects of decision-making. All else being the same, careers in which many students expect incomes above those in alternatives are likely to be especially attractive and to recruit many new entrants, while the opposite should be true in fields where students expect incomes below those in close alternatives.

A comparison between changes in degrees in the period 1965–1968 (or 1960–1968) and the fraction of survey respondents viewing income as high relative to that in close alternatives confirms this implication of the marginal analysis. Taking fields with roughly comparable nonpecuniary advantages — the sciences and engineering, for example — increases in the number of degrees is positively rank-correlated with "marginal income incentives," [8] with a coefficient of 0.70, significant at 1 percent.

Since the test relates to degrees in the late 1960s rather than to the 1970s and is limited to academic fields, it should be viewed as tentative or suggestive only. For a more rigorous test of the relation between student evaluations and changes in degrees, nonpecuniary factors must be held fixed in a better way and the time lag between evaluations and supply extended. A comparison of income evaluations and supply at two points in time is clearly desirable. As it stands, the limited evidence available suggests that marginal income incentives influence plans in the expected way.

Conclusion

This chapter confirms the favorable report on the micro-foundations of the economic theory of occupational selection given in Chapter 10. As far as can be told from the survey responses, the theory rests on a firm foundation at the level of the individual decision-maker.

12 Policy and Research Implications

Although not directed toward policy issues, the findings of the study necessarily have implications on labor market and manpower policies. In addition, they suggest some topics for future research on the operation of the labor market. Before considering these implications, the reader may find it useful to review the summary of findings with which the volume began.

12.1 High-level Manpower Policy

The principal conclusion of the study — that the market for college-trained specialists is governed by economic forces in a relatively direct way — has three implications for policy. First, and most obviously, it directs attention to a particular set of tools, those relating to the price system. In the market for college-trained specialists the manpower objectives of policy-makers may be attained through salary or stipend adjustments, with no recourse to extraordinary nonmarket policy tools.* Second, the observed responsiveness of the market validates the use of the "classical theory" as a norm for judging market performance and points to the need

* The evidence on the relative impact of stipends and salaries further suggests, moreover, that a salary policy may be more efficacious. Salaries have a greater effect on the supply of new entrants in the short run, do not lose effectiveness in the long run, and influence experienced as well as new workers. Moreover, students appear to be better informed about salaries than about the availability of stipends. On the other hand, however, stipends may be easier to manipulate on the margin, for increases in salaries may end up as rent to experienced workers. A benefit-cost study should be able to point to the most effective method for directing manpower to desired objectives.

for government intervention in submarkets where institutional or other rigidities hamper the adjustment mechanism. A priori, the markets for medical manpower, for college-trained women and for minorities may qualify for special treatment on this count. Third, since the market is a responsive mechanism, the chief policy problem is not to find ways to influence the behavior of suppliers and employers but rather to choose an appropriate set of manpower goals. This is a difficult task which requires evaluation of the *social worth* of complex activities like research and education.*

From more detailed findings come more limited and specific implications for education and manpower policy:

1) Lags in supply adjustment due to training delays and the responsiveness of students to stipends suggest consideration of "manpower scholarship" awards, as described in Chapter 6. These awards would be made on the basis of market conditions in high-level occupations to reduce temporary shortages due to the adjustment period. They would increase the efficacy of stipend spending and improve the responsiveness of the market mechanism.

2) The evidence that a sizable minority of students, particularly social science and humanities majors, needs additional information about careers and that the chief source of information is employment suggests the establishment of government or industry summer job programs. By offering jobs in "shortage" areas, a job program could alleviate shortages, create interest in these occupations, and improve the information network. Since students are mobile, a national computerized placement program is a reasonable possibility.

3) The importance of nonpecuniary income to high-level workers directs the attention of industry, which has had difficulty attracting top students in science or engineering, to greater reliance on nonmonetary incentives. It would be worthwhile for personnel directors to consider the impact of extended sabbaticals, periods of "free work," and related university-type incentives on the employment plans of young specialists.

4) The lags in salary determination suggest that a formal system of gathering and analyzing the hiring and salary plans of firms would help increase the flexibility of salaries and the speed of adjustment in the mar-

* More broadly speaking, the general finding that a market operates effectively does not eliminate the need for policy, as sometimes suggested by advocates of laissez-faire. Instead, it calls for an evaluation of the resultant output of the market in terms of social goals and possible use of income incentives to attain more desirable results.

ket. Long-term manpower planning by firms, educational institutions, and students would also be facilitated by such a system.

5) The existence of vacancies in universities in fields with good non-academic opportunities points to the need for greater efforts to circumvent the internal salary constraint. Greater use of differential rates of promotion and of especially favorable sabbatical or leave policy for men in shortage areas would be useful here. Leaves without pay have the advantage of allowing specialists to take advantage of industrial opportunities without increasing faculty salaries or budgets.

6) If desired, the current emphasis on research in universities could be altered by changing the economic incentive to teach. The evidence of economically responsive behavior by universities and faculty suggests that National Teaching Awards, offering the financial support and prestige to "good" teachers currently available only to researchers, would reorient university and faculty activities.

7) The economic behavior of students suggests that a loan bank method of financing education is a feasible alternative to current non-duty stipends and low-cost tuition, though not a fruitful competitive mechanism of support. Obligating students to pay the direct expenses of their own education is likely to have desirable effects on rational decision-making and on the distribution of incomes.

8) Finally, the existence of lengthy disequilibriums under incomplete adjustment directs attention to the value of manpower forecasts in the labor market. Since career decisions result from a rational consideration of alternatives, students are likely to react favorably to a comprehensive, high-quality set of forecasts.

In sum, the tools for directing investment in human capital to desired alternatives exist. It is possible to predict the response of the market to policy. The chief problem is to devise a rational set of priorities and goals.

12.2 Labor Market Research

In the course of the present study it became apparent that some topics could be examined fruitfully in greater detail and that others might profit from reconsideration in light of the findings. One issue on which further work is needed is the cross-elasticity of supply. A detailed study of the characteristics of occupations, their ability requirements, and the economic value of these factors could improve our knowledge of the occupational decision and of the meaning of work. The studies of job analysts, psychologists, and sociologists may be useful here. Another unresolved issue relates to the transmission of information about jobs to students with different family incomes or racial background. Experiments at various campuses with alternative methods of disseminating information could cast light on the process of learning about market conditions and on the best way to improve information networks.

More work is also needed on the operation of universities — especially on the goals of institutions and the income and educational production relations constraining actions. An industrial organization study of the education market, making use of financial data and possibly of surveys or interviews, would be helpful in developing more rigorous and useful models.

Some of the models and related analyses of this study could be fruitfully applied to other labor markets. One obvious application is to the analysis of labor mobility. By calculating the implicit value of job characteristics and the "disequilibrium income" in a market, it might be possible to explain the mobility of workers among industries. A more general line of research is to apply the basic labor market or the simultaneous allocation model to markets for other groups of workers — medical specialists, skilled craftsmen, junior college graduates, and technicians. A third area of application is to the markets for college-trained women, blacks, or other groups likely to face discrimination. By building explicit models of the operation of these markets it may be possible to determine some of the factors underlying discrimination and the way in which suppliers and firms adjust to discrimination. In the case of women, the ways in which marriage and child-bearing affect career plans and utilization deserve special study.

Finally, an important, possibly fertile, area of research just touched upon here is the determination of the social — as opposed to private — value of specialized work, in particular the activity of scientists and engineers, where external economies are important. There appear to be sufficient data on R & D, productivity, sales, profits, new products, and the employment and earnings of high-level specialists to merit a major research effort. Such research might delineate the role of technical expertise, managerial skills, and of high-level manpower in general in creating new technologies and advancing the use of best practice techniques. Studies of this kind would contribute to understanding the entire process of modern economic growth.

Appendices
Notes
Index

Appendix A | Computation of Incremental Taxes

The precise computations of incremental taxes paid by students is as follows:

1. For ease in analysis, the computations relate to male students only; a correction for female students is introduced in step 11.

2. The difference in mean incomes between male college and high school graduates was $4000 in 1966. Following Edward Denison, who attributes 40 percent of the difference in incomes to ability, family connections, and so forth, three fifths of this differential, or $2400, will be viewed as the result of college education. See E. Denison, "Measuring the Contribution of Education," *The Residual Factor and Economic Growth* (Paris: Organisation for Economic Co-operation and Development).

3. The $2400 difference is assumed to remain constant over time. This *underestimates* the advantage of college. In years past the *absolute* income difference between college and high school graduates increased markedly and is likely to continue to do so in the future.

4. Incremental taxes received by state and local governments are then calculated by taking 5.6 percent (the average fraction of personal income paid in taxes, exclusive of the property tax) of $2400. Assuming a 43-year working life and a 6 percent discount rate, the value of the extra taxes is $2050.

5. Federal tax collections in 1966 were 18 percent of personal income per capita. Eighteen percent of $2400 is $432. Discounted at 6 percent over a 43-year working life and net of taxes lost due to four years of income foregone, yields an estimate of incremental taxes of $4900.

6. Public educational institutions received subsidies of about $800 per student per year from state and local governments in 1966. All such institutions received governmental subsidies of approximately $650 per student in 1966. In terms of present values at the time of graduation, these subsidies cumulate over four years to $3500 and $2840, respectively.

7. The withdrawal of state and local support from public universities would increase tuition and fees from $200 to $1000. The withdrawal of *all* government

support of all educational institutions would increase tuition fees by 150 percent.

8. According to a time series study by R. Campbell and B. Siegal ("Demand for Higher Education in the U.S." *American Economic Review,* June 1967), the elasticity of enrollment to tuition is about 0.44. Preliminary results from a cross section study given in *Toward a Long-Range Plan for Federal Financial Support for Higher Education* show an elasticity of about 0.45 also. According to that report, a $100 change in tuition changes the proportion of the relevant age group enrolling in college by approximately 0.05. With current tuition and attendance, the elasticity is 0.45.

9. On the basis of 0.44 elasticity to tuition, approximately one half of the students in public educational institutions and one third overall would withdraw from college if tuition were raised to cover the subsidies.

10. This yields a final estimate of the incremental taxes received by state and local governments as a result of subsidizing public colleges and universities of $1025 per student. All governmental bodies received incremental taxes worth $2300.

11. These figures, however, are based on male incomes only. Females make up approximately 40 percent of the college population. The difference in the earnings of female college and high school graduates is about three fourths as large as the male differentials. Adjusted for females, the incremental taxes received by states and localities are worth $930 per student. The incremental taxes of local, state, and federal governments are worth $2070.

12. Finally, these figures are compared to the estimated cost of subsidies given in step 6. Approximately 28 percent of the state and local investment and 74 percent of the total governmental subsidy is repaid in additional taxes, discounted at 6 percent. The rate of return on the subsidy is in the neighborhood of 4 percent.

13. Since the effect of growth on real income differences has been ignored thus far, the estimate may be regarded as a minimum figure. With a 2 percent real growth in all incomes, the rate of return would be about 2 percentage points higher or 6 percent.

14. The calculations ignore the potential effect of subsidies on investments in human capital through on-the-job training. The limited information available on the relation between investment in education and in on-the-job training does not point to any substantial bias in the calculations.

Appendix B | Questionnaire and Representative Response

Dear Student,

What sort of knowledge do you have about the job market for college graduates? What are your career plans?

Enclosed is a questionnaire dealing with these topics. The questionnaire is designed to provide information on the relationships among education plans, career plans, and the job data available to students making career decisions. The findings from this study will be used to help formulate policy on providing career information to college students.

The questionnaire requires 15 minutes or so to complete. Your answers to the questions are completely confidential.

An analysis of the results will be available in late spring to interested students.

Thank you very much for your assistance.

Sincerely,

Richard B. Freeman
Manpower Project

Instructions:

The questionnaire begins on the reverse of this sheet. Most of the questions can be answered by placing a check (√) next to the appropriate response. When answering questions of this form, choose the statement closest to your circumstances, even if it may not fit exactly. If you are uncertain about the answer to a question, make the best guess you can.

Several questions require short written answers. Please be as specific as possible in answering these questions (*e.g.* if the question asks you to write in your field of study and yours is physiology, write "physiology," not "biological science").

When you have completed the questionnaire, place it into the enclosed self-addressed, stamped envelope and mail it.

I. Education and Background

1. What is your present status in school? (*i.e.* senior; 1st year law) *sophomore*

2. a. What is your major field of study at present? If you have not selected a major field yet give your prospective major.

   Major Field *chem engineering* Prospective Major ________

   b. If you have ever changed your major field of study, what was your previous major(s)? ________

3. Do you plan to attend graduate or professional school? (for undergraduates only)

   No ________ Yes, I plan to study in my present field ✓
   Yes, I plan to study in a different field which is ________

4. What do you consider to be the cost or sacrifice involved in attending graduate school?

   You sacrifice a year or two when you could be working

5. a. When you have completed your education, do you intend to seek employment in your major field of study?

   Yes, permanently ✓ Yes, but not permanently ________ No ________

   b. If you do not expect to be permanently employed in your present major field, why do you remain in this field?

   The field gives me good preparation for my career ________
   I enjoy the subject ________
   The field gives me a wide choice of future careers ________
   It was a mistake to choose the field, but it's too late to change ________

6. To what extent did (or will) your choice of career depend on your success or lack of success in college studies?

   Greatly ✓ Somewhat dependent ________ Not dependent ________

7. Where do you expect to be permanently employed when you have completed your education?

   Business ✓ Federal government ________ Self employed ________
   Academic ________ Other government ________ Other ________

8. What do you estimate your yearly (before-tax) earnings would presently be if you were not in school? Assume you were working today in a full-time permanent job.

Less than $4,000 ____	$5–6,000 ✓	$7–8,000 ____	$9–10,000 ____
$4–5,000 ____	$6–7,000 ____	$8–9,000 ____	$10,000 + ____

II. Career Choice

9. What is your anticipated permanent career? *chem engineering*

10. How definite is this career choice?
Definite ✓ Fairly definite but subject to change ____ Indefinite ____

11. Have you given serious consideration to a different career from that given in #9 since graduating from high school? Yes ✓ No ____

12. a. If you answered yes to the preceding question what other career(s) have you seriously considered. If you have considered more than one, circle the career you have considered most seriously.

accounting, teaching math

b. If you answered no to the preceding question, what other career(s) do you regard as being possible alternatives for you? If you have more than one possible alternative, circle the career which is the most likely alternative.

____

13. The following questions ask you to compare some characteristics of careers. Compare your chosen career with the career you gave as the answer to question 12 by checking the appropriate space. If you gave more than one answer to question 12, compare your career to the circled career.

	Chosen Career	Circled or Other	No Difference	How important is this factor to you in selecting a career? Very	Somewhat	Not
a. Which career requires more years of education beyond the bachelor's?	✓				✓	
b. On the average which career will provide higher earnings?	✓				✓	
c. In which career does the nation have a greater need for persons?		✓			✓	
d. Which career offers a wider variety of possible places of employment?	✓				✓	
e. In which career is the work of greater interest to you?	✓			✓		

f. Which career offers greater stability in employment or earnings?	√		√
g. In which career is the financial and personal sacrifice of entering greater to you or your family?		√	√

III. Earnings

14. a. What do you estimate are the *yearly* earnings (before taxes) that an individual might *on the average* expect in your chosen career. (Ignore possible changes in the price level, *e.g.* inflation, which may influence earnings in all jobs).

    1) At the start of his career (first full-time job) *$8,000*
    2) With about fifteen years of experience *$11,000*
    3) Near retirement *$15,000*

    b. If you expect *your* earnings to differ from the average, what do you expect to earn in your career?

    1) At the start of your career *$8,000*
    2) With about fifteen years of experience *$11,000*
    3) Near retirement *$15,000*

15. How do you think earnings in your career will change in the future, compared to earnings in other college level careers?

    In my career earnings are likely to increase { more rapidly √ / at the same rate ____ / less rapidly ____ } than elsewhere.

16. Which of the following statements do you consider to be applicable to prospective earnings in your career, compared to other college level careers?

	True	False
a. There is a great variation in earnings among people in my career.	√	
b. There is opportunity to become very wealthy in my career.	√	
c. Earnings in my career are higher than those in most college level careers.	√	

IV. Career Information

17. Which of the following possible sources of job information have been important in providing you with information about your career?

	Important	Slightly Important	Not Important
Family			√
Members of local community, friends of your family		√	
Guidance counselors		√	
College Professors	√		
Employment in the field		√	
General information sources: books, etc.		√	

18. a. When in your estimation did you make your final decision concerning your career?

Before college __√__ During college______ Am making decision now______

b. Do you consider the information available at the time you made (or are making) your career decision adequate for a wise decision?

Reasonably adequate ______ Barely adequate __√__ Inadequate ______

c. What is the possibility that additional information about your career choice and other careers would have led you (or would lead you) to a different choice?

Quite possible _____ Possible, but unlikely __√__ Not very possible _____

19. Here is a list of careers which are often selected by college students. These careers require advanced study beyond the bachelor's degree. In the columns to the right are a set of characteristics describing the careers. Rank the careers in terms of these characteristics, giving the rank 1 to the career you rate highest in the specific characteristic, the rank 2 to the career you rate second, etc.

Careers	Society's Need for More People in the Field	Initial Earnings in Career	Earnings After 15 Years	Job Opportunities Have Improved Greatly in Recent Years
Engineer with a Master's Degree	2	2	2	1
Lawyer	5	3	4	5
Doctor	1	1	1	4
College Professor with a doctorate degree	3	5	5	2
Businessman with a Master of Business Administration degree	4	4	3	3

20. Here is a list of fields in which the doctorate degree (Ph.D.) is common. Assuming the persons in the field have this degree, rate the fields in terms of the characteristics listed in the columns on the right. Rate the fields by checking (√) the three you rate highest in the characteristic and putting a zero (0) next to the three you rate lowest.

Field	Availability of Fellowships	Society's Need for More People in This Field	Average Earnings in the Field	Job Opportunities Have Improved Greatly in Recent Years
Chemistry	√	√	√	√
Engineering	√	√	√	√
History		0	0	0
Mathematics		√	0	
English	0	0	0	0
Genetics	0			
Botany	0	0		0
Economics			√	√
Physics	√			
Political Science				

Thank you for your assistance

Appendix C | Analysis of the Response Bias

This appendix seeks to discover the possible effect of the large number of nonresponding students on the validity of the survey findings. Slightly more than seven in ten students did not answer the questionnaire. Is it likely that the responses of these students would undermine the picture of the college labor market depicted in the text?

In the absence of a special check on the nonresponding students, indirect evidence is used to answer this question. The available indirect information indicates that a larger response rate would not have changed results to any great extent.

First, internal comparisons of the responses of students with high and low rates of response reveal no obvious bias in the pattern of answers. The responses of men from the Boston branch of the University of Massachusetts, for instance, who had the lowest response rate of any of the students, did not differ materially from those of Harvard students, for whom the response rate was highest. The few differences in the pattern of answers are due primarily to the economic background of students (for example, fewer Harvard men than University of Massachusetts men consider "sacrifice of entry" important in career choice) rather than to response bias. Even with the different background of students, however, the variations in answers are slight. Similarly, the responses of students in majors having high response rates, do not differ materially from the average response on nonmajor-related questions.

Second, the responses of students in individual classes where personal distribution of the questionnaire guaranteed a near-perfect response rate were similar to those for the average respondent. This was true among classes at several institutions, including some (such as Northeastern and Harvard Summer School) not included in the overall sample.

A third test of the potential effect of response bias requires a comparison of the answers of respondents in my survey to those elicited by similar questions in more carefully controlled national studies. I compared overlapping questions from the

National Science Foundation study, *Two Years After the College Degree,* and from Professor A. Davis's *Undergraduate Career Decision* (Chicago, 1965). Both of these studies covered students throughout the country, obtained higher response rates (at greater cost) than my survey, and made a careful follow-up of nonrespondents.

Since my survey focuses on the career and economic orientation of students, the most likely systematic bias is on over-representation of career or economically concerned persons. Hence I made a special check of the career and monetary orientation of respondents among questionnaires. These comparisons show no obvious bias in the reponses. The proportion of students intending to work in the area of their major field in the NSF study, for example, was 73 percent; in my study, 72 percent. Similarities in related questions also reveal a similarity in respondents. Analogous comparisons with the Davis study also show no obvious response bias to the findings of my survey. The fraction of students interested in income and their distribution by major in the Davis study mirrors the finding in this study.

From those limited comparisons it appears that response bias does not seriously mar the findings of the current study.

Notes

Chapter 1: Theory of Occupational Choice

1. For an analysis of the time input into the production of human capital see Y. Ben-Porath, "The Production of Human Capital and the Life Cycle of Earnings" *Journal of Political Economics,* August 1967.

2. The movement from engineering and the sciences into administration may result from the accretion of "maturity in decision-making" and the obsolesence of specialized knowledge learned in school.

3. T. Scitovsky, *Welfare and Competition* (Chicago: Irwin, 1962), p. 84.

4. Alfred Marshall, *Principles of Economics* (New York: Macmillan, 1936), p. 566.

5. The trade-off between nonmonetary and monetary incomes is examined in Gary Becker, *The Economics of Discrimination* (Chicago: University of Chicago Press, 1957), and in O. E. Williamson, "Managerial Discretion and Business Behavior," *American Economic Review,* December 1963.

6. This analysis follows closely the pathbreaking work of K. Lancaster, whose investigation of activity models in consumer choice includes a very general programing model of career selection. See K. Lancaster, "A New Approach to Consumer Theory" *Journal of Political Economy,* April 1966.

7. This point is made by Lancaster in "A New Approach to Consumer Theory" (n. 6 above).

8. The analysis of abilities is a modification of Benoit Mandelbrot's work on Paretian distributions and career choice. It differs from the Mandelbrot model by introducing the R vector and examining the determination of earnings potential. See B. Mandelbrot, "Paretian Distributions and Income Maximization," *Quarterly Journal of Economics,* February 1962.

9. Mandelbrot, p. 69.

10. Other factors are also likely to influence expectations. For example, the experience of workers in a field over time, as well as at a point in time, is likely

to have some effect on expected future earnings. In addition, young persons may have limited horizons and consider only part of the income curve — say, starting salaries or the earnings of men at the peak of their career. If such is the case, expectations equations different from the one suggested here are appropriate. Empirically, it is difficult to test related formulations of the expectations formation process. See T. W. Schultz, "The Rate of Return in Allocating Investment Resources to Education," *Journal of Human Resources,* Summer 1967.

11. An alternative behavioral hypothesis is that expectations are adjusted rather than behavior. Adjustment of expectations seems to be a common phenomenon: the adjustment of expectations over the life cycle is one aspect of maturation.

12. This aspect of variability is considered in M. Friedman and S. Kuznets, *Income from Independent Professional Practice* (New York: National Bureau of Economic Research, 1951), chaps. 7–8.

13. Marshall, *Principles of Economics,* p. 554.

14. Adam Smith, *The Wealth of Nations* (New York: Modern Library); M. Yaari, "Convexity in the Theorem of Choice under Risk," *Quarterly Journal of Economics,* May 1965.

15. Marshall, *Principles of Economics,* 535.

16. If moments properly reflect incentives, the skewness proposition follows directly from preference for more income. Certainly, individuals will choose an alternative offering greater positive skew, given equal mean and variability. However, distributions with identical first and second moments but with different skew coefficients must have different shapes, with the central part of the distributions shaped unfavorably to the skewed alternative. Thus the "skew proposition" follows from income maximization only if moments measure the entire incentive of a distribution.

17. See Daniel Ellsberg, "Risk, Ambiguity and the Savage Axioms," *Quarterly Journal of Economics,* November 1961; William Fellner, "Distortion of Subjective Probabilities as a Reaction to Uncertainty," *ibid.;* and Howard Raiffa, "Risk, Ambiguity and the Savage Axioms: Comment," *ibid.* Also K. R. W. Brewer, "Decisions under Uncertainty: Comment," *Quarterly Journal of Economics,* February 1963; Daniel Ellsberg, "Risk, Ambiguity, and the Savage Axioms: Reply," *ibid.,* May 1963, and K. R. W. Brewer and William Fellner, "The Slanting of Subjective Probabilities: Agreement on Some Essentials," *ibid.,* November 1965.

18. M. Friedman, *Price Theory* (Chicago: Aldine, 1962), p. 219.

19. This line of reasoning extends to the situation in which nonmonetary characteristics can be purchased with leisure. In Figure 1.2 equal dollar increases in income raise the points of maximum earnings for each occupation. The slope of the frontier becomes steeper, and the low-paying occupation benefits. In the extreme case in which both money incomes approach infinity, the nonmonetary career clearly dominates its competitor.

Chapter 2: Models of the Labor and Education Markets

1. A. Marshall, *Principles of Economics,* (New York: MacMillan, 1936), p. 571.

2. This assumes that the information-decision lag in demand is equal or less

than that in supply. A priori, equality seems to be the most realistic assumption. The only plausible argument for different-sized lags is that suppliers respond to wages that already reflect employer responsiveness. However, as long as suppliers react to non-wage information as well as to wages, there need be no difference in the lag pattern. There is, at any rate, no indication that the supply response is so rapid as to balance out the training lag.

3. The need for pre-college training of scientists and engineers is stressed in A. Alchian, K. Arrow, and W. Capron. *An Economic Analysis of the Market for Scientists and Engineers,* (Chicago: Rand, McNally, 1958), pp. 85–86.

4. In 1961–1962, 572,000 students took mathematics courses in their senior year of high school. First degrees in mathematics in 1964 were awarded to 19,000 people.

5. See G. J. Stigler, "The Economics of Information," *Journal of Political Economy,* October, 1962.

6. See E. Denison, "Measuring the Contribution of Education to Economic Growth" (Paris: Organisation for Economic Co-operation and Development, 1964).

7. Substitution of past wages for the stock of labor in equation (7B) yields:

$$W_t = -1/a_0Q_t + (1 - \delta)\, W_{t-1} + (a/a_0)\,[A_t - (1 - \delta)\, A_{t-1}] + b/a_0\,(Y_t - (1 - \delta)\, Y_{t-1}).$$

Note that the depreciation term (δ) can be estimated from this equation.

8. The active labor market hypothesis has been suggested by Reder, among others. See M. W. Reder, "Wage Differentials: Theory and Measurement," in *Aspects of Labor Economics.* National Bureau Committee for Economic Research (Princeton, N.J., 1962).

9. Equilibrium can also be defined as *steady-state* growth, in which all variables increase at a proportionate rate. There is no conceptual advantage to this formulation.

10. Substitution yields the following difference equations, which can be solved by the usual techniques (see G. Goldberg, *Introduction to Difference Equations,* [New York: John Wiley, 1961]):

(1) With equation (2A):

$$N_t = (1 - \delta - \alpha_0 r/a_0)\, N_{t-1} + K_1;$$

(2) With equation (2B):

$$N_t = [2 - \delta - B_0(1 + \alpha_0 r/a_0)]\, N_{t-1} + (B_0 - 1)\,(1 - \delta)\, N_{t-2} + K_2;$$

(3) With equation (2C):

$$N_t = [(2 - \delta) - r\alpha_0/a_0(B_0 + B_1) - B_0]N_{t-1} + [(1 - \delta)(1 - B_0) + r\alpha_0 B_1/a_0]N_{t-2} + K_3,$$

where K_1, K_2, and K_3 are constants dependent on output (Y_t) and income in other occupations (A_t).

11. This can be easily seen by noting that equilibrium salary must be between

the actual and expected salary by factors related to the slopes of the supply and demand schedules. Algebraically,

$$\overline{w} - w^*_{t-1} = \left(\frac{r\alpha_0}{a_0}\right)(\overline{w} - w_{t-1})$$

12. Shortages or surpluses of manpower have received much public attention in years past. In the mid-1950s, attention focused on an alleged shortage of scientists and engineers; in the early 1960s on a shortage of teachers; in the late sixties, on a doctor shortage. Concern over a surplus of engineers was expressed in the late 1940s, and Seymour Harris worried about a general surplus of college graduates in his book *The Market for College Graduates* (Cambridge, Mass.; Harvard University Press, 1949).

13. K. J. Arrow, and W. M. Capron, "Dynamic Shortage and Price Rises: the Engineer-Scientist Case," *Quarterly Journal of Economics,* (1959).

14. For a discussion of educational production functions see Samuel Bowles "Towards an Educational Production Function" (unpubl. paper, September 1968).

15. For example, the Tinbergen-Bos-Correa model used by the OECD. See *Econometric Model of Education* (Paris: Organisation for Economic Co-operation and Development, 1965).

16. In the long run, of course, both funding and the number of applicants are endogenous variables, determined by the education system and thus are not fixed constraints.

17. Gary S. Becker, in *Human Capital* (New York: Columbia University Press, 1964), has shown the effect of specific investments on the employment and disemployment decisions of firms. See also Walter Oi, "Labor as a Quasi-Fixed Factor of Production," *Journal of Political Economy,* December 1962.

Chapter 3: Developments in the Market for Highly Specialized Workers after World War II

1. OECD figures show Sweden (11.5 percent) with a larger proportion of professionals than the United States (10 percent). See *Resources of Scientific and Technical Personnel in the OECD Area* (Paris: Organisation for Economic Co-operation and Development, 1963).

2. Alternative estimates of the number of natural scientists in the United States by the Bureau of Labor Statistics and Naional Science Foundation report twice as many scientists as in the Census. Part of the difference in the estimated science population is due to different classification of occupations and part to different treatment of older scientists performing administrative tasks.

3. See D. Blank and G. Stigler, *The Demand and Supply of Scientific Personnel* (Washington, D.C.: National Bureau of Economic Research, 1957), pp. 10–11.

4. *The Education of Management in American Manufacturing*: Preliminary Report on a Questionnaire Survey with Special Emphasis on Scientists and Enginers Conducted for the Science and Public Policy Program, Graduate School of Public Administration (Cambridge, Mass.: Harvard University, 1960).

5. This does not mean that all college graduates enter nonunionized labor markets. A minority — e.g., pilots, some teachers, newspapermen, and government workers — are union members. However, most college men are not union members.

6. These differences are also due to different systems of education. An American high school or college graduate has a different training from that of a European graduate from a *lycée, gymnasium,* or university.

7. It is interesting that European methods for training craftsmen and other skilled workers also differ from American methods, with greater reliance in Europe on apprenticeship. The reason for different modes of training ought to be examined further.

8. The discussion of growth in this chapter focuses on percentage rates of increase and changes in share of degrees. It is also reasonable to view the changes in terms of absolute figures. The different size of the various fields creates some inconsistencies in the picture of growth given by these two methods of measurement — especially at the "subspecialty" level. In terms of analysis, measurement by percentage change or absolute change depends on the form of the supply function: percentage changes are relevant when the function is best fitted in logarithmic form; absolute changes are relevant when a linear-dependent variable fits the data better.

9. In contrast to occupational mobility there is relatively little field-of-study mobility over the life cycle. Few persons return to school to study a new subject (and even if they do they can still be classified in the initial field). For this reason, occupational classifications may be less stable and meaningful than classification by area of specialization.

10. One problem with these matrices was that the original source failed to distinguish graduate students with part-time jobs from full-time workers. To check on the possible bias due to this classification, I estimated the number of students in each graduating class. Except in psychology, where 44 percent of 1958 B.A. graduates enrolled for further study, the fractions were small. Thus the matrices are a meaningful picture of ultimate career selection.

11. U.S. Department of Labor, *Formal Occupational Training of Adult Workers,* Manpower Research Monograph No. 2 (USGPO Washington, D.C.: U.S. Government Printing Office, December 1964).

Chapter 4: The Cobweb Pattern: B.S. Engineering

1. Adjusting for the higher quality of recent graduates by weighing graduates according to wages reduces slightly the drop in stock-flow ratios. The dominant trend is still a sharp reduction in the relative number of college engineers.

2. Albert Shapero, "Government R and D Contracting" in *Factors in the Transfer of Technology,* ed. W. H. Gruber and D. G. Marquis (Cambridge, Mass.: The MIT Press, p. 198).

3. Note that specifying equal coefficients for freshman and sophomore salaries has the desirable effect of reducing the terms to changes in salaries over a two-year period (that is, $\ln[ESAL_{t+2}] - ln[ESAL_t]$).

4. This specification ignores the possibility that some potential engineering students decide against college when they reject engineering.

5. The "veterans" hypothesis is developed in the report of the Committee for the Analysis of Engineering Enrollment, American Society for Engineering Education, *Factors Influencing Engineering Enrollment* (Washington, D.C., 1965).

6. The correlation here is greater than that between changes in enrollment and changes in the size of the student population ($r = 0.59$), indicating a larger effect for economic than for demographic factors in determining the number of future engineers.

7. See any of the reports by F. S. Endicott on salaries entitled *Trends in the Employment of College and University Graduates* (Evanston, Ill.: Northwestern University).

8. The Los Alamos data are contained in *National Survey of Professional and Scientific Salaries* (Los Alamos Scientific Laboratory, Los Alamos, New Mexico). The Endicott data, published since 1949, are from F. S. Endicott, *Trends in Employment of College and University Graduates.*

9. This finding is supported by additional experiments with Koyck lags.

10. The bias on the engineering salary coefficient due to incorrect measurement of alternative incomes can be estimated as follows: Assume that the true equation is $\Delta \ln \text{ENR} = b\Delta ln\ \text{ESAL} - b\Delta \ln \text{ALT}$, where *ALT* is the true alternative income available to engineering majors, while the estimated equation is $\Delta \ln \text{ENR} = b_0 \Delta \ln \text{ESAL} - b_1 \Delta \ln PSAL$.

Let R_{ES} = the correlation between ENR and ESAL;
R_{EA} = the correlation between ENR and ALT;
R_{EP} = the correlation between ENR and PSAL;
R_{SA} = the correlation between ESAL and ALT;
R_{SP} = the correlation between ESAL and PSAL;
S_A = the standard deviation of ALT;
S_S = the standard deviation of ESAL;
S_P = the standard deviation of PSAL.

Then assume that $S_A = S_S = S_A$, so that $R_{ES} = -R_{EA}$. This means that

$$b = (R_{ES}/1 - R_{SA})/(S_E/S_S),$$

while the estimated coefficient, b_0, is

$$(R_{ES} - R_{EP}R_{SP})/(1 - R_{SP}^2)/(S_E/S_S).$$

But $R_{EP} = -\lambda R_{ES}$, where λ is the ratio of b_1 to b_0; so that

$$b_0 = (R_{ES} + \lambda R_{SP}R_{ES})/1 - \lambda^2 R_{SP}^2,$$

again divided by S_E/S_S. The ratio of b_0 to b is then simply the ratio of $(1 - R_{SA})$ to $(1 - \lambda R_{PS})$. Empirically, λ is about 0.15 and R_{PS} about 0.10, so that the estimated coefficient differs from the true coefficient by approximately $1 - R_{SA}$. If R_{SA} equals R_{PS} the estimate is biased downward by 10 percent. If

R_{SA} is much greater than R_{PS}, the bias is also much greater. As long as the correlation between actual salary and the true alternative is positive, the estimate is biased downward.

11. In preliminary calculations one highly significant cross-relation was uncovered. Starting salaries for chemists had a well-defined negative impact on engineering enrollment. Given the relative size of engineering and chemistry, however, and the crudity of the chemist salary series, this finding was omitted in the final calculations.

12. Because of the absence of a series on veterans in freshman programs, VET was estimated in two ways: by the total number of enrolled veterans and by the number of "original" entrants into college (of whom perhaps one half are freshmen). The results reported give the "best fit" variable in order to provide the maximum measure of the veterans effect. Even so, it is obvious that only a small fraction of the variation in engineering enrollment can be attributed to demobilization of the military.

13. D. R. Coombe, *High School Seniors and the Engineering Career* (San José State University, February 1966), p. 17.

14. To be precise, 49 percent of all males cite vocational reason as the primary motive for selecting an undergraduate major, compared to 66 percent of engineering students. *Two Years after the College Degree* (Washington, D.C.: National Science Foundation, 1963), p. 228.

15. The precise adjustment is as follows: Let $G_t =$ number of B.S. graduates; $\hat{G}_t =$ number on the market; $N_t =$ net increase in post-B.S. enrollment; $E_t =$ gross enrollment in post-B.S. training; $M_t =$ number of M.S. graduates. Then we have, by definition, $\hat{G}_t = G_t - N_t$, *and* $E_t = E_{t-1} - M_t + N_t$. By substitution we obtain an equation for G_t in terms of available data: $\hat{G}_t = G_t - (E_t - E_{t-1}) - M_t$. This is the equation used to adjust the gross number of B.S. graduates for the number actively seeking work.

16. Probably the most serious misspecification is the treatment of demand for new B.S. engineers as an independent phenomenon, unrelated to other factor inputs. Although it is perhaps reasonable to ignore the impact of production workers and capital in analyzing the short-run demand for engineers, it is less defensible to ignore non-B.S. engineering inputs (M.S., Ph.D., and other engineers). Hence, an attempt was made to estimate the effect of these inputs on the demand for new B.S. engineers. First, the number of non-B.S. engineers was added to the regression equations, with no significant results, suggesting that in the short run it is legitimate to treat demand for new B.S. engineers as an independent phenomenon. Factor substitution may be a long-run process with only modest influence on the annual variation in changes in salaries. Second, the salary determination process was completely respecified under the hypothesis that the *total stock* of engineers, not the flow of new entrants, determines starting salaries (e.g., I employed the original basic model of Chapter 2 rather than the simplified new entrants model). An annual stock series was estimated, using the number of new entrants and various postulated depreciation rates. The results are comparable to those in Table 4.5. The "best fit" equation using stock variables was

$$\Delta \ln \text{ESAL} = 0.020 + 0.201\ \Delta \ln \text{RD} + 0.102\ \Delta \ln \text{DUR} - 0.234\ \Delta \ln \text{STK} - 0.904\ \Delta \ln \text{STK}_{t-1} + 1.35\ \Delta \ln \text{STK}_{t-2} - 0.310\ \Delta \ln \text{STK}_{t-3}.$$
$$R^2 = 0.876 \qquad \text{D.W.} = 2.53$$

where STK = stock of engineers

This equation provides a tolerably good explanation of changes in salary and, more important, confirmation of the lag in salary determination found in the regressions of Table 4.4. The new entrants model is emphasized in the text because it is based on more reliable data, yields better statistical results (in regressions with stock and graduate terms, only the latter are significant), and is conceptually preferable in analyzing starting salaries.

17. This explanation of market disequilibrium and shortage is similar, though not identical, to the Arrow-Capron "dynamic shortage." In the present model, disequilibrium is due to lagged response of salaries to changes in supply rather than to changes in demand. (See K. Arrow and W. M. Capron, "Dynamic Shortages and Price Rises: The Engineer-Scientist case," *Quarterly Journal of Economics,* 1959.

Chapter 5: The Income of Doctorate Specialists

1. The economics of information has been developed by G. S. Stigler in two interesting papers: "The Economics of Information," *Journal of Political Economy,* June 1961, and "Information in the Labor Market," *ibid.,* Supplement, October 1962.

2. Bifurcation of the market for loans means that two discount rates ought to be used in calculating discounted incomes. It also suggests that the *availability* as well as the value of awards will influence decisions, especially if non-stipend financing is hard to come by.

3. Part of "nonpecuniary income" may be attributed in empirical work to measurable job characteristics, such as opportunities, vacations, sabbaticals, consultantships, or the risk and skewness of income possibilities. For the present these factors are all under the rubric, "nonpecuniary income."

4. Kenneth Arrow, "Economic Welfare and the Allocation of Resources for Invention," in *The Rate and Direction of Inventive Activity,* National Bureau of Economic Research (Princeton: Princeton University Press, 1966), p. 615.

5. It should be stressed that these normative statements relate to abstract economic systems and involve a comparison of the free market with an ideal optimizing system. In the United States the government and nonprofit foundations support research, and it is not immediately apparent whether this support is excessive or deficient. Different institutional mechanisms for funding R & D need not be better than present methods nor preferable to a reliance on the free market only. The papers of Harry Johnson, "Federal Support of Basic Research: Some Economic Issues," and Carl Kaysen, "Federal Support of Basic Research," in *Basic Research and National Goals* (Washington, D.C.: U.S. Government Printing Office, 1965), discuss the problems of determining the appropriate allocation of resources.

6. See, for instance, the study of P. E. Cullen, "The Interindustry Wage Structure" (*American Economic Review,* June 1956), or that of Sumner Slichter, "Notes on the Structure of Wages" (*Review of Economics and Statistics,* February 1950).

7. The rank correlation for salaries and growth from 1948 to 1964 was 0.53. A higher correlation is obtained when the salaries of young scientists are used (0.75). The 5 percent significance level is 0.714.

8. While there are some differences in the ranking of fields by rate of change in salaries according to the NSF data (Table 5.6) and the NAS-NRC data (Table 5.5), the general picture of developments is similar. For comparable intervals (1948–1960 in the NSF figures and 1950–1960 in the NAS-NRC data) the rank correlation of the two indicators of change is 0.79 for the natural sciences. Since the NAS-NRC data were obtained at the same time, these figures are probably less subject to problems of incomparability and more reliable than the NSF figures.

9. This comparison is not quite appropriate, for the Ph.D. data relate to salaries in individual occupations while the industrial wage figures are a mixture of wages for different occupations. The rate of increase in industrial wages will exhibit less variation than the increase in occupational wages if changes in the occupational structure of industries are fairly similar and if the occupational component of wage changes dominates the "industrial component."

10. While there are differences among fields in the time spent studying for a degree, the data have not been adjusted for the complication. As a first approximation, the time lapse between B.S. and Ph.D. is assumed to be five years. This estimate is in line with National Academy of Science studies, which indicate that students earn a Ph.D. within 5–6 years of entering graduate school, on the average. A B.A. at 22 would, according to their calculations, receive his doctorate at age 27.

11. This can be seen by taking the Taylor expansion of the discounted income series, adjusted for growth, and dropping higher-order terms:

Let $D = \Sigma_t Y_t (1 + g)^t/(1 + d)^t$ be the adjusted discounted income,

where: Y_t = income,
g = growth rate,
d = discount rate.

Then, by expanding, we obtain for the $(1 + g)^t/(1 + d)^t$ term

$$1/(1 + d - g - dg + \text{higher-order terms})^t$$

For reasonably small values of g and d — say $g = 0.03$ and $d = 0.10$ — this is approximately equal to

$$1/(1 + d - g),$$ as asserted in the text.

12. The income and cost-of-schooling figures were taken from a survey by the National Opinion Research Council Center, Chicago), *Graduate Student Finances,* and an Office of Education study, *The Academic and Financial Status of Graduate Students* (Washington, D.C.: U.S. Government Printing Office, 1969). Both surveys report that a full-time graduate student receives $4,000 per year. The NORC

survey estimates the cost of education to be $600. The Office of Education figure is slightly higher, $800. The higher cost estimate yields a net income of $3,200 during the years of schooling. If five years (from age 22 to 27) are spent in school, this accumulates to $19,100 (at 6 percent compound interest). The figure in the text is the sum of $19,100 and the income earned after the Ph.D.

13. The median income is used in this calculation because it is the rough equivalent of the geometric means used earlier. In lognormal distributions, the median equals the geometric mean. Most income distributions are approximately lognormal.

14. Analytically it is preferable to use arithmetic means in calculating lifetime incomes. The NAS-NRC survey, which provided the data for the computations, did not calculate means. An estimate of the arithmetic means of Ph.D. income in each cohort can be made from the NAS-NRC data if it is assumed that Ph.D. incomes are lognormally distributed. In a lognormal distribution, the log of the arithmetic mean is equal to the geometric mean plus one half the variance of the geometric mean. Estimates of lifetime incomes based on this adjustment show few differences among fields beyond a general increase in the *level* of income. The ranking of fields by DLIs is unchanged.

15. Gary Becker, *Human Capital,* p. 79.

16. *Ibid.,* p. 82.

17. The income figures underlying these calculations are a "stylized" summary of the results of several income surveys for scientific and engineering specialties. According to the College Placement Council, starting Ph.D. scientists in industry earned $13,800 in 1967 compared to $8,200 for starting B.S. scientists. In electrical engineering, the incomes were $14,850 and $8,750 respectively. In both cases, the Ph.D. earned 59 percent more than the B.S. — roughly $5,000 per year. The Engineers Joint Council reports a smaller differential for engineers at the start of their careers — 47 percent, of $4,000. Later in life, the EJC statistics show an increase in the absolute value of the differences to $5,000–$6,000. The American Chemical Society reports that starting Ph.D. chemists earned $11,900 in 1967 compared to $7,200 for B.S. chemists. The order of magnitude of all the figures suggests a 50–60 percent difference.

18. The regression equations are:

(a) for Ph.D.'s DLI = 248,000 − 990 EDUC $\quad R^2 = 0.60$
(b) for Master's DLI = 197,000 − 750 EDUC $\quad R^2 = 0.36$
(c) for Baccalaureate DLI = 100,000 − 1010 EDUC $\quad R^2 = 0.22$

when EDUC = fraction of specialists working in the education sector.

The fraction in education explains a significant part of income differences among doctorate and master's graduates. Because of the small number of bachelor's graduates in education, it is less important in that case. The slopes of the regressions are not significantly different — they range from $750 to $1010 — and thus can be used to value work in universities, regardless of level of education. In the text, $750 and $1000 are taken as bounds on the values.

Chapter 6: Stipend Income and Educational Subsidies

1. *Graduate Student Finances* 1963 (Chicago: National Opinion Research Center, 1965).

2. Casual observation suggests that at least some graduate students marry in order to finance an education. Available data do not permit a test of this hypothesis.

3. *Graduate Student Finances,* chap. 3.

4. *Report of the President; 1957–58, 1964–65,* Harvard University, Cambridge, Mass.

5. The data for this comparison are taken from the stipend income awarded Yale graduate students.

6. The higher correlation for the income of stipends results from the relatively large income of federal awards.

7. It is rational for a monopsonist to pay for the training of potential employees. The enormous federal support given to meteorology and oceanography by the government may be a particular reflection of this kind of behavior.

8. Ordinary least-squares are used in these calculations on the hypothesis that stipends are an exogenous variable. To test for the possibility that the number of awards is partly determined by the number of graduate students — i.e., for a simultaneous relationship between stipends and enrollment — we also ran two-stage least-squares regressions, using as instrumental variables the number of graduates in the base year and federal support. These regressions confirm the findings reported in the test.

9. The following argument shows that the coefficient on the stipend term is the same whether or not stipends are "deflated" by Ph.D.'s:

Let $\mathrm{GRD}_t =$ graduates;
$\mathrm{STP}_t =$ stipends;

then the per-Ph.D. equation is: $\mathrm{GRD}_t = (\mathrm{STP/GRD})^{\alpha}\ (\mathrm{GRB})^{\beta}$, while the total stipend equation is: $\mathrm{GRD}_t = (\mathrm{STP})^{\alpha}\ (\mathrm{GRD})^{\beta-\alpha}$. In both cases, the stipend term has a coefficient α.

10. *Graduate Student Finances,* p. 203.

11. John A. Creager, A Study of Graduate Fellowship Applicants in Terms of Ph.D. Attainments, Technical Report No. 18 (Washington, D.C.: National Academy of Sciences-National Research Council).

12. These figures *exclude* federal contributions to research and "auxiliary enterprises" Miscellaneous categories account for the missing 10% of income. See *Toward a Long-Range Plan for Federal Financial Support for Higher Education* (Washington, D.C.: U.S. Department of Health, Education and Welfare), Table A-1.

13. *Ibid.*

14. *Educational Opportunity Bank.* A Report of the Panel on Educational Innovation to the U.S. Commission on Education, the Director of the National Science Foundation, and the Special Assistant to the President for Science and

Technology (August 1967). See also Karl Shell et al., "The Educational Opportunity Bank: An Economic Analysis of a Contingent Repayment Loan Program for Higher Education," *National Tax Journal,* 21:1–45 (1968).

Chapter 7: The Incomplete Adjustment Pattern: Doctorate Manpower

1. Statement of the President, The White House, Washington, D.C. (December 13, 1962).

2. The derivation of the substitution relation is described in Chapter II, note 10.

3. Changes in alternatives have been omitted on the assumption that changes in income are compared with the average change for doctorate fields.

4. The National Academy data were kindly given to me by Dr. Lindsay Harmon. Some of these data have been published in Dr. Harmon's *Profiles of Ph.D's in the Sciences* (Publication No. 1293, National Academy of Sciences-National Research Council). The NSF data are contained in National Science Foundation, *American Science Manpower,* 1964. Comparable data for 1948 are from the Bureau of Labor Statistics (Bulletin 1027).

5. The exact computation was as follows: First, I added together the number of persons who left a specialty (say field A) to work in other fields and the number who entered from all other alternatives into A. This produced a series of figures telling the gross number of "movers" between A and other specialties. The number of movers was then divided by the number of persons in specialty A and applied to the alternative incomes to produce the weighted average.

In terms of the theory of occupational choice outlined in Chapter 1, this weighting procedure is closely related to the linear programming model of behavior. In that model, fields with few "neighbors" are expected to have relatively small supply elasticities. Weighting incomes by observed postgraduate mobility patterns is a crude adjustment for the relation of one field to another.

6. Note, however, that because the demand parameter enters the incomplete adjustment equation, this is not an estimate of the supply elasticity.

7. Additional experiments, using the *stock* of Ph.D.'s as the dependent variable and alternative estimates of disequilibrium income, show the model to be "robust" with regard to different specifications.

8. The amount of field-switching inevitably depends on how specialties are defined. Some of the findings may accordingly be distorted by the particular definitions used in the NAS-NR survey. The main results are still probably valid.

9. For computations of rates of return on the bachelor's degree in the period 1949–1959, see the unpublished paper "Trends in the Return on Investment in Higher Education, 1949–1959," by M. Borland and D. E. Yetts. Since 1961 the rate of increase in the salaries of young college graduates has been less than that of young high school graduates according to the Current Population Survey, which reverses the 1949–1959 pattern. This may indicate that the rate of return declined slightly in the 1960s.

10. John L. Chase, *Doctoral Study,* Office of Education Circular No. 646, (Washington, D.C.: U.S. Government Printing Office, 1961).

11. The survey suggests some differences among fields in the importance of constraints. In biology, only 4 percent of the deans thought that lack of faculty was a serious barrier; in physical sciences, 17 percent. Similarly, lack of financial aid was thought by more deans to be a barrier in the humanities (72 percent) than in the biological or physical sciences (42 percent).

12. The one-third estimate is derived by (1) applying the ratio of Ph.D. to master's degrees (about 1:5) to the total number of graduate students in 1960 (314,000) to obtain the approximate number of doctorate candidates (63,000); and (2) dividing the number of available places (20,000) by this estimate, Note that the calculation assumes that all of the available places are filled with doctorate students in accord with the Office of Education questionnaire.

13. Loose entry, the existence of product differentiation among institutions, absence of profit motives, reliance on subsidies, and the importance of prestige and invidious comparisons in the education market are suggestive of these "monopolistic competition" inefficiencies.

Chapter 8: Cobweb and Incomplete Adjustment in Other College Markets

1. National Science Foundation, *Two Years After the College Degree* (Washington, D.C.: U.S. Government Printing Office, 1963).

2. Discounted lifetime incomes for accountants by level of schooling indicate that the large number of noncollege accountants and the small number of post-bachelor's accountants are consistent with economic incentive. With a 6 percent discount rate, the DLI from high school graduates in accounting is relatively high and that for graduate school accountants, relatively low:

Level of education	*Discounted income*
High school graduate	162,400
College, 1–3 years	157,300
College, 4 years	166,400
College, 5+ years	163,600

3. According to the model, the coefficient on the lagged share term should be unity. It is, however, less than one in regressions in which a constant term is also introduced into the model. Apparently, the constant picks up part of the effect of the relative fixed share of degree term. In equations without a constant the lagged term is unity. A more complex model, taking explicit account of the equilibrium share of degrees, should be able to adjust for this inconsistency.

4. For example, using sophomore and freshman-year salaries separately yields the following equation:

$$\begin{aligned} \ln(\text{ACCT/GRAD})_t = {} & 1.00 + \underset{(5.73)}{1.49}\,\Delta\ln \text{ASAL}_{t-3} + \underset{(1.88)}{.32}\,\Delta\ln \text{ASAL}_{t-4} \\ & -\underset{(7.65)}{3.06}\,\Delta\ln \text{YSAL}_{t-3} - \underset{(2.18)}{0.72}\,\Delta\ln \text{YSAL}_{t-4} \\ R^2 = {} & .819 \\ \text{D.W.} = {} & 1.52 \end{aligned}$$

5. Experiments with the number of graduates in the period to which plans refer show, moreover, no relation between salaries and supply at that time. This supports the expected supply model of salary plans.

6. National Science Foundation, *Two Years After the College Degree.*

7. For a detailed analysis of top executive salaries and their relation to MBA salaries, see W. G. Lewellen, *Executive Compensation in Large Industrial Corporations* (New York: National Bureau of Economic Research, 1968).

8. The principal study of the relation between executive salaries, profits, and sales is J. S. McGuire, J. S. Chui, and A. O. Elbing, "Executive Incomes, Sales, and Profits," *American Economic Review,* September 1962.

9. Over the long run, from 1900 to the 1960s, the position of chemistry as a baccalaureate specialty fell markedly: in 1901–1905, 5.2 percent of bachelor's degrees were awarded in chemistry, compared to 2.0 percent in the 1960s. The decline in the field as a doctorate specialty, on the other hand, is strictly a postwar phenomenon. Until the 1950s the share of Ph.D.'s in chemistry rose steadily.

10. In the B.S case, the acceleration of supply is rank-correlated with changes in relative salaries three years earlier at 052. The velocity of supply is also correlated with changes in salaries at 0.52. Since the relative decline in chemistry degrees is moderate at the B.S. level, the similarity in coefficients is to be expected.

11. Regression calculations for the lifetime income of doctorate chemists yield somewhat different results. In this case the lagged degree term has a negative coefficient:

$$\begin{aligned}\Delta\ln \text{LI} &= \underset{(4.41)}{0.04} - \underset{(1.39)}{.04}\ \Delta\ln \text{DEG}_{t-1} - \underset{(1.48)}{0.02}\ \Delta\ln \text{DEG}_{t-2} \\ &\quad + \underset{(1.66)}{0.05}\ \Delta\ln \text{INV} + \underset{(0.62)}{0.04}\ \Delta\ln \text{RDC}_{t-1} \\ R^2 &= .447 \\ \text{D.W.} &= 2.57\end{aligned}$$

Where $\Delta\ln$ LI = percentage change in discounted lifetime income of specialists in the chemical industry.

Not surprisingly, the determination of changes in the income of experienced and starting specialists differ somewhat, with increases in new entrants reducing the salaries of the former, irrespective of expectations of the number of graduates.

12. These figures come from the American Mathematical Society survey of starting Ph.D. salaries. See *Notices of the American Mathematical Society.*

13. These figures are reported in the 1968 National Survey of Compensation of U.S. Atomic Energy Commission (previously the Los Alamos Salary Survey).

14. See National Science Foundation, *Employment of Mathematicians in Industry and Government* (Washington, D.C.: U.S. Govt. Printing Office, 1963).

Chapter 9: Demand for Education and the Market for Faculty

1. The "elasticity of places" has a dual meaning. It can refer to the change in faculty with respect to changes: enrollment or to changes in the faculty : student ratio. Here we are concerned with the former meaning in the text.

2. It might be argued in this regard that, as the principal employer of Ph.D.'s, universities are a "monopsony sector" facing an upward sloping supply curve, while as only one of many industries employing non-Ph.D. workers, they face an elastic schedule.

3. The elasticity from cross-sectional data was estimated by comparing Ph.D. and master's degree salaries for faculty with relative employment on major specialties.

4. For additional vacancy data see National Education Association, *Teacher Supply and Demand in Universities* (April 1965).

5. National Educational Association, *Salaries in Higher Education,* 1967–68, Higher Education Series Research Report 1968–R7. This study shows that only one third of the universities permit deviations in salary "to obtain teachers in fields of scarcity."

6. In a more complete model the changes in resources are endogenous variables.

7. The data underlying these calculations were gathered by John T. Dunlop for the Harvard study of faculty in 1968.

8. These figures are from the U.S. Office of Education, *Teaching Faculty in Universities and Four-year Colleges* (Washington, D.C.: U.S. Government Printing Office, 1966).

9. A proper interpretation of the independent role of income in the determination of employment requires a more general model of university decision-making, in which the impact of enrollment and other variables on income is explored. In the absence of such an analysis it is useful to bear in mind two facts about university financing: 1) student fees constitute only 25 percent of educational and general income (excluding income from enterprises); and 2) about 20 percent of total current fund income. Thus part of the income effect — perhaps most — is due to the enrollment-induced increase in income.

10. The reduced-form equations do not yield unique estimates of the parameters because the system is overidentified.

11. The analysis of bias follows that developed in Chapter 4, n. 11. It is shown there that when salaries in a field and in an alternative have equal absolute effects on supply, the bias due to faulty measurement of the alternative is $(1 - r_{SA})/(1 - \lambda r_{PS})$, where r_{SA} = correlation between salaries in the field and in the true alternative; λ = the ratio of the coefficient estimated on the salary variable to that on the alternative variable; and r_{PS} = correlation between salaries and the measured alternative. In the current situation, $\lambda = 0.13$, $r_{PS} = 0.44$, so that the bias reduces to $(1 - r_{SA})/(0.94)$. If $r_{SA} = 0.50$ (maximum estimate), the bias is 47 percent; if $r_{SA} = 0.25$ (minimum estimate), the bias is 20 percent. Thus the estimate in the text probably understates the true elasticity by 20 to 47 percent.

12. Blank and Stigler also found that the number of graduate students has a mixed effect on faculty:student ratios. See D. Blank and G. Stigler, *The Demand and Supply of Scientific Personnel,* chap. 5.

13. L. Harmon, *Careers of Ph.D.'s,* Career Patterns Report No. 2, National Academy of Sciences-National Research Council (Washington, D.C.).

Chapter 10: Career Plans and Occupational Choice

1. For an interesting discussion of this methodology in the theory of the firm, see the Presidential Address of Fritz Machlup, *American Economic Review,* March 1967.

2. In general, statistical analysis with aggregate time series or cross-sectional data is not a sufficiently fine tool to validate social science theories. It is almost always possible to explain regressions in more than one way.

3. National Academy of Sciences–National Research Council. Publication 1142, Appendix 12.

4. The one fourth cited in the text is an unweighted average of percentages for the ten nonscientific occupations.

5. Obviously this is a crude categorization, for even general channels such as public media or jobs may be more readily available to students from upper-income families.

6. The precise increase was from 27 percent in 1947 to 47 percent in 1967. Because of the peculiar composition of the 1947 student body, with many veterans, the trend may be partly spurious. On the other hand, employment rates were roughly the same in 1947 and 1967, so that the cyclic bias is probably slight.

7. Because of problems in interpreting "starting salaries" for medicine — mixing salaries of full-time doctors and interns — comparisons for starting salaries produce a lower correlation.

8. This result can be compared to the evidence gathered by Reynolds, Meyers, and Schultz that shows considerable ignorance about opportunities in "blue collar" labor markets. Two factors may explain the divergent results between the studies of the blue collar worker and of college students. First, the blue-collar studies refer to inter-firm or inter-industrial differentials rather than to occupational differentials. Second, greater skill and investment in human capital may make college students better informed. See L. G. Reynolds, *The Structure of Labor Markets: Wages and Labor Mobility in Theory and Practice* (New York: Harper & Row, 1951); C. A. Meyers and G. P. Schultz, *The Dynamics of the Labor Market: A Study of the Impact of Employment Changes on Labor Mobility* (Englewood Cliffs, N.J.: Prentice-Hall, 1951).

Chapter 11: Expectations and Marginal Decision-Making

1. These estimates are *not* based on the average income expected by students themselves relative to the average income expected for the career. Rather, for each student expecting to do better, a ratio of ability rent was computed and the mean ratio calculated.

2. Adam Smith, *The Wealth of Nations* (Modern Library edition), p. 107.

3. Since the questions are worded as true–false, it is possible that uneven distributions of responses do not, in fact, reflect incorrect perceptions of the market. Some students may view their career as exactly average and thus be required to make a false comparison.

4. Exaggerated perceptions of characteristics are not infrequent in economic

life. Professors, for example, have an exaggerated view of the quality of their departments. Cartter reports that they "lean over backwards in rating their present university attachment . . . rating it on the average 17% higher than outsiders did." A. Cartter, "Economics of the University," *American Economic Review,* May 1965, p. 487.

5. These estimates are backward extrapolations of the income of men with those levels of training in the age bracket 25–34. The basic data are from U.S. Bureau of Census, *Current Population Reports,* ser. P–60, no. 56. "Annual Male Income, Lifetime Income, and Educational Attainment of Men in the U.S. for Selected Years, 1956–1966" (Washington, D.C.: U.S. Government Printing Office, 1968).

6. The compensating differential was calculated by the formula $R = 100(1 + i)^t - 100$, where $t =$ the number of years of training and R is the compensating difference in income in percentage terms. See H. G. Lewis, *Unionism and Relative Wages in the United States* (Chicago, 1963), p. 122.

7. The principal noncomparability occurs between the final level of education foreseen by survey respondents and used in the income data. For example, our survey mixes M.A.T. and Ed.D. students in the graduate education category and compares their expectations with the income of Ph.D. graduates. This probably explains the low rank of the field in expected income in the table.

8. The comparison described in the text can be improved in two ways. First, nonpecuniary income could be held fixed by focusing on the marginal incentive of students preparing the work in particular sectors of the economy — e.g. business or academic. Second, students could be surveyed in the future and their expression of marginal income incentive compared to that of the 1967 students. Presumably, changes in incentive will be correlated with a changed pattern of career choice.

Index

Ability
effect on rates of return, 91–92
role in career choice, 6–8
student perceptions of ability and economic rent, 219–223
Accountants
cobweb model, 140–144
demand for, 142–144
education, 34–36, 41–45, 140
employment, 34–36, 51–52
in education-occupational matrix, 51–52
supply of, 141–143

Bachelor graduates
degree awarded, 44–45
discounted lifetime income, 93–96
employment, 47–52
stipend support, 101
training lag, 17

Career information
chance for wealth, 219–223
income information, accuracy of, 196–216
sources, 195–196
subjective adequacy, 194–195
variability of income, 218–223
Career plans
alternative career possibilities, 187–193
marginal suppliers, 223–226
return to college studies, 183–188
timing, 181–185
Chemists
demand for, 154–156
discounted lifetime income, 88, 93–96
education, 34–35, 41–45, 149
employment, 34–35
faculty, 161–166
salaries, changes in, 80–85
salaries, level of, 150
stipend support, 103–107
supply of, 119–125, 150–154
supply of Ph.D.'s, 119–125
Cobweb equation, 72–74, 148
Cobweb model
accounting case, 140–144
basic structure, 22–26
engineering case, 58–65
MBA case, 144–148

Demand
for accountants, 142–144
for chemists, 154–156
for engineers, 62–64
for mathematicians, 158–159
for MBA's, 144–148
for Ph.D.'s, 77–79
Discounted lifetime incomes. *See also* Salaries; Starting salaries
adjusted for abilities, 91–93
Bachelor's graduates, 90–96
corrected for nonpecuniary factors, 88–90
effect of stipends, 111
Master's graduates, 90–96
pay-off for Ph.D., 99
Ph.D.'s, 87–96
risk and variability, 96–99
use in analysis, 86

Dropout rates
in engineering, 68–71
role in career choice, 16–17

Economic man, 14, 225
Education market
adjustments to disequilibrium, 28, 165–167
constraints on, 29–30, 165–166
education production function, 29
faculty-student ratio, 29
financing, 111–115
graduate capacity, 134–136
income differentials, 84–85, 130–134, 165–166
link to labor market, 28
mobility of Ph.D.'s, 130–134
new programs, 136
stipend support, 101–107
Education-occupation matrix
chemists, 154
class of 1958, 47–54
class of 1967, 188–189
mathematicians, 157
Ph.D.'s, 53, 123–130, 177–178
shape of, 46–47
Education of workers
postwar changes, 39
professionals, 35–36
U. S. and Western Europe, 37
Educational adjustment process, 44–45, 130
Educational Opportunity Bank, 113–114
Employment
professionals, 34
sectors, 36–37
Engineers
cobweb equation, 72–74
cobweb model, 58–65
demand, 62–64
discounted lifetime income, 88, 93–96
dropout rate, 68–70
education, 34–36, 57–58
employment, 34–36, 41–45, 51–52, 55–57
enrollment, 65–68
faculty, 161–166
non-degree workers, 58
salaries, changes in, 80–85
stipend support, 103–107
supply of B.S.'s, 59–61, 65–70
supply of Ph.D.'s, 119–125
Expectations. *See also* Perceptions of market
income, 202–208
income, by specialty, 209–216
relative incomes, 205–206, 217–218
rules for models, 20–21
theoretical considerations, 8–11

Faculty
demand for, 171–172
doctorate faculty, 175–178
employment equations, 169–170
faculty model, 30–32, 168–177
faculty-student ratio, 29
hiring standards model, 164
interfield composition, 161–164
mobility of experienced Ph.D.'s, 177–178
salary equations, 169
supply of, 171–173, 175–178

Humanities
career plans, 183–184
degrees awarded, 40–45
discounted lifetime income, 88, 93–96
employment, 53
faculty, 161–166
information on market, 194
salaries, change in, 80–85
stipend support, 103–107
supply of Ph.D.'s, 119–125

Income. *See also* Salaries
expectations of, 196–206
expectations of relative income, 205–206, 217–218
expected over life-cycle, 215–216
in student decisions, 207–208
Income foregone
in educational costs, 112–113
in student decisions, 207–208
Incomplete adjustment
basic model, 22, 26–27, 117–118
chemist case, 149–156
doctorate case, 119–223
mathematics case, 156–159
sectoral case, 130–134
Incremental vacancy rates, 164–165
Information decision lags, 17–18, 181–186
Information about careers. *See* Career information
Internal labor market, 29, 165–166

Labor market models
basic lagged model, 19–20
cobweb, 22–26, 58–65, 112–118
disequilibrium behavior, 23–26
educational adjustment, 44–45, 130
equilibrium, 22
faculty model, 30–32

incomplete adjustment, 22, 26–27, 148–159
new entrants model, 21–22
simultaneous allocation model, 30–32
stipend model, 109–110
Life cycle income, 215–216

Marginal decision makers
anomalous supply behavior, 13
in economic theory, 13–14, 223
students with marginal characteristics, 183, 223–226
Marshall, A., 1, 2, 16
Master's graduates
degrees awarded, 42–44
discounted lifetime income, 93–96
employment, 47–52
Mathematics
demand for, 158–159
discounted lifetime income, 88, 93–96
education, 34–36
employment, 34–36
faculty, 161–166
incomplete adjustment, 156–159
salary changes, 80–85
stipend support, 101–103
supply of Ph.D.'s, 119–125, 156–158
training lag, 17
M.B.A.
cobweb model, 144–148
demand of, 147, 148
salaries, 144
stipend support, 102
supply of, 146–147
Mobility
among sectors, 130–134, 177–178
among specialties, 53, 123–130

Nonmonetary income
effect on careers of wealthy, 3
effect on return to Ph.D., 89–90, 93–96
in Ph.D. incomes, 87–89
problems in analysis, 12–13
use in faculty market, 167

Occupational choice
abilities, 6–8
college studies, role of, 183–188
distinctive aspects, 1–2
economic theory, 1–11, 141
expectations, 8–10
income, subjective role of, 207–208
individual choice, 2–11
linear activity models, 5–7
marginal suppliers, role of, 223–225
nonmonetary factors, 3, 12–13
preferences, 5–6
risk, 10–11, 96–99
social science analyses, 14–15
timing, 181–185
Occupational mobility. *See* Education-occupation matrix, mobility

Perceptions of market
chance for wealth, 219–223
change in income, 219
income, 202–218
variability, 218–223
Ph.D.
capacity of universities, 134–136
career information, 200–201
characteristics of market, 76–77
chemists, 149–156
degrees awarded, 40–42
demand for, 77–79
discounted lifetime income, 93–96
effect of stipends on supply, 107–111
employment, 53, 123–130
faculty, 175–178
mathematicians, 156–159
occupational mobility, 53, 123–130, 177–178
relative ability, 91–92
salaries, by sector, 84–86
salaries, changes in, 77–87
salaries, level of, 156
sectoral allocation, 130–134
stipend support, 101–107
supply, 119–123
training lag, 17
Policy
financing education, 111–115
implications of research, 227–228
labor market stipends, 114–115
stipend awards, 105–107
Professionals
postwar growth, 34

Research, future, 229–230
Risk
in career choice, 10–11
in doctorate training, 96–99
student perceptions of, 218–223

Salaries. *See also* Discounted lifetime incomes; Starting salaries
engineers, 62–64
Ph.D. workers, by sector, 84–86, 132
Ph.D. workers, changes in, 77–87
Ph.D. workers, levels, 81–85, 87–88, 93–96
Shortages and surpluses

chemist market, 148–149
in basic model, 27
mathematics market, 156–157
Ph.D. market, 89–90, 121
Social science
career plans, 183–184
degrees awarded, 40–45
discounted lifetime income, 88, 93–96
employment, 53
faculty, 161–163
information on market, 194
salaries, changes in, 80–85
stipend support, 103–107
supply of Ph.D.'s, 119–125
Starting salaries
accountants, 142–144
chemists, 154–156
engineers, 70–73
expected, 62–65, 209–216
mathematicians, 158–159
M.B.A.'s, 144–148
Ph.D. workers, 77–79, 82
use in new entrants model, 21
Stipends
change in support, 102–103
effect on career choice, 107–108
effect on labor supply, 109–111
effect on years of study, 108–109
federal support, 105–107
information about, 198–201
methods of subsidization, 100–102
support by field, 102–105
value of awards, 102–104
Supply
acceleration rule, 26
aggregation of individual decisions, 11–13
anomalous results, 12–13
educational and occupational adjustments, 44–45
effect of stipends, 107–111
of accountants, 140–144
of chemists, 150–154
of engineers, 59–61
of faculty, 171–173, 175–178
of mathematicians, 101–103
of M.B.A.'s, 144–148
of Ph.D.'s, 119–134
short-run adjustments, 18
time lags, 16–17

Training facilities. *See* Education market